BEFORE BABYLON, BEYOND BITCOIN

PERSPECTIVES

Series editor: Diane Coyle

BEFORE BABYLON, BEYOND BITCOIN

From Money That We Understand
To Money That Understands Us

REVISED PAPERBACK EDITION

David G. W. Birch

LONDON PUBLISHING PARTNERSHIP

Published by London Publishing Partnership
www.londonpublishingpartnership.co.uk

Published in association with
Enlightenment Economics
www.enlightenmenteconomics.com

Revised paperback edition, June 2019
ISBN: 978-1-907994-91-3 (paperback)

First published in hardback by
London Publishing Partnership, June 2017

A catalogue record for this book is available
from the British Library

This book has been composed in Candara

Copy-edited and typeset by
T&T Productions Ltd, London
www.tandtproductions.com

Cover image by Austin Houldsworth:
www.austinhouldsworth.co.uk

Author photograph by Ewan Mackenzie:
www.ewanmackenzie.co.uk

Cover design by James Shannon:
www.jshannon.com

This book is dedicated to Gloria Benson, Stuart Fiske and Neil McEvoy, my business partners at Consult Hyperion for more than three decades. Without them, I might never have discovered the worlds of digital identity and digital money that obsess me today!

Everything, then, must be assessed in money: for this enables men always to exchange their services, and so makes society possible.

— Aristotle (384–322 BCE) in *Nicomachean Ethics*, Book V, Chapter 5

Contents

CONTENTS

Foreword by Andrew Haldane

O FTEN, THE MOST interesting issues in economics arise from the intersection – sometimes the collision – between technology and society. To take an example, there is no more topical, and vexed, an economic issue right now than the impact of new technologies (such as robots, artificial intelligence and big data) on the world of work (individuals, sectors, communities, societies). Indeed, history makes clear that this creative friction between technology and work has existed for many millennia.

Money is another issue that, through the ages, has illustrated vividly this complex tango between societies and technologies. Money is a technology – indeed, a key one for discharging obligations between people, for keeping score in the economy, for facilitating trade, finance and commerce. But money is also a social good – indeed, a key one as an emblem of civic identity, as a measure of societal trust and order.

Technology and society have, in the main, operated in harmony when it comes to monetary issues. As money technologies have improved, this has tended to enhance trust in money, thereby boosting its supply and enhancing its public good properties in society. For example, one of the most transformative shifts in monetary technologies was from commodity to fiat monies. This not only freed up resources for more productive uses but over time enhanced the attractiveness of money.

But new monetary technologies have not always been trust boosting, certainly not immediately. Indeed, in the hands of the wrong government or private entrepreneur, some money technologies have been trust busting. Some of the relative tranquillity in fiat monies over recent centuries can probably be put down to the stabilizing role of central banks.

Now a new technological wave may be about to break over money. For some, this could herald a completely new monetary epoch – perhaps one where money is fully digital rather than physical, where the structures that engender trust in money are distributed rather than centralized, where central banks' role is changed fundamentally or even circumvented.

This issue is shaping up to be every bit as vexed as those of robots and jobs. Passions around cashless societies run high. If nothing else, this tells us that money is, always has been and always will be much more than a cryptographic code; it is a social convention. Old conventions tend to change slowly. And it is society, rather than technology, that tends to choose the destination.

This book by David Birch brings out in rich and lucid detail the full historical journey money has been undertaking and the technological revolutions it has encountered en route. More speculatively, it also sketches the possible contours of future monetary paths, given the possibility of transformative technological change.

Historical scholars, technologists, monetary economists and policy makers will all find something in here to hold their attention, to reshape their view of history or technology, finance or policy. They may or may not agree on what the next chapter in the history of money holds. But this book provides a well-researched and engaging account of the story so far, of money in retrospect and money in prospect.

Andrew Haldane
Chief Economist and Executive Director for Monetary
Analysis, Research and Statistics at the Bank of England,
and member of the Monetary Policy Committee

Foreword by Brett King

Before Babylon, Beyond Bitcoin makes several points that are absolutely essential to understanding why money, banks and money markets are set to be massively disrupted over the next century. The first critical framing in the book is the undeniable truth that money is just a technology in and of itself, and as such it cannot possibly be immune from the broad technology shifts that we're witnessing.

From the first recognizable coin in Lydia 2,500 years ago through sea shells, shekels, wooden tally sticks, Mondex and Bitcoin, Dave Birch takes us on a journey through how and why money and value exchange work the way they do. More importantly though, he examines why various currencies, money exchange systems and value stores have succeeded while others have failed. The book's second critical framing is the idea that capitalism took money from a system of control largely at the whim of the owner of a currency (such as a feudal lord) to a system based on titles to assets, and leverageable debt.

The third critical framing I took away from the book is one for those that argue about the stickiness of cash and how hard it will be to displace. We are given plenty of examples to show that this is not the case, including the fact that the payment card itself is clear evidence of rapid change across technical, social, business and regulatory lines.

An additional point Dave Birch makes is about how the use of the term 'unbanked' is obviously part of the problem, because forcing people to use banks is demonstrably no longer a precursor to financial inclusion – look, for example, at what is happening in Kenya, India and China. Let us just get the argument for the longevity of cash out of the way: it doesn't have a future because technology will simply force us to change the way we pay for things and store value. That said, the book does make a case for why cash might still hang on for a few years yet.

The secret to the readability of *Before Babylon, Beyond Bitcoin* is the wry sense of humour, which brings us a take on the history and the future of money that is unique. An example is this quote from the book about Sir Thomas Gresham, one of the leading merchants in the era of Henry VIII: 'He went on to die of apoplexy – which may well be a common fate for those who truly understand money – and left an astonishing legacy.' Or this one about the bankers behind Overend & Gurney, a British Bank that collapsed in 1866: 'The directors were, incidentally, charged with fraud, but they got off as the judge said that they were merely idiots, not criminals.'

Birch has an insatiable appetite for just the right story to describe what is happening and to make his point. Whether it is Internet-powered underpants or the disruption of the Pony Express by the first transcontinental telegraph line, it's the story that matters. He is a natural narrator for the story of money, especially when it comes to the changes being thrust on this ancient mechanism by rapid technology and behavioural shifts. There are so many insights in *Before Babylon, Beyond Bitcoin* that I came away with a lot more ammunition to use when talking to stalwarts who don't get the significance of technology in financial services and the chaos it is currently unleashing – and the chaos that new technologies have consistently unleashed over the centuries.

This is a book that will help bridge the conceptual gaps between the world we think we have come from and the role that money, banks and regulation have played in the past, and the near-future world in which we will actually use money in a purely digital form. It is a book I'm proud to endorse, not only because it's well written, funny and full of great facts and history, but because the author is about the smartest guy on the planet when it comes to the future of money.

If you're in financial services and you don't read *Before Babylon, Beyond Bitcoin*, you'll be walking into a minefield blindfolded... and you'll likely face the same ignominious end.

Brett King
Best-selling author of *Augmented: Life in the Smart Lane*, host of the 'Breaking Banks' radio show and founder/CEO of Moven

Preface to the paperback edition

SHORTLY AFTER THE first edition of the book came out, I noticed that the concept of 'smart money', which may have seemed somewhat futuristic to many readers, was receiving serious attention and attracting informed debate. Therefore – and in response to kind reviews and constructive comments on the first edition – I have changed the final section to focus less on the general issue of cashlessness and more on exploring the issue of smart monies in greater depth.

Another concept that has developed in interesting directions since my original draft is that of 'tokenization'. In this context, tokenization means taking assets and creating 'money-like' claims on those assets that can be traded without clearing and settlement. In response to this evolution I have also expanded on the topic of tokens as private currencies.

I have also attempted to explain in more detail the technologies of cryptocurrencies and how they might be used to bring smart money to the mass market in a practical way. I hope that these explanations are accessible and that they will help the general reader to understand cryptocurrencies such as Bitcoin in a wider context.

Preface to the first edition

The creation of money is a political act.

— Martin Mayer in *The Bankers* (1998)

WHEN I was invited to give a talk in my home town for the very first TED×Woking way back in January 2015, I decided to return to the topic of money. I had been thinking a great deal about transformation in the electronic payments world for a couple of decades, and because Bitcoin had become a topic of polite conversation, I chose to talk at that event about the future of money. More specifically, I returned to explore the idea that technology might be taking money back to its past, back to a more local and diverse version of money than we are used to, something I had touched on in my previous book, *Identity Is the New Money* (Birch 2014). When I was subsequently invited to prepare a piece on the future of money for the *Kings Review* in July 2015, I expanded on the ideas from that TED× talk to create a two-part series and then took the plunge and used those articles as the starting point for this book. Having been inspired by the sociologist Nigel Dodd's landmark *The Social Life of Money* to reconsider the interplay between the technological evolutionary tree of money and its social context, I thought it would be interesting to look to ideas from the social sciences in conjunction with technology forecasting to develop perspective on *where technology is taking money*.

At one level that question cannot be answered, because the trajectory of technology is ever-better tools. How society chooses to utilize those tools is a different matter entirely. I hope that this book will help you think about money in a useful and structured way so that you can generate ideas around how we – society – should be using the new tools to evolve money.

One might argue that, while neutral about the tools, technology does create a direction of travel and nudges society along. Given that the direction of travel is broadly towards decentralization, distribution and an overall lessening of state power, it is possible to bring input from disciplines including social anthropology and the study of 'palaeo-futures' (that is, what people used to think about the future) to make an informed and, I hope, surprising prediction about the future of money, which is that we will return to the multiple, overlapping community monies of the past but that they will be smart monies, monies with values, monies that know about us.

Acknowledgements

It goes without saying that this book would not have been possible without the support of my wife, Hara, who never got annoyed with me sitting up typing at all hours – whenever an idea came to me.

Sincere thanks also to the journalist Wendy Grossman. Even though she hates me misusing her phrase 'from money that we understand to money that understands us' in this way, it describes the direction of this narrative so perfectly that I could not resist it.

Introduction

Money is the instrument and measure of commerce.
— Nicholas Barbon in *A Discourse Concerning Coining the New Money Lighter* (1696)

HERE'S A STORY I came across. It has a 'guy falls asleep under hypnosis and awakes a century later to find a model society, then finds it's all a dream' narrative arc that is hard to read with modern eyes, because the perfect society that the author imagines is a communist superstate that looks like Disneyland run by Stalin. Everyone works for the government, and since government planners can optimize production, the 'inefficiency' of the free market is gone.

The time traveller at the centre of the narrative is told by his host in the modern era, the good Doctor Lette, that cash no longer exists. Instead, the populace use 'credit cards'.* This strikes me as rather unusual for a utopian vision since, as Nigel Dodd observes (Dodd 2014), utopias from Plato's *Republic* to *Star Trek* don't seem to include money at all, never mind chip and PIN.

While the author does not talk about phones, the Internet, aeroplanes or the knowledge economy, he does make a couple more insightful predictions about the evolution of money. When talking about an American going to visit Berlin, the good doctor notes how convenient it is to use cards instead of foreign currency:

> 'An American credit card,' replied Dr Lette, 'is just as good as American gold used to be'.

---

* He then goes on to describe what are in fact offline pre-authorized debit cards, but that is by-the-by.

What an excellent description of the world after the end of the gold standard. However, I think that the most fascinating insight into the future of money comes later in the book, when the time traveller asks his twenty-first-century host 'Are credit cards issued to the women just as to the men?', the answer comes back: 'Certainly'.

The answer might alert you to the age of the text, which contains the first mention of a credit card that I have found as part of a fictional narrative. The book is by Edward Bellamy and is called *Looking Backward, 2000–1887*. It was written in 1886, a century before the credit card became the iconic representation of money, and it was one of the best-selling books of its day. I have a 1940s edition in front of me as I write (Bellamy 1946), so it was still being reprinted sixty years later!

The discourse on money in that book is a wonderful example of how science fiction is not about the future but about the present: the retort *'Certainly'* is clearly intended to surprise the Victorian reader as much as the prediction of glass tunnels that surround pavements when it rains. In this book I hope to develop a narrative just as surprising to contemporary audiences and I intend to do so (while using technology as the driver of and infrastructure for change) by following Bellamy's example and looking to the social sciences to make my predictions.

Looking for narrative

At the heart of this narrative there are two relationships: that between the technology of money and wider technological evolution, and that between the technology of money and the way that society thinks about money. To use a famous illustration of this, scientists would have found it hard to imagine a clockwork universe if they hadn't first seen a clock.

You can't invent coins unless someone has already invented smelting, you can't invent banknotes without printing, you can't have Western Union without the telegraph, and so, rather obviously, on. But what is the technology of the *present* that will helps us to think about the money of the *future*? Most people, I imagine, think about money as $100 bills and gold in Fort Knox, €500 notes and plastic cards, £50 notes and the Bank of England. This is the present paradigm, so far as the public and the politicians are concerned. I think they are wrong. We are already living in the future, because the future of money began back in 1971 when the US government severed the link between the world's reserve currency and anything physical at all (in that case, gold).

We need to adjust our mental models of money and start exploring the future paradigm, both to shape it and to see where it might take us. Money existed before records began in ancient Babylon and money will continue to exist when Bitcoin is long forgotten. But the money that the Babylonians used, the money that we use today and the money that we will use in the future are all different. The way money works now is the result of particular arrangements and institutional structures, not a law of nature.

The answer is 42

A while back, The Atlantic magazine published a list of the fifty greatest breakthroughs since the wheel (Fallows 2013). They asked a variety of eminent scientists, historians and technologists to rank a list of innovations and then put them together into a feature. Number 1 was the printing press, but what caught my attention was the appearance of paper money at number 42. It made me think that in the great sweep of things the replacement of stuff of some kind by records of some kind goes back a lot further – to the grain banks of ancient Babylonia and to the marks made on cuneiform clay tablets – and extends right up to the present day, where there are fascinating discussions going on around the use of cryptography to manage distributed ledgers. Was paper money as big a technological breakthrough as the clay tablet was to ancient Babylon or the blockchain may be to the pervasive Internet?

The interaction between money and the technology of money is more complex and less well understood than you might think, given just how long both have been around. As Jevons wrote, back in Victorian times (Jevons 1884):

It is a misfortune of what may be called the science of monetary technology, that its study is almost of necessity confined to the few officers employed in government mints. Hence we can hardly expect the same advances to be made in the production of money as in other branches of manufacture, where there is wide and free competition.

Well, that was then and this is now. The 'science of monetary technology' is becoming more widely studied, and with the arrival of smart cards, mobile phones and Bitcoin it has become easier than ever to create your own money and experiment with it. Years ago my son was already trading World of Warcraft Gold via his iPhone with insight and dexterity to match the best of Wall Street's high-frequency traders. Now you can download an app for the Brixton Pound on your smartphone and, even as I write, there are kids in basements dreaming up the next DogeCoin and Drachma.

Money eras

It is difficult to see the trajectory of money when technologies that were invented in the 1960s (like the magnetic stripe) or indeed the 1860s (like uniformly valued, nationally based paper US dollars) exist alongside technologies that haven't yet been fully invented (Maurer and Swartz 2014). It seems to me that the credit crunch, the recession, the collapse of 2008 and a variety of debt and currency crises are forcing many people to think about money, banking and the economy in a way that they had not before. This in turn means that people are beginning to think about using the technology of money to create new kinds of money, rather than using it to implement digital versions of the money we have had for a generation.

When the economy is pottering along nicely, no one (least of all the politicians who are 'in charge of' the economy) stops to wonder what money is, what banks do or what the disruptive impact of technological change might be. I spend much of my working life looking at ways for banks, payments companies and governments to exploit new technologies, and I often therefore have to think about how the digital economy will evolve. Money is an essential part of that economy, but a common assumption seems to be that it will carry on at it is now, as if the post-Bretton Woods fiat currency is a natural phenomenon or the final stage of a directed evolutionary process.

Christine Desan, Leo Gottlieb Professor at the Harvard Law School, asks why, if industrial-age capitalism was the result of the seventeenth-century 'redesign' of money, we do not debate the design of money more, and I agree with her wholeheartedly (Desan 2014a). We should. The structure of central banks, commercial banks and international institutions that we have in the present comes from another age and must change. We did not have them in the past and we will not have them in the future.

The past: Money 1.0

The first great innovation in the world of finance – banking – predates money by some considerable time, having its origin in the grain banks of the ancient Assyrian and Mesopotamian kingdoms. Five-thousand-year-old cuneiform tablets refer to banking and foreign exchange, as well as secured and unsecured lending. I imagine there are more, presumably lost to history, that refer to the Ishtar Bank being bailed out after unwise speculation on bronze futures at the dawn of the Iron Age. Some 4,000 years ago the temples of Babylon were taking deposits and making loans, and by 750 BCE there was a sort of 'Basel –1' in *The Code of Hammurabi*.

Money by that time was entries in a not-at-all-shared ledger, recorded on clay tablets. Money as a commodity itself is a more recent innovation. The first recognizable coins date from Lydia (in modern Turkey) more than 2,500 years ago.* These were made from electrum, an alloy of gold and silver, and their central features (standardized weights for specie and some form of maker's mark) spread rapidly from there. King Alfred had a working system of mints up and running in ninth-century England.

---

* One of the only twelve of these coins known to still exist was acquired by a Texan collector in August 2016 for an undisclosed sum.

Figure 1. Sumerian cuneiform-inscribed baked clay coins,
c. 2900 BCE. (*Source*: The National Museum, Baghdad.)

The next revolution – paper money – came from China. Noted financial visionary Kublai Khan created a paper money system through the simple expedient of capital punishment, instituting the death penalty for anyone who tried to use gold or silver instead of accepting his paper money. As Marco Polo noted in *The Travels of Marco Polo*:

> Furthermore all merchants arriving from India or other countries, and bringing with them gold or silver or gems and pearls, are prohibited from selling to any one but the emperor [who] pays a liberal price for them in those pieces of paper... And with this paper money they can buy what they like anywhere over the empire.

Subsequent Chinese rulers, unburdened by Kublai's fiscal rectitude, were responsible for the most dangerous implementation of the technology of paper money: the fractional reserve. They calculated that so long as the merchants believed in the paper money, it didn't actually matter if there was any gold or silver or gems or pearls in the imperial strongroom. They therefore succumbed to the inevitable temptation of quantitative easing and began to print money willy, and very probably, nilly. Their paper currency system eventually collapsed in hyper-inflation (as I suppose they all do in the end) in the fourteenth century and was not independently rediscovered by the next great crucible for monetary experiment – the New World – until the Massachusetts Bay Colony began to issue fiat paper in 1698.

Around the same time as the technology of paper money was rebooted, the last great monetary innovation of the pre-modern age, central banking, arose around the coffee houses of Amsterdam. What were they smoking? But the idea spread, and in 1692 the Bank of England was created for the admirable purpose of financing wars against France. France, incidentally, went on to become the source of all sorts of crazy money experiments that ended in disaster: the assignats, John Law's land bank, the Latin Monetary Union and the euro.

The *past* begins with money as debt in commodities and then a commodity (anything from grain to seashells to gold) or a claim on such. The agricultural revolution led to the rise of cities and the dawn of banking and, eventually, to coins. Stretching from antiquity to early modern times, the technological implementations went from cuneiform to banknotes to printed cheques. The Industrial Revolution then allowed these claims to move faster, by steam train rather than by horse, until technology freed them from the constraints of physicality. The past is about *money as atoms*.

The present: Money 2.0

The present era began in 1871, when Western Union started formal electronic funds transfer (EFT) by telegraph and thus helped us to distinguish properly between invention and innovation. At the time, Western Union's management team turned down the invention of the telephone, rather famously commenting:

> The 'telephone' has too many short-comings to be seriously considered as a means of communication. The device is inherently of no value to us.

That's management for you, you might say, but there was no more reason for a telegraph company to catch the telephone wave than there was for Microsoft to invent Google or, for that matter, for a bank to invent the successor to the payment card. But were they crazy? It took twenty-five years for the telephone to make any serious dent in their telegraph business (a business that peaked in 1929), and while Western Union sent their last telegram a few years ago they still make serious money from EFT. Incidentally, just to reinforce the point that money innovation can come from communications companies, rather than banks, in 1914 Western Union gave some of their best customers a charge card for deferring payment (without interest). I have a suspicion – although googling has failed to either confirm or deny it – that the reason that payment cards are the size and shape they are today can be traced back to that Western Union 'metal money'.

Innovation in banking is about sustained business change. It is not delivering the same business using new technology (Gardner 2009). Throughout this period, the business of finance and payments and investment changed utterly, yet money remained the same, however loosely tethered to the physical by the bonds of Bretton Woods. Personal wealth shifted from bank deposits to mutual funds. Cash shifted from bank branches to ATMs. Payments went from cheques to credit cards. But the money stayed the same.

This period I classify as the *present*. It arrived with electronic communications – when even paper became too substantial and too slow for society, and the invention of the telegraph spurred the innovation of electronic money – and it still dominates the way that the man in the street thinks about money. It is the prevailing paradigm, but it is not the truth (a paradigm is a model, remember, not reality). The present, therefore, is about money as information about physical things (paper that represents gold), or, to put it another way, *bits about atoms*.

The future: Money 3.0

The steps to dematerialize money for consumers – those major postwar innovations of payment cards and money market accounts – began to separate payments and banking, just as money separated from value starting with the end of the gold standard in the 1930s and finishing in 1971 when Nixon ended the US dollar's convertibility. These processes will be completed soon and the final step will come with the transition to the mobile phone as the basic platform for financial services, for the simple reason that mobile phones can accept payments as well as make them, thus ending the need for cash to pay individuals. What kinds of innovation will this invention trigger? When money is completely dematerialized, the cost of introducing new currencies will fall to zero: who will stick with sterling when Facebook credits, electronic gold and the Brixton Pound are only a click away?

Thus, I claim that the *future* began back in 1971, when money became a claim backed by reputation rather than by commodities of any kind. At this point, *money became bits*. The atoms have gone. The only bodies able to provide reputational currencies to implement all the functions of money (especially as a mechanism for deferred payments) were nation states, so the idea of national fiat currencies as the only form of money became embedded. This kind of money is now middle aged and its midlife crisis is just beginning. Its central dynamic is no longer connectivity (since everything is connected to everything else) but community. We can see a glimmer of the future in Facebook and eBay, Zopa and Zcash, PayPal and Craigslist. It is the age of Reed's Law, disconnection technology and the decoupling of currency from the nation state.

The pace of change

You might well wonder why, if that future began a generation ago and we are shifting to a cashless world where reputation is the prerequisite for transactions, we are still using SWIFT to send US dollars from one bank account to another. Well, people have always overestimated the speed of impact of new technology in money. More than fifty years ago, in April 1965, an article in *New Scientist* magazine about the automation of cheque clearing predicted that in a generation the transfer of money would be completely automatic and 'the payment of a birthday fiver from an uncle to a favourite nephew merely a matter of direction and timing of electronic impulses' (Sayers 1965). Within a year of this, the first British credit cards were in customers' hands, and a year after that Barclays launched Britain's first ATM (in Enfield, North London). A year later, in 1968, the precursor to the Bankers' Automated Clearing Services (BACS) was formed and direct debits were launched. Yet that birthday fiver was still sent by post. As it still was in 1975. And 1985. And 1995. Perhaps, just perhaps, it went by PayPal in 2005, by which time BACS was processing two billion direct credits per annum. But today? Today it could well be sent by PayM or Internet transfer, WeChat or Venmo, Facebook or M-Pesa. So how will that birthday £500 (adjusted for inflation) wend its way in 2025 to celebrate the diamond anniversary of that *New Scientist* prediction?

Futurology

How can we begin to think about this redesign of money for a post-industrial age? Well, we can begin with a modest step and then try to work forwards. While sketching the outlines for this book in 2015 I was challenged to envisage the payments landscape in 2025. I thought this challenge would be a good platform to stand on to try to see what impact the new technology of payments might have on money itself.

The first question to tackle was what approach to take, just to reach that more limited goal of trying to picture payments at the modest distance of a decade from now, when we can see that so much is going to change on the technological, social, business and, most importantly of all, regulatory fronts? Well, one of the techniques of futurologists trying to assess the magnitude and direction of technology-induced change is to find an appropriate point in the past to compare with. If you want to imagine the changes coming a generation from now, they would argue, you must look back two generations into the past to correct for the accelerating pace of change.

That line of thinking suggests that if we want to imagine digital money a decade from now, we need to look back two decades into the past and understand the landscape and dynamics of change. A simple way of doing this (see figure 2) is to look at the technologies that support products in the marketplace and, particularly, at the security needed to make them useful.

Cheque clearing	Credit card	MOTO	ATM	Debit card		CNP	Paypal	Mobile money	Instant payments	???
1965	1975		1985		1995		2005		2015	2025
Mainframe	Telecommunications			Magnetic stripe	PC		Smart card	Internet	Mobile phone	Wearable
	Online authorization		Hologram	EMV		One-time passwords		Biometrics	Analytics	

Figure 2. A payments timeline: products, technologies, security.

This perspective-led approach makes good sense for the topic at hand because the mid 1990s were a cusp in the co-evolution of payments, technology and security. Twenty years ago, the world was experimenting with different kinds of debit proposition, smart card technology, offline operation and 'electronification' in the mass-market (salaries, benefits, bill payments and so on). Some debit systems failed and some succeeded, but the experimentation began a period of growth that saw the debit card rise to become the consumer's instrument of choice while prepaid solutions began to spread in the mass market. The march of electrification means that the direct debit has become the way that most consumers pay most regular bills (eight out of ten UK adults have at least one). The rise of the web led consumers and businesses to want new solutions, yet it was another decade before the United Kingdom led the world in introducing instant payments (i.e. real-time transfers between payment accounts held by regulated institutions). Despite 'typically British' scepticism, the Faster Payments Service (FPS) has been an outstanding success (IBSintelligence 2013), bringing us to the point where British consumers expect to be able to use their mobile phones to send money from one account to another, instantly and reliably. Around the world countries are following in these footsteps and evolving that infrastructure still further by bringing in more sophisticated data representation and management to add the ability to carry value-adding data along with the payment.

Technology and timeline

The timeline in figure 2 also provides a useful lesson about the interaction between payments and technology that we should keep in mind as we attempt to look forward: in 1995 the financial sector was focusing on making the most effective offline payment system possible (which led to the Europay–MasterCard–Visa (EMV) standard that is used in all 'chip and PIN' cards) and using it to displace cash. It was doing this just as the whole world went online, with the mobile phone already in use and the web around the corner.

In Europe, the smart card was used in a variety of electronic purse schemes with the intention of displacing cash at retail point of sale. Most failed and had no impact on the world of retail. In the United States, by comparison, we saw myriad efforts to create Internet alternatives to cash and cheques, and while most of those also fell by the wayside, one of them did not: PayPal. PayPal rode the existing rails to deliver a more convenient service to consumers, something that the established players could have done, but didn't. Speaking simplistically, online won! But note that while the electronic purse failed, the technology that was being used to deliver it to the mass market (the smart card) became so widespread it is now unremarkable.

It is very tempting when looking at the current landscape – in fact it is irresistible – to see the current flurry of experimentation around Bitcoin through this lens. It may well be that the new payment mechanism never obtains traction, any more than Mondex or DigiCash did, and we will never use Bitcoins at the corner shop, but that the evolution of the underlying technology, the 'shared ledger', turns into an infrastructure so pervasive that it becomes as unremarkable as the smart card did. The World Economic Forum certainly sees things this way: it says that new financial services infrastructure built on shared ledger technology will 'redraw processes and call into question orthodoxies that are foundational to today's business models' (Bruno and McWaters 2016).

We know where not to look, and that's on our desks. We are already past that inflection point. The installed base of smartphones and tablets is already bigger than the installed base of desktop and laptop PCs. The installed base of iOS devices alone will soon exceed the installed base of all PCs. By 2020, global shipments of PCs will be lower than global shipments of tablets (according to a Statista prediction made in July 2015). But perhaps we should be looking beyond smartphones? Just as the designers of 1995 set about building for an offline world just as it went online, we should be thinking about the next infrastructure, not the current one. And this, I strongly suspect, is the 'Internet of Things'. The Thingternet (as I cannot resist calling it) will naturally stimulate entirely different business models. As figure 3 shows, we can already see these growing around us.

	Internet	Thingternet	What does it mean?
Value creation			
Customer needs	React to existing needs	React to emergent needs	*Payments become a constant flow between devices and the data around payments becomes more valuable than the fees earned from the payments*
Offering	Stand-alone products; obsolescence	Products always-on and refreshed	
Role of data	Single point data used for future product requirements	Information convergence creates services	
Value capture			
Path to profit	Sell the next product	Enable recurring revenue	*Payments are no longer a product managed by banks but part of multiple overlapping ecosystems that transfer many kinds of value*
Control points	IP and brand	Network effects between products	
Capability development	Leverage core competencies and existing resources	Create platforms to help partners to build their businesses	

Figure 3. The Thingternet mindset. (With acknowledgement to Smart Design/*Harvard Business Review*, July 2015.)

The impact of these changes will of course extend to retail. The US Food Marketing Institute predicted that by 2025 customers would no longer wait in lines to check out at grocery stores but would walk out of the door while a 'frictionless checkout' would automatically account for products in their carts – and this prediction was even made before AmazonGo's pilot store was unveiled. This is certain to impact the payments business and not only drives us on towards cashlessness but also drives payments further 'underground' in retail environments.

These trends pivot on the mobile phone of course, shifting to an app-centric model, in which mobile devices coordinate fast, safe and transparent solutions. As I write, one in five payments in Starbucks is already mobile, so this is hardly a radical view. Now we have Android

Pay and Ford Pay, Walmart Pay and CVS Pay, Tesco Pay and Chase Pay. The trend is clear, cash drawers and tills are vanishing from retail, and this means that retail transaction flows will be reconfigured.

Using money in shops, over the phone, on the web and to pay a friend will all become the same experience. Connected devices, instant payments, strong authentication to a token held in tamper-resistant memory will be the converged infrastructure for the invisible payment and will form a platform for the next money.

Where next?

Think for a moment about the *Cutty Sark*, the famous old sailing ship that is dry docked in Greenwich, London. It was a vessel known as a 'tea clipper', built for speed, and at one time it was the fastest ship of its size afloat, famously beating the fastest steamship of its time and doing the Australia-to-United Kingdom run in sixty-seven days. (Yes, I know there's no tea in Australia but the Suez Canal meant that she only carried tea for a few years and was then set to work bringing wool up from down under.) When she was built, high speed was economically important and there was considerable pressure from the tea companies to get the fastest ships: they weren't built just for the fun of it, or to show off technology, but because of economic imperative.

She was commissioned in 1869. Note the timing: the fastest sailing ship was built well *after* the first steamships arrived. The first iron-hulled steamship, the *Aaron Manby*, had crossed the English Channel in 1822. The first steamship with a screw propeller, the *Archimedes*, had been built in Britain in 1839. Brunel's iron-hulled, screw-driven *SS Great Britain* had crossed the Atlantic in 1847. Christopher Freeman and Francisco Louca (2001) summarize this crossover well:

> However, it had taken a fairly long time for the steamship to defeat competition from sailing ships, which also began to use iron hulls. The competitive innovations in sailing ships are sometimes described to this day as the 'sailing ship effect', to indicate this possibility in technological competition for a threatened industry.

In the long run, the sailing ships vanished, except for leisure, and the steamships took over. But when the steamships first came onto the scene they stimulated a final burst of innovation from the sailing ship world, which then stimulated the building of some great ships as a kind of last hurrah.

Perhaps this 'sailing ship effect' can be applied to money. The Bitcoin blockchain is one kind of shared ledger: one of the first steamships, the equivalent of the *Archimedes*. It isn't the kind of liner that eventually transports passengers across the Atlantic in unparalleled luxury and it isn't the kind of tramp steamer that transported most of the world's goods to global markets and it isn't the kind of dreadnought with which Britannia used to rule the waves. It's the kind of steamship that shows that steamships work and sets off a chain of innovation that triggers a sustainable change in the way that the world works.

Let us imagine for a moment that this tortured analogy holds and that the invention of the shared ledger will, just as the steamship did, trigger one final round of innovation in the 'legacy' financial services infrastructure (push payments exchanging fiat currencies between accounts held at regulated financial institutions). Well, if Money 2.0 is going the way of the tea clipper, what will that Money 3.0 steamship look like?

Many years ago my colleague Neil McEvoy and I argued in *Wired* magazine that while the new technologies for the medium of exchange were being deployed in a reactionary fashion to bring improvements to the current money system of national fiat currencies (i.e. the sailing ship effect, although we did not think of it in those terms at the time), they would in future drive such decentralization and be used to create non-fiat currencies (Birch and McEvoy 1996). Our argument was that emerging technologies – particularly the synthesis of cryptographic software and tamper-resistant chips – would, we said (as did many others), make the cost of entry into the currency 'market' quite small.

Many organizations beyond central banks and commercial banks might then wish to create private money. This could be as a means of supplying credit, as envisaged by the Nobel-winning economist Friedrich Hayek in 1970s, or it could be a means of encouraging customer loyalty, as explored by lateral thinker Edward de Bono in the 1990s. There might also be idealistic reasons, as explored by 'Satoshi Nakamoto', the mysterious inventor of the cryptographic asset Bitcoin (Vigna and Casey 2015), and others since 2008. I will explore all these possibilities in my '5Cs' of money creation (central banks, commercial banks, companies, communities and cryptography) in more detail later in this book, before settling on a narrative for the 'next money' that is likely to surprise you.

PART I

THE PAST: MONEY THAT WE UNDERSTAND

Money is technologically equivalent to a primitive version of memory.
— Narayana Kocherlakota when at the Federal
Reserve Bank of Minneapolis (1997)

Where did money come from? Money and banking go back together as far as written records exist, and yet the origins of money are not entirely economic: from tribute as well as from trade, from blood-money and bride-money as well as from barter, from ceremonial and religious rites as well as from commerce, from ostentatious ornamentation as well as from acting as the common drudge between economic men.

As Yuval Noah Harari discusses in his sweeping history of the human race *Sapiens: A Brief History of Humankind*, it is easy to remember who owes what obligation to whom in a kinship group but an economy of favours and obligations is impossible to scale, especially once you add strangers. As we moved from tribes and clans to settlements and king-doms we needed technology to augment our memories. At some point civilization reaches a point where technology takes over from memory. This is the point where the past begins in our narrative.

Chapter 1

Money is a technology

Money talks because money is a metaphor, a transfer, a bridge...
Money is a specialist technology, like writing.

— Marshall McLuhan (1964)

ONEY IS NOT a law of nature: it is a human invention. What is more, the kind of money that we use today is a relatively recent construct. It is in its forties and having something of a mid-life crisis. When Richard Nixon ended the convertibility of the US dollar into gold in 1971, we entered the world of fiat currency described in the introduction. From that day on, dollars have been backed by the full faith and credit of the United States and nothing more. All the world's currencies are now 'pure manifestations of sovereignty conjured by governments' (Steil 2007b). That is why the talk of 'virtual currency' is misplaced. *All* currency is now virtual (i.e. bits): there is no gold in the Bank of England to back my £5 note, and the $100 bill in my wallet has no claim over the gold in Fort Knox.

How did we end up with this kind of money? I'm not going to present a detailed history. There are hundreds of good books about the history of money and I have no intention of attempting to compete with them, or even summarize them here, but I do want to draw out a specific thread around the historical impact of technology on money, and that is about the way in which technology allows for the 'moneyfication' of debt (Graeber 2011a), converting a store of value into a mechanism for deferred payment and then a medium of exchange that can in turn become a unit of account. *Moneyfication* is a horrible word, but I hope you will come to see why I use it to start the story of money's past.

The functions of money

The usual place to begin in an examination of the impact of technology on something – and I am nothing if not conservative in this respect – is to consider what that thing does. What does money do? Since a great deal of the discussion about money is confused because of a lack of understanding about the nature of money, let me begin by being clear on this topic. As most texts about money begin by stating, money has four basic functions.

- It is a *unit of account*. The unit of account does not, of course, have to have any physical reality. The European Currency Unit (ECU) and the Special Drawing Right (SDR) are examples. Brazil's transition from the *cruzeiro* to the *real* began by establishing 'units of real value' as market-based units of account, and gradually adding other functions as the currency moved to have status as a legal tender.
- It is an acceptable *medium of exchange*. Whether it is packets of data or packets of Marlboro, money is useless as a medium of exchange unless it is acceptable to both parties to a transaction.
- It is a *store of value*. Unfortunately, inflation can erode the value of stored money no matter what medium is chosen!
- It is a *means for deferred payment*. For a society to function, it must support contracts between parties that include provision for future payment even when the store of value is subject to inflation or other changes.

Each of these functions may be implemented in a different way. A favourite example of mine is that of the American colonies at the turn of the eighteenth century. The colonists used sea shells (known as 'wampun') for their medium of exchange: a form of cash borrowed from the Native Americans (who were, in effect, the central bankers of this monetary system, converting the shells into animal pelts that were used to store wealth and for external trade). The unit of account was the English pound (despite most of the colonists having never even seen one) and the means for deferred payment was bullion.

A contract, then, might run like this: person A would contract with person B to pay '£10 in gold per annum for rent of the field' or whatever. When the rent fell due, it would be commuted to a £10 beaver pelt (since no one had any gold or silver, as the English refused to export bullion to the colonies). The beaver pelt was purchased with wampum and barter goods. The economy worked and the 'money supply' was based on commodities (pelts) and was stable for many years, until over-harvesting led to a decline in the beaver population: as pelts became scarce, the 'exchange rate' for wampun against pelts rocketed.

Money as memory

Money didn't start as coins manufactured to ease the burden of barter. Money existed long before coins, as did banking (Davies 1995a). Five thousand years ago the societies of the Near East were becoming civilizations and were already using money in the form of tokens representing deposits, taxes due and so forth (Pringle 1998). These tokens initially seem to have represented just three basic 'currencies', representing labour, grain and livestock (goats and sheep), but as cities developed so new currencies soon emerged to represent manufactured and finished goods (e.g. textiles). For the working stiff in the early Near Eastern pre-metropolis, grain (barley) was the most important commodity, because that was how wages were paid. (Barley was used to make both beer and bread: the staples of the ancient diet.)

Around the world a great many kinds of token have been in use at different times. Cowrie shells, whale teeth and the stones of Yap have all served as tokens. Many of these tokens became currencies: units of account against which other tokens were measured. These currencies did not need to be a physical part of transactions to be useful.

The currency in our North American example above was the pound sterling. No one in North America had one of these, almost no one had ever even seen one, and yet it functioned as an agreed unit of account.

This illustrates the important distinction between a money and a currency. Today, we tend to associate currencies with nation states, and their values are, in essence, determined by the ability of those states to obtain revenue. This idea – that decisions on currency are ultimately driven by questions of state power – is what Charles Goodhart has called the 'cartelist' theory of money: that the evolution of money is linked to the needs of the state to increase its power to command resources through monetization of its spending and taxing power (see Kahn 2015). Currencies did not begin this way.

To use just one illustration of this point, note that there was a chocolate standard operating in central and southern America far longer than there was a gold standard. In the *Codex Mendoza* – a manuscript commissioned in 1541 by Antonio de Mendoza, the first Spanish Viceroy of the newly conquered Mexico, and now in Oxford's Bodleian Library – there is a wonderful exhibit from economic history. It is a copy of the 'Tribute Roll', listing 400 towns paying annual dues to the Aztec emperor. The unit of account was cocoa beans and we even know roughly what they were worth because a list of commodity prices from the area in 1545 gives the exchange rates:

- 1 good turkey hen = 100 cacao beans,
- 1 turkey egg = 3 cacao beans,
- 1 fully ripe avocado = 1 cacao bean and
- 1 large tomato = 1 cacao bean.

The first people to grow cocoa were the Maya, who used the beans as a barter currency to exchange for food or clothes, as well as for preparing the bitter drink *xocoatl* (apparently nothing like today's hot chocolate). The Aztecs eventually seized the Mayan land and adopted the beans for trade.

Why did it catch on? To be used as a currency, so that tokens representing a claim on it have value, a commodity needs to be rare or precious. Cocoa owed its value to the difficulties inherent in growing the tree and producing the beans (the low yield made it an expensive commodity) and this made the beans a useful means of exchange. They were fungible (that is, any bean could function in the place of any other bean) and could be divided up. It was a money that had the advantage of encouraging profit without causing miserliness, since the beans did not function as a standard of value and were not hoarded. Those accumulating beans of their own were more tempted to eat them than plant them. For a standard of value, the Aztecs instead tended to use large white cotton cloths (*quachtli*) that represented, in essence, a 'proof of work' (a precursor to the Bitcoin blockchain, I suppose).

The beans provided a stable, widespread and long-lived currency even though they were not a store of value. Henry Hawks, a merchant who spent five years in Central America, wrote in 1572 that in Guatemala the beans 'goeth currently for money in any market or faire, and may buy any flesh, fish, bread or cheese, or other things' (Einzig 1966). In 1712 a royal decree in Brazil listed cacao beans, cloves, sugar and tobacco as commodities that legally circulated as money and noted that troops were paid in these commodities. In nineteenth-century Nicaragua, 100 beans would have bought you a slave.

The cacao beans must have worked well as money: they were observed still being used as 'small-change' money in Central American markets in the mid 1850s. And, as the final confirmation that they were real money, they were counterfeited: fraudsters would extract the chocolate from inside the beans and replace it with mud of an equivalent weight!

Debt

What did these currencies, from barley to gold and from cocoa to sterling, measure? David Graeber makes a case for a simple answer: debt (Graeber 2011b). He observes that the difficulty in the 'chartalist' position (from the Latin *charta*, or token) is to establish why people would continue to trust a token, rather than a commodity, as society develops and points out that the chartalist version of currency (see the later discussion about the Irish bank strike) means providing sufficient token claims against different commodities, whether those are cocoa beans, sea shells, copper axes or anything else.

However, in order to allow everyone even in a medium-sized city to be able to carry out a significant portion of their transactions in such a currency would require millions of tokens and associated guarantees (Graeber 2011b). I should say that while I agree that this would have mitigated against the continued use of tokens in the cities of the pre-industrial and industrial economies, I do not see this as a practical barrier to economic activity in a world of social networks, mobile phones and cryptography, but that is a discussion we will return to later in the book. The key point is that once civilization reaches a certain complexity, money emerges as a claim on debt rather than as a representation of tokens, and it is this debt money that is the origin of our money today.

We know that debt accompanied civilization. We know that interest rates were set in three primary civilizations – Bronze Age Sumer, classical Greece and Rome – at the beginning of their commercial evolutions and remained remarkably stable over the course of each society's development. On an annualized basis, the rate for each new society was lower than that for its predecessor, beginning with 20 per cent for Mesopotamia, where archaeological finds of clay tablets show a remarkably liquid market in personal promissory notes (Goetzmann 2016). Later, in classical Greece, rates fell to around 10 per cent; and then in Rome they were a little over 8 per cent (Hudson 2000). Debt and interest were part of the warp and weft of civilization from the very beginning.

Debt makes for a different perspective on the use of technology to provide money. Money as debt is measured in a unit of currency that, to the credit theorists, is not the measure of the value of an object but an implicit measure of one's *trust* in other human beings. This element of trust, of course, makes everything more complicated. As society evolves, and trust does not scale, these values begin to diverge.

Economic history provides many examples in which the debt used as a medium of exchange was never short-maturity or demandable and therefore must have integrated that measure of trust. The type of longer-maturity notes known as bills of exchange were widely used as a form of payment among merchants until the twentieth century: they were, in effect, instruments created as means for deferred payment that then became stores of value because people would hold them as well as use them to facilitate trade.

Rich as Croesus

Broadly speaking, then, we can see that the idea of money (as a store of value) originated as debt but that tokens were not a practical means of using that debt in commercial transactions. Hence, as we might reasonably expect, ancient societies began to develop a medium of exchange and, for a variety of well-understood reasons, they opted for precious metals, which could additionally serve as a store of value and a mechanism for deferred payment. In the Near East, it was silver that became the standard against which currencies were measured. The shekel, which is something like 5,000 years old, originated as a term for a specific weight before it became a unit of account for reckoning prices.* In Biblical times, standard weights of silver were the trade currency throughout the region, but they still lacked the key ingredient of modern cash: authenticity (Pringle 1998). This problem was tackled, in the West, with the invention of coins in Lydia in the seventh century BCE. Standardized, carrying recognizable images of authority and readily exchanged, within a relatively short time (a few decades) coinage spread throughout the Western world. It was, note, already familiar in the East. There are ancient bronze coins in China (marked 'good for gold') that suggest that cash was well established in the Far East long before it was in the West (Mar 1885).

After coins were introduced, shekel became a general term used to describe silver coins that weighed a shekel, and then later it became the official name for the coin, completing the path from a stable store of value through medium of exchange to unit of account.

We had debt, then we had banking, then we had money, and then, a couple of thousand years later, we invented coins. In inventing coins we invented cash: a medium of exchange that did not need to be redeemed against anything, but that could be self-assayed (within bounds) and passed from person to person indefinitely. Cash is just one form of money, although it dominates mental models because of its simplicity and familiarity, but it is not obviously the best form. Yes, cash

---

*The weight, incidentally, was not that standard: the Canaanite shekel weighed more than the Babylonian shekel, for example (Hockenhull 2015).

is convenient and anonymous, but it bears an implicit tax and is subject to theft and illicit use – another subject that we will return to.

Minted

Throughout early modern times, coins became the standard of value even though they might not have been used a medium of exchange by the majority in a feudal economy. The history of coins in England illustrates this rather well. Guildford, the home of Consult Hyperion (the consulting company that I helped to found many, many years ago), was first mentioned as a Saxon village in the will of King Alfred (who died in 899 and left it to his nephew Ethelwold). It had a few hundred inhabitants but it already had its own mint, one of a number established by England's greatest monarch to mint his silver pennies. He did this because he knew, as other economically aware rulers did, that good-quality coinage has beneficial economic effects. It was not, by itself, the route to economic success (regulated markets, punishment of fraud, witnesses to sales and so on were also components), but it played a part in stimulating trade and, therefore, wealth.

England was, even then, a wealthy country. Bearing in mind that a cow cost a couple of shillings (i.e. twenty-four silver pennies), note that between 991 and 1012 the Anglo-Saxon kingdoms paid £137,000 in tribute to the Danes to buy them off from invading (the 'Danegeld')! Estimating from the number of dies used by moneyers and the quantity of coins produced by each of them, something like three or four million pennies were being struck every year (Dyer 2002a). And we can tell from the wear and tear on the coins found around the country that they were in circulation, not simply being hoarded as a store of value.

Coins remain a remarkably successful technology, as evidenced by the fact that we still use vast quantities of them today. In 2010 the United States produced more than six billion coins, including about four billion pennies and half a billion nickels. In 2011 it produced more than eight billion coins, including five billion pennies and a billion nickels. It loses money on every single one of them (a penny costs around 1.5 cents to make) and a great many of them are simply thrown away.

The Mondex story

A diversion from the Wessex of the ninth century to the Wessex of the twenty-first century will show you where my fascination with the relationship between technology and money stems from. A generation ago, banks in many countries had their first stab at cash replacement with a variety of electronic purse schemes. We can learn from that era. Although it used some new technologies, that first wave of cash replacement was firmly rooted in the paradigm of the present, not the future, using cards to implement electronic fiat currency.

Figure 4. Mondex cards and wallet.

The story of the most 'cash like' of those efforts, Mondex, is I think illustrative, and personal, because I was there on 3 July 1995 in Swindon town centre when a vendor of the *Evening Advertiser* (the local newspaper) made the first ever live Mondex sale! It was a very exciting day because by the time this launch came, my colleagues at Consult Hyperion had been working on the project for some years. Mondex was one of the family of electronic purses based on a tamper-resistant chip (this chip could be integrated into all sorts of things, one of them being a smart card for consumers) but it was unique in that value was transferred directly from one chip to another with no intermediary and therefore no cost. In other words, people could pay each other without going through a third party and without paying a charge. It was designed to be a true cash replacement.

Mondex was invented by Tim Jones and Graham Higgins at the National Westminster Bank (NatWest) in 1990. Swindon was where the public launch of the product took place, in a pilot with Midland Bank (now part of HSBC) and British Telecom (BT). Swindon had been chosen as, essentially, the most average place in Britain, and since I'd grown up there I was rather excited about this!

When the day came, there was good geographic coverage despite the hassle of fitting out the retailers to take the purse. The shops needed special point-of-sale (POS) terminals but they also need special 'unlock' terminals. The cards could be locked using a four-digit pass code, something that customers had requested in focus group discussions, but the only way to lock the cards was by using the custom-built electronic wallets – devices that looked a little like electronic calculators – and the telephones that few customers had. All the shops that accepted Mondex had to be fitted with a lock/unlock device. As it turned out, customers never bothered locking their cards and never used the lock/unlock stations, but it was the fact that the lock existed and that the lock/unlock stations were visible that gave them confidence in the system.

More than 700 of Swindon's 1,000 retailers adopted Mondex, which was an impressive testament to the team effort behind the launch. By and large, the retailers seemed positive (Leighton 2014). The shops and pubs didn't particularly want to mess around with change or take bags of coins to the bank for deposit. Many of the retailers were enthusiastic because there was no transaction charge and for some of them the costs of cash handling and management were high for non-transaction cost reasons. I can remember talking to a hairdresser who was keen to get rid of cash because it was dirty and she had to keep washing her hands, a baker who was worried about staff 'shrinkage', and so on. But while 'from a retailer's point of view it's very good', news-stand manager Richard Jackson said, 'less than one per cent of my actual customers use it'. As he went on to explain, 'Lots of people get confused about what it actually is, they think it's a Switch card or a credit card' (Whittaker 1996).

It just never worked for consumers. It was a pain to get hold of. I can remember the first time I walked into a bank to get a card. I wandered in with £50 and expected to wander out with a card with £50 loaded onto it but it didn't work like that. I had to set up an account and fill out some forms and then wait for the card to be posted to me. Most people couldn't be bothered to do any of this so ultimately only around 14,000 cards were issued.

I pulled a few strings to get my parents one of the special Mondex telephones so that they could load their card from home instead of having to go to an ATM like everyone else. BT had made some special fixed-line handsets with a smart card slot inside and you could ring the bank to upload or download money onto your card. I loved these and thought they were the future! My parents loved it: not because of Mondex but because, in those pre-smartphone days, it was a way of seeing your account balance without having to go to the bank or an ATM or phone the branch.

For the people who didn't have one of those phones (everyone, essentially) the way that you loaded your card was to go to an ATM. Now, the banks involved in the project had chosen an especially crazy way to implement the ATM interface. Remember, you had to have a bank account to have one of these cards, and that meant that you also had an ATM card. If you wanted to load money onto your Mondex card, you had to go to the ATM with your ATM card and put your ATM card in and enter your PIN and then select 'Mondex value' or whatever the menu said and then you had to put in your Mondex card. Most people never bothered. If you go to an ATM with your ATM card then you might as well get cash, which is what people did.

A couple of months after the retailer launch, Mondex ticket machines were installed in six of the town's car parks, and a few months after that card readers were installed in eighty buses that offered reduced fares for electronic cash users. I do remember these as places where the hassle of getting the electronic cash was outweighed by the hassle of using physical cash. My dad liked using the card in the town centre car park instead of having to fiddle about looking for change but it often didn't work and he would call me to complain (and then I would call Tim Jones to complain!).

I remember talking to Tim about this some years later and he made a very good point, which was that in retrospect it would have been better to go for what he called 'branded ubiquity' rather than for geographic ubiquity. In other words, it would have been better to have made sure that all of the car parks took Mondex or that all of the buses took it or whatever. Sadly, the car parks still take cash to this day (and the last time I pulled in to park, I didn't have any, so I had to leave the car and go to a shop to get change and then come back to the car).

So Mondex didn't take a chunk out of cash. Cash is still around. Cash accounts for just under half of all retail transactions. At the time of the Mondex launch, it accounted for more than two-thirds of them. There is progress towards cashlessness, but not because of the electronic purse.

Lessons from Mondex

I learned lessons from all of the many different Mondex pilots: not only the original in Swindon but also the further launches in the United States, Canada and the West Country.

The first lesson is that banks are very probably the wrong people to launch this kind of initiative. Our experiences with (for example) M-Pesa suggest that a lot of the things that I remember that I was baffled and confused by at the time come down to the fact that it was a bank making decisions about how to roll out a new product: the decision not to embrace mobile and Internet franchises, the decision about the ATM implementation, the stuff about the geographic licensing and so on. I was told that when the publicans of Exeter asked the banks to install Mondex terminals in the pubs since all of the students had cards the bank refused on the grounds that the university's electronic purse was only for use on campus. Normal companies don't think like this.

There were many people who came to the scheme with innovative ideas and new applications: retailers who wanted to issue their own Mondex cards, groups who wanted to buy pre-loaded disposable cards, and so on. They were all turned away. I remember going to a couple of meetings with groups of charities who wanted to put 'Swindon Money' on the card – an idea I was very enthusiastic about. But the banks were not interested.

The second lesson is that the calculations about transaction costs (which is what I spent a fair bit of my time doing) did not matter: they had no impact on the decision to deploy or not deploy in any specific application. I remember spending ages poring over calculations to prove that the cost of paying for satellite TV subscriptions would be vastly less using a prepaid Mondex solution than it would if a subscription management and billing platform was built, but nobody cared. I went to present the findings to a bank that was funding satellite TV roll-out at the time, to BT, who were providing the backhaul, and to the satellite TV provider. Nobody cared. The guys at the bank told me that they didn't have the bandwidth for it (which meant, I think, that they had no interest in spending money so that another part of the bank might benefit). The banks with big acquiring operations were being asked to compete against themselves and they didn't care either. The transaction cost, which I thought was the most important factor, was not the main driver.

Now, of course, we know that those tamper-resistant chips are in the iPhone and in Samsung and other Android phones and that they are nothing to do with the banks (or, for that matter, the mobile operators either). We were right about the architecture and the need to anchor digital money in physical security, but we were wrong about who the builders would be.

The third lesson is that while the solution was technically brilliant, it was too isolated. The world was moving in the direction of the Internet and mobile phones and to online in general and Mondex was trying to build something that did not use of any of those things. At the time of the roll-out, I had an assignment for the strategy department of the bank to provide technical input to a study on the future of retail banking that one of the big management consultancies was working on. I remember being surprised that it didn't mention the Internet, or mobile phones, or (and here's something that I thought would be big!) digital TV. As far as I could see, most of their work was on redesigning the furniture in the branches. Mondex was designed to be the lowest-cost peer-to-peer offline electronic cash system at exactly the moment that the concept of 'offline' began to fade. It was not alone in failing to react to this fundamental change and it is an interesting point to ask with hindsight why systems such as Danmont, Proton, Geldkarte, Mondex, SEMP, VisaCash and all the others were determined to compete with cash in the physical world rather than focus on the virtual world where there was no cash?

Figure 5. In twenty years, the futuristic retailers of Swindon went from not seeing any Mondex transactions to not seeing any Bitcoin transactions.

This was clear to me very early in the experiment. This is not hindsight: I drew the same lesson from the Mondex pilots in Canada and the United States as well. The banks put Mondex terminals in places where they already had card terminals that worked perfectly well. You could use Mondex cards in Swindon in the places that acquired bank-issued payment cards (e.g. supermarkets) but not in places where digital cash had a real competitive advantage: on the Internet, in vending machines and in corner shops and newsagents.

I hope I'm not breaking any confidences in saying that I can remember being in meetings discussing the concept of online franchises and franchises for mobile operators. Some of the Mondex people thought this might be a good idea but the banks were against it. They saw payments as their business and they saw physical territories as the basis for deployment. Yet as *The Economist* said in an article titled 'Dreams of a cashless society' back in 2001, 'Mondex, one of the early stored-value cards, launched by British banks in 1994, is still the best tool for creating virtual cash'.

At the same time as this was going on at Mondex, my colleagues and I were working on other projects for mobile operators who had started to look at payments as a potential business. These were mobile operators who already had a tamper-resistant smart card in the hands of millions of people, so the idea of adding an electronic purse was being investigated. Unfortunately, there was no way to start that ball rolling because you couldn't just put Mondex purses into the SIMs: you had to get a bank to issue them. And none of them would: I suspect they were waiting see whether this mobile phone thing would or would not catch on.

Look at how it's gone trying to get banks to use operator SIMs for near-field communication (NFC). Mondex didn't begin to experiment with the Internet for another year, and even then it was severely hampered by the lack of standards for online commerce and payments. I remember many happy hours around the table with a variety of organizations working on what became the Internet Open Trading Protocol (IOTP) in an attempt to get something going here, but it never took off. And besides, alternatives were already up and running: DigiCash went live a year before Mondex. In a fragmenting market, which now had Visa and MasterCard backing different horses, the proposition started to disintegrate.

For a variety of reasons, therefore, Mondex never caught on. It never got even half of the 40,000 hoped-for users in Swindon, and usage remained low. Two decades on, the debit card and the mobile phone (and the combination of the two in Apple Pay, Android Pay, WeChat, Walmart Pay and all the rest) continue to displace cash, we still don't have a mass market cash alternative on the web (yes, I know,

Bitcoin, whatever), and prepaid card propositions, while still expensive (because they use the existing debit rails), are widespread. A decade from now strong authentication, privacy propositions, push payments and immediate settlement networks will achieve what Mondex set out to do: reduce cash to the rump payment mechanism (down to perhaps a third of transactions by volume and a tenth by value) and make person-to-person electronic payments safe and simple.

On 3 July 1995 I thought I was witnessing the dawn of a new era in financial services. In fact that happened a month later with the Netscape IPO on 9 August.

Chapter 2

1066 and all that

The old practice of using tallies as a virtual currency made out of public debt.

— Christine Desan in *Making Money: Coin, Currency and the Coming of Capitalism* (2014)

COINS WORKED WELL in the pre-modern age, but of course once trade reaches certain levels and complexity, coins become a burden. At the beginning of the eleventh century, rents in England were collected in goods, services and (least importantly) coin. By the end of the of the century rents were being collected as money, starting a commercial revolution (Spufford 2002). This transition in time resulted in a shortage of coin, and a particular and recurrent lack of coins of small denominations – a theme we will return to in discussions about two revolutions: the French one and the Industrial one. Growing prosperity and trade meant a 'bullion famine', as it has been dubbed by historians, which was an outflow of silver to the east that was not matched by new supplies from mining. Governments were faced with hard decisions on how to keep the economy running on diminished quantities of silver. In England, the mint, which had been accustomed to producing coins worth at least £1,000 a year, was reduced to producing only £182 per year by the early fifteenth century (Dyer 2002b).

Across medieval Europe, then, a money economy was developing, but there wasn't that much money in circulation. Remember Graeber's comment that money is a yardstick that measures debt? Focusing on

England, the case of the tally stick makes this real. Tally sticks came into use in England after the notorious war criminal William the Bastard's illegal invasion and regime change of 1066. Tax assessments were made for areas of the country and the relevant sheriff was required to collect the taxes and remit them to the king. To ensure that both the sheriff and the king knew where they stood, the tax assessment was recorded by cutting notches in a wooden twig and then splitting the twig in two, so that each of them had a durable record of the assessment. When it was time to pay up, the sheriff would show up with the cash and his half of the tally to be reckoned against the king's half. As the system evolved, the taxes were paid in two stages: half paid up front at Easter and the rest paid later in the year at Michaelmas, when the 'tallying up' took place.

The technology worked well. The tally sticks were small and long-lasting (after all, they still exist!), they were easy to store and transport, and they were easily understood by those who couldn't read (i.e. almost everyone). As a new technology, however, they soon began to exhibit some unforeseen characteristics (in the context of their record-keeping function). During the extended period of use of any technology, creative people come along and find new ways to use the technology in different times and in different cultural contexts. Tally sticks were a form of distributed ledger to record debt, and were soon being used as money.

Tally-ho!

By the time of the reign of Henry II (who died in France in 1189) the exchequer was already a sophisticated and organized department of the king's court, with an elaborate staff of officers. The use of tallies to enable this operation had an interesting consequence. Since (as is generally the case) the king couldn't be bothered to wait until taxes fell due, and could not borrow money at interest, he would sell the tallies at a discount. The holder of the tally could then cash it in when the taxes fell due, making it (in effect) a fixed-term government bond. Since paying interest was forbidden by the church, selling tallies at a discount became a key means for the Crown to borrow money without God noticing what was going on.

The discount on the tallies, being equivalent to the interest rate for government debt, varied just as one would expect. As economic circumstances changed, so did the discount rate. As Adam Smith notes in *An Inquiry into the Nature and Causes of the Wealth of Nations* (Book V, Chapter 3: 'Of public debts'), in the time of William of Orange the discount reached 60 per cent when the Bank of England suspended transactions during a debasement of the coinage. Clearly, then, the tally system could be (and was) abused by the exchequer selling tallies that they would not redeem, but the Crown soon learned not to renege on tallies since doing so meant that the discount on future tallies would increase and the exchequer would be hit hard.

In summary, then, by the middle of the twelfth century there was a functional market in government debt centred on London. The Crown allowed the tally sticks to circulate as a functioning medium of exchange insofar as it gave a present value to the tallies that people held (Desan 2014b). No wonder the London money markets are so sophisticated: they've been doing it for a thousand years. I often fall into the trap of thinking that there's never been a revolution in monetary technology before, so I forget how rapidly previous significant developments were co-opted by the financial 'establishment' and taken for granted or just how old some aspects of the apparently modern financial infrastructure are. And it's not just government bonds. When the Doge of Venice died in 1238 he left an estate indistinguishable from a modern portfolio: 7 per cent in cash (coins) and the rest in negotiable municipal bonds and 'partnerships', a precursor to equities (Wood and Buchanan 2015).

The market for tallies evolved quickly. Someone in (say) Bristol who was holding a tally for taxes due in (say) York would have to travel to collect their due payment or find someone else who would, for an appropriate discount, buy the tally. Thus, a market for tallies grew, arbitrating various temporal and spatial preferences by discounting. It is known from recorded instances that officials working in the exchequer helped this market to operate smoothly (Davies 1995b). The distributed ledger technology of the tally had been used to convert a means for deferred payment into a store of value and then into a means of exchange, and the sticks remained in widespread use for hundreds of years.

The Bank of England, being a sensible and conservative institution naturally suspicious of new technologies, continued to use wooden tally sticks until 1826: some 500 years after the invention of double-entry bookkeeping and 400 years after Johannes Gutenberg's invention of the printing press. At this time, the Bank came up with a wonderful British compromise: they would switch to paper but they would keep the tallies as a backup (who knew whether the whole 'printing' thing would work out, after all) until the last person who knew how to use them had died.

Figure 6. Medieval tally sticks. (*Source*: Winchester City Council Museums (Flickr), via Wikimedia Commons.)

Thus, tally sticks like the ones shown in figure 6 were then taken out of circulation and stored in the Houses of Parliament until 1834, when the authorities decided that the tallies were no longer required and that they should be burned. As it happened, they were burned rather too enthusiastically and in the resulting conflagration the Houses of Parliament were razed to the ground (Shenton 2012), which is why they are now the Victorian Gothic pile designed by Sir Charles Barry, built from 1840 onwards, rather than the original mediaeval palace. I find this an incident so loaded with symbolism about the long-term impact of innovations in the technology of money that had it occurred in a novel no one would have believed it.

Technology and markets

The technology of money, like all technologies, exhibits the law of unintended consequences, and this stands square in the way of anyone who claims that they can clearly see the direction that a new technology will take (Postman 1993). The story of the tally illustrates this point well: what began as a technology for the record keeping of debts soon went on to become the basis of a money market; and then it went on to remain in use long after 'better' alternatives were available. As historian David Edgerton nicely phrases it, the modern world is a world of 'creole' technologies: technologies transplanted from their origins to find use at a greater scale elsewhere (Edgerton 2006). It is impossible to say what the unintended consequences of current innovations in financial technology will be, but we can observe that there will be some.

While not the subject of this book, I do find it interesting to note the role that the City of London played in shifting the new technology of the tally from debt to medium of exchange. London has always survived and thrived through the introduction of money technologies: ranging from banknotes and bills of exchange, through derivatives and EFT. The City has always been associated with financial innovation and, crucially, the creation of markets. Look at insurance, where it is preeminent. London didn't invent insurance: the preamble to the Insurance Act of 1601 talks about it as a long-established business (Raphael 1994). Indeed, it starts with the words: 'Whereas it hath bene tyme out of mynde an usage amongste Merchantes...'.

What London did invent was the insurance *market*: Lloyd's. Today, the City of London is still good at being a market. It handles 41 per cent of world foreign exchange dealing (more than New York and Tokyo combined) and 17 per cent of global bank lending (Home Office 2016). Nearly two-thirds of all international bonds are issued in London, and three-quarters of the trading of them takes place in the City. The City is the world centre for settling gold trades, and at the millennium half the world's oil cargoes were fixed up on the Baltic Exchange (Jacomb 1998). London is the principal wholesale market for the euro, even though the United Kingdom has never been part of the eurozone (and soon will not even be part of the European Union). All things considered, there doesn't seem to be any reason for the City to be worried about the blockchain or quantum computers, provided it does what it always has and takes advantage of technological change.

To be fair, recent governments have done much to advance the City's position as a 'fintech' crucible, and Brexit or no Brexit I am sure that London will remain a place of monetary experiment and innovation.

A warning from history

From wooden tally sticks we move on to the first great paper money experiment in China. That it was in China is unsurprising: they were the first to invent paper and printing, the precursor technologies. But it took real innovation to turn paper into money, and that came from the Mongols.

Mongol fiscal policy was initially confused: when Genghis Khan took control of China in 1215, his pacification plan was to kill everyone in China – no small undertaking since China was then, as now, the world's most populous country. Fortunately, one of his advisors, a man who ought to be the patron saint of finance ministers everywhere, Yeliu Ch'uts'ai, pointed out (presumably via a primitive abacus-based Treasury model of some sort) that dead peasants paid considerably less tax than live ones, and the plan was halted.

The economy grew. In 1260 Genghis's grandson Kublai Khan became emperor of China. He decided that it was a burden to commerce and taxation to have all sorts of currencies in use, ranging from copper 'cash' to iron bars, to pearls to salt to specie, so he decided to implement the paper currency noted by Marco Polo.

His legal tender policy was refreshingly straightforward and more robust than we are used to today. If you didn't accept his paper money in full and final settlement for debts incurred, he would kill you. Naturally, in a short time, the new single currency was established and the paper money began to circulate instead of gold, jewels, copper coins and metal bars.

Unfortunately, this paper money ended in disaster because the money supply was not managed: it collapsed in hyperinflation because in the days after Yeliu Ch'uts'ai the temptation to print money was just too great for the monetary authorities to resist. In effect, the Chinese rulers were printing their own counterfeit money.

Experimenting and experiences

Let us accept counterfeiting as a manageable risk and return to the story of paper money. It is interesting to note that the fledgling United States, which had strongly resisted the notion of a central bank (the Federal Reserve was not created until 1913 – a direct consequence of the banking collapse of 1907), was the home of the first great monetary experiment of the industrializing world and ended up with the world's reserve currency. So can we continue with the story of the colonies to see if we can find any useful analogy between Britain's view of North America in the early eighteenth century and our view of the virtual world today that might tell us something about future trends in money?

How about this one? A superpower is bogged down in a distant guerrilla war. The superpower must resupply its army (victorious for a generation) thousands of miles from home, and that has become a costly exercise. Support for the war is tentative, dividing both the people and the political leadership. The guerrillas are supported – financially and militarily – by the superpower's greatest enemy. The war drags on as casualties mount and generals are disgraced. The rebels continue to gain momentum, even though they are occasionally beaten. Are we talking about Iraq? Vietnam? No. This is historian Kenneth Davis's brilliant description of British North America in 1782. The analogy, worth serious examination, tells us that unenforceable unfair legislation causes disputes that will lead to secession. It is easy to see the roots of these disputes emerging:

- a distant colony where conditions are different;
- politicians taking actions they feel constrained to implement even while they are being advised that they are acting against the nation's best interests (in 1774 Viscount Rockingham, Britain's 'Minister of War', had said that a land war in America would be useless, costly and impossible to win);

- legislators trying to fit something they don't understand into existing models (British politicians operated in almost complete ignorance of America: none of them had ever been there, they knew no Americans, unlike the merchant classes, and made no effort to learn anything about it).

The colony analogy also tells us that the world of banking and finance may be changed as much as the world of politics and commerce. In the American colonies, as discussed earlier, bullion for coins was scarce because Britain wouldn't export any, an action that led to one of the great revolutions in money: the issuing of banknotes not as a means of substituting for some otherwise inconvenient means of exchange but as a means of *creating* money. Starting with the Massachusetts Bay Colony in 1690, banknotes were issued by impoverished authorities to avoid the high costs and uncertainties associated with borrowing and the need to impose taxation.

What would it mean to create new stores of value? We looked at the chocolate standard earlier. Out in the British colonies the store of value was related to some physical good: often, but not always, gold. The United States was on a tobacco standard for twice as long as a gold standard. Tobacco was made legal tender in Virginia in 1642 – by the outlawing of contracts calling for payments made in gold or silver – and remained so for two centuries. The US gold standard, as noted, lasted only from 1879 to 1971.

In an era of blockchains and smartphones, entry barriers to virtual financial businesses are low, so one might today expect to see monetary experimentation on a par with the young United States. It is possible that the most revolutionary impact of new technology will come from its ability to monetize new forms of debt rather than from its ability to act as a useful means of exchange, thereby creating new stores of value that are claims over that debt. This is one of the reasons that I remain sceptical about the new virtual currency Bitcoin (this is, again, something that we will return to in Part III of the book).

If the colony analogy holds, we would expect just such a development and the emergence of not only new forms of money but a whole new virtual finance industry, as different from our existing finance industry as fractional reserve banking was from the striking of electrum coins in Lydia. Who would bet against a new standard emerging – an energy standard, as for example envisaged by the artist Austin Houldsworth in chapter 15 – that is not related to first- or second-wave commodities but to claims against the future production of goods or the delivery of services?

Writ large

As an aside there is a further interesting parallel with the old New World to be found between the row going on about encryption and spying on people on the Internet and the row that went on in the colonies about taxation. In the 1760s the British government introduced the Writs of Assistance to clamp down on the evasion of customs duties. These didn't work, of course, because the cost of enforcement vastly outweighed the revenues collected. The writs were not peculiar to America and similar legislation was introduced in England, such as the hated Cider Tax, which prompted William Pitt's famous tirade in opposition:

> The poorest man in his cottage may bid defiance to all the force of the Crown. It may be frail; its roof may leak; the wind may blow through it; the storms may enter; the rain may enter – but the King of England cannot enter; all his forces dare not cross the threshold of the ruined tenement!

This is as good a call for privacy as anything since. Back then, the British government was still concerned that the colonies might be overrun by their eighteenth-century equivalent of today's terrorists, money launderers, drug dealers and child pornographers: namely, the French, who still had a toehold in Louisiana. Britain tried to get the colonies to pay for their defence from these menaces, but they would not.

Things went from bad to worse. As American historian Barbara Tuchman observed, a consistent feature of the dealings between the British and the Americans in this period was that each side overestimated the goals of the other. The Americans thought that the British were concocting a huge conspiracy to enslave and subdue them when in fact the British were just being stupid. The British thought the Americans were aiming to subvert the Crown when they just wanted fair treatment. British intransigence, when compromise was both sensible and feasible, created rebels where there were none before. Is this that different from the current situation, where the netiscenti suspect the NSA and GCHQ of wanting to read their email while the Home Office sees subjects that are suspicious of this as agents of anarchy.

There's no need to labour the analogy: as we all know, the colonists decided against the many benefits of British rule. This was a disaster because, as Edmund Burke was later to observe, the retention of America was worth far more to the mother country economically, politically and even morally than any sum that might have been raised by taxation, or even any principle of so-called constitution. Will we be thinking the same about 'cyberspace' a generation from now, taxing fiat currencies to scratch out an existence while the new wealthy have their money in Facebook Credits, Kilowatt-Hours or Parking Places?

Chapter 3

Money and markets

> There is required for carrying on the trade of the nation, a determinate
> sum of specifick money, which varies, sometimes more, sometimes less
> as the circumstances we are in requires.
>
> — Sir Dudley North in *Discourses upon Trade* (1691)

NEW TECHNOLOGY BRINGS along new opportunities. In the Western, capitalist tradition, new technology works with long cycles of change in a well-understood way. The recession that follows the collapse of a bubble once again creates conditions for the emergence of a new economics and of new policies. In the context of financial innovations, these policy tools will have to conform closely to the characteristics of the current technological revolution and its paradigm (Perez 2005), which is why I think it important to separate the present paradigm from the present time, if you see what I mean.

Thus, technological evolution often leads to crises as the technology races ahead of institutions and legal systems, but the crises may be an indispensable part of the co-evolution of financial services, because they in turn lead to regulation that puts markets onto a firm footing and allows them to grow even more. Money needs regulation. When money is produced by the temple or the local mint or the sovereign, this regulation is straightforward. But what happens when the production of money drifts beyond those centralized and controlled options?

The production of money does not have the properties of a natural monopoly and there is no technical necessity for money to be produced by a monopolist, let alone by the state (Glasner 1998), something we will discuss in more detail later in the light of new technology. But as the feudal system faded in the thirteenth century, the typical European money-issuing authority was still a feudal mint under the control of a local lord, or sometimes a bishop, serving the needs of the mainly rural population. The main object of the monetary policy of such a ruler was to raise revenue, whether honestly by seigniorage or dishonestly by debasement. Although he might be constrained in some ways, the deeds of trade or the benefits of stable prices would not concern him (Chown 1994a).

This was about to change, however. The great invention of capitalism is the creation of titles to assets – bank accounts, bonds and stocks – that can be cashed in with varying degrees of ease and that make money available to enterprise (Mayer 1998a). Those titles, like the tally sticks, become money. Whereas the debt underlying the tallies was tax debt, there are plenty of other forms of debt that could be turned into money.

Empire and states

In the middle ages the great trade fairs of Europe (that grew up in France to facilitate trade between Italian and Flemish merchants) saw the emergence of new forms of debt, turned by paper into new forms of payment. These fairs, which lasted about six weeks, began with commercial trading and then ended with financial trading as, during the last two weeks, the bankers and other intermediaries managed their loans, did their foreign exchange trading and traded letters of exchange. At that time, the Lombard, Low Country and Jewish bankers were the most widely represented and transactions were carried out on the basis of mutual trust between them. As the fairs wound down, the bankers would offset transactions through an informal clearing system.

In the fourteenth century the fairs declined in importance as commercial transactions were replaced by direct trading between the Flemish, English and Mediterranean ports. However, even after the fairs declined in importance as far as the sale of goods was concerned, they gained importance as money markets. They became times and places where loans could be raised, payments for goods sold elsewhere could be made, and buyers and sellers of bills of exchange could be sure to find one another (Spufford 2002).

The bankers no longer needed to meet each other in person because, with the rise of literacy, signatures on paper could be recognized by all the correspondents, who undertook to honour the accompanying financial transaction. The creation of private postal services made the carrying of bills of exchange easier, and they became de facto means of moving money and capital.

In time, the trade fairs were completely replaced by financial fairs and they moved (because of the power of the Genoese bankers) from France down to Piacenza, near Milan, where they became the largest financial fairs in Europe from the end of the sixteenth century and into the seventeenth. The Genoese had established the function of the bank as a money merchant and separated this function from that of the 'merchant banker', who invested in trade and industry. The finance and wealth based only on paper astonished traditional Italian bankers and those of northern Europe, but they all had to adapt to the new reality so as not to be swept aside by this technological revolution in banking and finance (Giraudo 2007).

Bankers from Flanders, Germany, England, France and the Iberian peninsula came together four times each year to meet with the Genoese, Milanese and Florentine 'clearing houses' at the Piacenza fairs. The clearing houses put down a significant deposit to participate and in return they fixed the exchange and interest rates on the third day of the fair. As well as the bankers and clearing houses, there were moneychangers, who presented their letters of exchange, as well as representatives of firms and brokers.

During the fair, everyone tried to clear the transactions in such a way as to limit the exchange of actual coins and I cannot help but see a mimetic echo of this in the current development of payment channel technology around the blockchain, such as the Lightning network that has counterparties clear off-chain tokens and then net settle in Bitcoin. Any outstanding amounts were either settled in gold or carried forward to the next fair with interest. This was the first structured clearing system in international finance and it made international trade far more efficient, greatly increasing the prosperity of all involved. The system lasted until 1627, when the Spanish Empire went bankrupt (again) causing serious losses to the Genoese bankers who were its principal financiers (and who, sadly for them, had no access to a taxpayer-funded bailout). As a result of this collapse, the financial centre of Europe was drawn by the strange attractor of innovation first to Amsterdam – which, as we will see, already had a new kind of bank for efficient inter-merchant transfers and was developing newer instruments including futures and options – and then onto London.

The growing international trade facilitated by bills of exchange had a political significance as well as an economic one. Felix Martin refers to the seventeenth-century writings of Claude de Rubys, a man who understood clearly that the creation and use of bills drawn on the banks, a private form of money, was not only an economic innovation but also the seed for revolution because it put money beyond any one sovereign's jurisdiction (Martin 2013). And, crucially, it was a private form of money that was substituting trust for bullion.

Gresham's law

There was, in essence, a war brewing. This was a war between bullion and paper, a war between the state and commerce. It was a war between kings and bankers, and the bankers won, as evidenced by the story of Sir Thomas Gresham, a story I was reminded of a few years ago when I was pottering around Barclays Bank's splendid headquarters in London's Canary Wharf and came across a fascinating artefact. In a glass display case up on the top floor there is a ring given by Sir Thomas Gresham, one of the most important people in the history of money, a man who ought to be on the fourth plinth in Trafalgar Square, on every banknote printed in England and universally revered as the patron saint of monetary innovation.

Thomas the Bank Engine

What does Sir Thomas's ring have to do with Barclays? He was a pioneer of lending and borrowing money in England and became the greatest of the London merchants. In fact, he is seen as the 'Father of English Banking'. He served Henry VIII, Edward VI, Mary I and Elizabeth I and founded his own bank, which eventually became Martins Bank. This, via a series of mergers including that with the Liverpool Bank in 1918, ended up as the only major UK bank with headquarters outside London. Martins was at the forefront of banking advances and in 1967 unveiled the first 'automatic cashier' in the north of England, in Church Street, Liverpool.

Figure 7. Sir Thomas Gresham.

Meanwhile, Barclays Bank had been incorporated as a joint stock bank in 1896 by the amalgamation of twenty private banks, based mainly in East Anglia and the home counties. Further important amalgamations followed, with the United Counties Bank in 1916 and the London Provincial and South Western Bank in 1918, and in 1919 controlling interests were purchased in the British Linen Bank and the Union Bank of Manchester, complete amalgamation with the latter being effected in 1940. In 1969 Martins Bank was merged into Barclays Bank: hence the chain from Sir Thomas to Canary Wharf and the display of the ring on the thirtieth floor.

But that's not the only reason why he's important.

Let me take you back to the City of London in the sixteenth century: the time of Henry VIII. Henry is quite famous to many people, primarily because of his ground-breaking approach to marriage and his pioneering work on interfaith relationships, but he's famous to me because of his economic incompetence. Like a great many dictators throughout history, he mistakenly thought that the laws of supply and demand could be suspended in the case of money. Therefore, he abused the prerogative of 'seigniorage'. Seigniorage is, essentially, the profit that accrues to the issuer of money (a £10 note does not cost £10 to make!). We'll discuss it further in Part III.

Henry had been adulterating the English shilling, the basic coin of the realm, by replacing 40 per cent of the silver in the coin with base metals. This was a clever way, he thought, to increase the government's income without raising taxes. This 'Great Debasement' began in 1542 and, as is so often the case on this sceptr'd isle, it was initially undertaken for a good cause (war against France), but it was economically illiterate and ultimately led to a collapse in the commerce that was the real source of England's wealth.

Henry told the mint to add six ounces of copper to every ten ounces of sterling silver it used to make pennies. A few months later, the amount of copper was increased to seven ounces per pound, then to ten, then to twelve and finally, under Edward VI, to thirteen.

It was, in short, a sneaky devaluation device. Henry hoped the people wouldn't notice but, of course, they did, and this 'bad money' drove out the pure silver shillings then in circulation because people kept the good shillings as a store of value and used the bad shillings as a medium of exchange in the marketplace, thereby damaging commerce for many years until Good Queen Bess called in the debased coinage, melted it down, separated out the copper and reissued a pure silver coinage.

This episode led Sir Thomas to derive his eponymous maxim: 'bad money drives out good' (although it should be noted that he was far from the first person to understand the principle). It might be more accurately rendered as 'bad money drives out good money at fixed exchange rates', since at floating exchange rates the market will simply adjust: thus, one Zimbabwean dollar used to be worth considerably less then one World of Warcraft gold piece. If an economically illiterate dictator (in Zimbabwe, for example) had set the exchange rate between Zimbabwean dollars and gold pieces at one-to-one, then sane citizens would offload all their dollars for worthless trinkets as soon as possible while hanging on to their gold pieces. This is because even though the rate is one-to-one, no rational consumer would really believe that a Zimbabwean dollar is really worth the same as a gold piece, so they wouldn't want to make them a store of value.

No one studies history

Henry's Great Debasement was, of course, just one of a multitude of debasements that began with the invention of money and continue to this very day. Consider the example of the Democratic People's Republic of North Korea, under the stewardship of the Korean Worker's Party and the divine tutelage of Kim Jong-il, the Dear Leader. The Dear Leader was famous for being the greatest golfer in history but was also a top-notch economist. In 2009 he caused chaos in North Korea by revaluing the country's currency and sharply restricting the amount of old bills that could be traded for new ones and wiping out personal savings.

When the North Korean people were not eating tree bark to stay alive, they must surely have noticed that the revaluation of the unit of account had not made the slightest difference to the supply and demand for goods and services. It had made a difference to the market, though. The revaluation and exchange limits triggered panic, particularly among market traders with substantial hoards of the worthless old money. Gresham's law took immediate effect: the new currency disappeared from the marketplace and people began to use whatever hard currencies they could get their hands on, forcing the Dear Leader to grab hold of the invisible hand. He banned everyone from using dollars or euros and the national TV network began exhorting the populace to immediately report counter-revolutionary elements using dollars.

I'm not saying that it's only dictators who don't understand how money works, and I'm certainly not trying to imply that money cannot be debased under a democratic government, as it was under Henry VIII, but I do want to emphasize the point that the marketplace needs a circulating medium of exchange and that it is the marketplace that is the source of wealth – something that Sir Thomas Gresham understood very well.

Exchange and market

Something else that Sir Thomas understood very well was the relationship between the market and sovereign power. He learned about borrowing, lending and foreign exchange while living in Antwerp. In 1587 he was responsible for an act of economic terrorism for which he should be celebrated by financiers everywhere. He 'cornered' bills of exchange drawn on Genoan banks so effectively that he was able to disrupt the build-up of resources for Phillip II's Great Armada, demonstrating how sophisticated economic warfare had become by the 1580s.[*]

Sir Thomas's role in the City of London was of lasting consequence: he founded the Royal Exchange and I cannot resist including the following description of the act:

> Sir Thomas Gresham, an opulent merchant of London, actuated by a laudable desire to facilitate commercial transactions, made a noble offer to the corporation, of erecting, at his own expense, a convenient bourse or exchange, for the accommodation of merchants, to meet and negotiate their business in; if a proper situation was provided for him. The city accordingly purchased fourscore houses, which composed two alleys leading out of Cornhill into Threadneedle-street, called new St. Christopher's, and Swan alleys, for 3532 pounds. They sold the materials of these houses for 478 pounds and Sir Thomas Gresham, with some of the aldermen, laid the first bricks of the new

---

[*] For further reading, I heartily recommend Neil Hanson's excellent book *The Confident Hope of a Miracle: The True History of the Spanish Armada* (2004).

building, June 7, 1566, each alderman laying one, with a piece of gold for the workmen: and the work was pursued with such alacrity, as to be roofed in by the month of November, in the following year. The queen would not have it called, as in other countries, the Bourse; but, when it was finished, came and dined with the founder, and with the heralds at arms, by sound of trumpets, proclaimed it by the name, of the Royal Exchange.

He went on to die of apoplexy – which may well be a common fate for those who truly understand money – and left an astonishing legacy.

Thus we move on to the critical point in this story. The development of banking institutions posed a threat to the existing sovereign state monopoly over money. If the benefits from banking and financial intermediation were not to be lost, the emergent nation state had to cope with the threat without actually suppressing the banks (Glasner 1998).

Tulips from Amsterdam

I cannot help but imagine that the London bankers of the early seventeenth century looked at free-thinking Amsterdam – the epicentre of innovation in financial services – as they look at the blockchain now: as a strange and exotic place where all sorts of bizarre experimentation in finance and financial services is underway, with outcomes that can only be guessed at. Close your eyes and you can hear the London traders of four centuries ago laughing about the idea of ledger money as ridiculous while considering tulip speculation to be a perfectly reasonable commercial venture. After all, tulips are in the end pretty and people like them, whereas no one would accept marks on paper rather than bullion. Yet it was in Amsterdam that an entirely new kind of bank was founded: the Amsterdam bourse began to develop new kinds of trading supported by that bank, and the well-known crisis caused by tulip mania led to regulated derivatives markets (Jay 2000).

This came about because of an innovation in the relationship between banks and markets. There had been calls for some sort of 'payments bank' (that is, a financial institution that did not extend credit, and therefore could not fail, but that could facilitate value transfers between people) as far back as the fourteenth century in Venice. This was in recognition of the difference between a bank to facilitate transfers in space and a bank to facilitate transfers in time (which involves the provision of credit). The two are not the same thing at all (and I have every reason to think that the recent temporary conflation of the two will not last).

It took a couple of hundred years for a payments bank to actually happen, and a number of experiments with local institutions to clear interbank payments took place in a number of different cities. The first central bank, the Bank of Amsterdam (the Amsterdamsche Wisselbank, founded in 1609), was, essentially, one of these municipal banks that provided a reliable and trusted payment mechanism but with an important difference: there were legal restrictions on settlement outside of the bank (Norman *et al.* 2011). The Amsterdam merchants were forced to open accounts there because of the law demanding that commercial payments had to be through the bank. They could deposit all sorts of different coins to credit their accounts and then make payments by instructing account-to-account transfers (Jay 2000). The result was that Amsterdam supported a vibrant commercial marketplace with access to safe, efficient and very inexpensive payments.

In parallel, the bourse was growing and experimenting with the trading of, well, everything, as Amsterdam became the Amazon.com of the seventeenth century, where everything was available to everyone (Shorto 2013). The existence of this marketplace gave the city an immediate comparative advantage because of its access to information. In modern terms it meant that merchants were able to allocate their capital in the most efficient ways. Among other things, the bourse traded derivatives. Futures trading in the Amsterdam markets had its origin in the sixteenth century and futures were traded on the Amsterdam exchange just like any other commodity.

Derivatives fed the tulip mania and the subsequent crash, although the reasons for the crisis and crash are not as clear as you might think. Some observers see the tulip market's collapse as a response to financial regulation, not market fundamentals (see 'Was tulipmania irrational?', *The Economist*, 4 October 2013). Government officials, who were themselves speculating on the markets, were planning a rule change to convert futures contracts into options, which would mean that people who had undertaken to buy tulip bulbs in the future could pay a small amount to cancel the contracts if the price was not in their favour. This, of course, tipped the market in favour of the speculators and led to a rise in the price of options (which then collapsed when the government decided not to go ahead with the rule change).

It is fascinating, looking back, to see how the Dutch government eventually gave up trying to outlaw futures trading, deciding instead, in the later seventeenth century, to regulate and tax it. As a consequence, by the 1680s there were futures contracts, options (puts and calls), margin trading and even index trackers available to Dutch investors. While the English were busy with the early Industrial Revolution the Dutch were busy with the early financial revolution, and they had Europe's most efficient economy for a hundred years until the French and the British began to attack their domination of trade by sea.

Newtonian mechanics

Queen Elizabeth I's coinage reforms had taken England into a new monetary age, with gold and silver in circulation. Unfortunately, since England couldn't control the price of gold or silver, this wasn't a particularly stable arrangement and led to a severe lack of silver coinage, which was needed for everyday transactions. England had an industrial revolution, but it didn't have industrial money.

Towards the end of the seventeenth century the government gave up passing pointless laws about money (such as the 1660 act forbidding the export of bullion) and instead of asking investment bankers or celebrities for advice in the modern fashion, they decided to ask someone clever instead. And so it was that the smartest man that ever lived, Sir Isaac Newton, then the Lucasian Professor of Mathematics at the University of Cambridge, was appointed the Master of the Mint. Newton quickly figured out what was wrong and changed money in such a way as to set England on a path of economic growth (Levinson 2009).

Newton looked to harness more technological innovation to transform money. First, he suggested that the mint should use machines to
make coins instead of people. This would vastly reduce the cost of production (and therefore increase mint profits) and would also introduce
uniformity and consistency to the coinage. Second, he suggested that
the machines 'mill' the edge of the coins to prevent further clipping.
The King himself agreed to these changes, with his proclamation of
19 December 1695, referring to 'the great mischiefs which this our
kingdom lies under, by reason that the coin, which passes in Payment,
is generally clipped'.

Newton's conclusions were correct (matching an industrializing
economy to industrial production of money) but it still took a generation (thirty years, in fact) to replace the old, clipped, hand-made coins
with shiny new emblems of the nascent Industrial Revolution.

Figure 8. Post-medieval clipped silver coin: probably a shilling of Elizabeth I.
(*Source*: The Portable Antiquities Scheme/The Trustees of the British Museum.)

But think about the magnitude of the changes. By the time Newton
died in 1727, a generation after the currency crisis, Britain had a central
bank (the Bank of England), banknotes in wide circulation, a proto-gold
standard (another of Newton's innovations) and a functional coinage
based on both gold and silver coins. At the time of the Glorious Revolution of 1688 none of these had existed. I make this point just to illustrate
how quickly change can come: we can't imagine anything other than

central bank currency, bank money and payment cards any more than the citizens of Stuart England could have imagined £5 notes.

One more point, and one that was well made by Milton Friedman (1992). Without a shadow of a doubt, Britain's later decision to fix on a monometallic gold standard (in 1816), largely because of the inconvenience of having heavy silver coins in daily use, was the key factor that made gold the dominant monetary metal, making it yet another example of the law of unintended consequences. The economic history of the world would have been very different if Britain had chosen instead to retain bimetallism or to resume convertibility on the basis of silver.

Chapter 4

Crises and progress

The bourgeoisie ... has pitilessly torn asunder the motley feudal ties that bound man to his 'natural superiors', and has left remaining no other nexus between man and man than naked self-interest, than callous 'cash payment'.

— Marx and Engels in *The Communist Manifesto* (1848)

N O ONE KNEW THERE was an Industrial Revolution under way at the time, but the transition to a society of urban anonymity instead of rural reputation – an economy of cash wages instead of feudal obligations – meant that there had to be a new kind of money for the new kind of economy just as there will have to be a new kind of money for the post-industrial economy.

The settlement

It is hard to tell whether the foundation of the Bank of England was inevitable or accidental. The private banking system was developing nicely and there was no public demand for a public bank (Chown 1994b). No matter how it happened, the creation of the Bank in 1694 announced a revolutionary settlement between the City and the state and, in effect, the creation of capitalism in its modern sense. The government shared its monopoly on money creation with a private institution and in return obtained a debt manager and access to finance.

Both the Tories and the Whigs hated the idea, by the way, as did goldsmiths and pawnbrokers, although luckily their lobby was not strong enough to prevent it (Thornbury 1878). Politicians were concerned that the 'power of the purse' would be transferred from the House of Commons to the governor and directors of the Bank (today we think that that is a good thing!) but they needed the cash. What came about as a result of 'a long-running guerrilla war between sovereigns and the private monetary interest that neither side could win' (Martin 2013) was the basis of the modern monetary system. Following the Glorious Revolution of 1688, the Dutch revolution in finance and the English revolution in industry collided to recreate money.

When the Bank's notes began to circulate as a medium of exchange, this was a by-product of the Bank's activities, not its purpose. Note that the smallest banknotes it issued were more than the average annual wage, so most people went through life without ever seeing one. The Bank did not issue its first £5 note for another century

We had reinvented paper money and it never went away again.

Cheque mate

We also had other kinds of paper payments coming into use at this time, one of which may well vanish in my lifetime: cheques. The earliest surviving European cheques are Tuscan, although the word itself appears to derive from the Arabic 'sakk', a written order for payment made through a banker. The oldest extant European cheque was drawn on the Castellani Bank in Florence in November 1368 (it was to pay for black cloth for a funeral). Within a hundred years cheques were in common use (Spufford 2002). Around about the time that paper money, central banks and America were being invented, the cheque in its modern form (that is, a cheque that could be endorsed and circulated) was invented, and we still use those today (some of us, such as the French and the Americans, more than others). But their end is in sight.

Cheques and clearing

The earliest of these modern cheques in the UK dates from 1659: it instructs a London goldsmith to pay £400 to a certain Mr Delboe

(Sinclair 2000). Not long after these cheques were invented, cheque clearing was invented. London bank clerks, tired of running round to every bank to clear cheques, began to meet (unofficially) at a coffee house to clear and settle between themselves. Some years later the banks realized that their clerks' idea was a good one and in 1833 they established a clearing house at 10 Lombard Street in the City of London.

In those days, of course, everything was accounted for with quill pens on paper and the clerks physically walked the cheques around to the clearing house. It therefore took three days for money to move from the payer's account to the payee's account: impossible to imagine in our electronic age (unless you live in America of course).

Figure 9. Cheque signed by Thomas Jefferson during his second term as president of the United States. (*Source*: National Numismatic Collection, National Museum of American History.)

Three centuries on a great many British retailers no longer accept cheques, and have not done so for a while (Daley 2008). In the United Kingdom, George Osborne, when he was the Chancellor of the Exchequer, set out a firm mandate to energize the British economy by forcing the payments industry to reduce cheque clearing from three days to two – this may well usher in a new economic age, although I frankly doubt it. The cheque's days are numbered, no matter how efficiently they are processed.

It seems that the cheque may well be the first payment instrument to vanish in my lifetime because the existence of instant payment systems means it no longer has an economic function. I'll return to this later in the book when we move on to the spread of instant payments and the potential for a 'push for push' in retail payments.

Buttons and bank acts

Industrializing Britain saw more changes in the way that money worked as it strove to reinvent money for its new economy. As the nature of that economy had changed, so the nature of money had needed to change too, but it lags. At the time, it was not clear exactly what needed doing. People could see that there were problems but not what do to about them.

Naturally I refer to this time because the Internet, mobile phones and online commerce are creating a vortex that is sucking in monetary innovation at an accelerating rate, my point being that we have been here before. Consider the relationship between private and public provision of small change (coins, essentially), which has been brought back into focus by discussions about micropayments in an online world (Selgin 2008).

When the Industrial Revolution caused an explosion in population and commerce in Georgian England, the lack of small change shifted from being an annoyance to being a major national problem, holding back growth and development. Factories had no coins to pay their workers, workers had no coins to buy their essentials and the economy was suffering. Furthermore, by the end of the eighteenth century most of the coins in circulation in Britain were counterfeits. Gresham's law meant that there was widespread acceptance of counterfeits because there were few legal coins in circulation. A shopkeeper might have four copper trays in his till: pennies, ha'pennies, good counterfeits of same, and 'raps' (counterfeits that could not easily be passed on).

Transaction costs were climbing and commercial exchange was often accompanied by disputes over the money used in payment. Merchants began to stipulate the weight of coin needed to settle a transaction and workers' pay days were often the basis of disputes about the value of wages. Rarely was any transaction made without an argument. Quarrels over money values were continuous; market days and fares were regularly scenes of brawls. Wages paid by employers to their workers were the cause of many Saturday-night disputes regarding the value of their money: 'such was the result of the apathy and ignorance of the government in so neglecting the currency' (Josset 1962).

While government did nothing, the private sector took action. The people involved were those at the centre of the industrialization storm, largely from Birmingham. The nascent metal-bashing industry there, the emergence of organized production (Matthew Boulton's factory) and the expanding skill base meant that the supply chain for medals and buttons and the machines to make them could be readily adapted to coins. The industrialists used the latest technology of steam presses, whereas the government did not. At the same time, the supply of copper (the world's largest copper mine was in Anglesey at the time) meant that the right raw material was in the right place at the right time.

What was the result of this technological change? It was that coins changed from commodity money (i.e. gold and silver to the face value) to token money (i.e. base metals and alloys worth a fraction of the face value). And it was, crucially, the private sector that caused the shift, with the public happy to accept the token money that, presumably, no one in government thought worth providing. There was money for the wealthy (banknotes and gold and silver coins) but there was no money for the masses. You couldn't buy a loaf of bread or a pint of beer with a banknote or a silver coin so private industry stepped in to mint copper token money, and this token money circulated particularly in industrial centres to (very successfully) facilitate wage payments and retail spending. A remote example? Not at all, and not only on the web. It's exactly the situation in, for example, Zimbabwe today, and it looks as if private industry is going to have a go! There are several mobile money schemes there, with many banks connecting to the 'ZimSwitch' mobile banking platform.

(As an aside, in his splendid book *Good Money* George Selgin asks why the private mints put so much effort and invention into creating such high-quality tokens and suggests that marketing was one of the key reasons: because high-quality tokens were good publicity – adverts for the skills of the companies involved. I wonder if mobile money services will similarly serve to advertise the competencies of mobile operators?)

These tokens gained rapid acceptance and by 1795 the problem of small change was almost solved with the official (or 'Tower') coins trading at a discount against the private alternatives. What happened then? Well, around two decades later the official government mint adopted token currency and began issuing modern coins. Could we see a similar trajectory in the post-industrial economy? This would suggest that private operators might step into the market to fill the void and then, when the competition had run its course and the 'best' coinage had been established, the government would step in and provide it as a public good. Perhaps, as we will discuss later when we talk about digital currency, the Bank of England should run its own version of PayPal and the government should insist that everyone has an account if they want to receive state payments of any kind: welfare, pensions, wages and so on? Once all money is digital, as opposed to the current 96.3 per cent of it (in the United Kingdom), who knows where that will take us? At some point in the future the government might adopt a digital payment technology that is in widespread use in the private sector (let us set aside exactly which technology for the time being) and make the final shift of cash from atoms to bits – a subject we will return to in Part III.

The last major money innovation of that age was the conclusion of the relationship between banks and the state through the monopolization of currency by the central bank. In short, the government took control of monetary policy and the central bank became the sole backer of currency, and in return the commercial banks became responsible for money creation. At this point the commercial banks, the money system and the modern state became fused together: all, in effect, aspects of one another (Lanchester 2016).

It was quite a big step. If you look at the United Kingdom as an example, the Bank of England has not always been the sole issuer of banknotes in England and Wales, as it is now. Acts of 1708 and 1709 had given it a partial monopoly by making it unlawful for companies or partnerships of more than six people to set up banks and issue notes. The ban did not extend to the many provincial bankers – the so-called country bankers – who were all either individuals or small family concerns. The Country Bankers' Act of 1826 allowed the establishment of note-issuing joint-stock banks with more than six partners, but not within sixty-five miles of London. The Act also allowed the Bank of England to open branches in major provincial cities, which gave it more outlets for its notes.

In 1833 the Bank's notes were made legal tender for all sums above £5 in England and Wales so that, in the event of a crisis, the public would still be willing to accept the Bank's notes and its bullion reserves would be safeguarded. Later, the 1844 Bank Charter Act was the key to the Bank achieving its gradual monopoly over note issue in England and Wales. Under the Act no new banks of issue could be established and existing note-issuing banks were barred from expanding their issue. Those whose issues lapsed – because, for example, they merged with a non-issuing bank – forfeited their right of issue. The last private bank-notes in England and Wales were issued by Fox, Fowler and Company, a Somerset bank, in 1921.

Figure 10. Barings circular letter of credit from 1892.

While the central bank was reorganizing the currency, the commercial banks were reorganizing deposit taking. The first joint-stock bank in Britain, the London & Westminster, opened in 1834 (Ellinger 1940). Note that the Bank of England refused to open an account for it or extend private banking facilities!

From joint-stock banks the next step was limited liability banks. Limited liability banking was made legal in 1858 but it was only after 1878 that it began to take off. You can probably guess why. When the City of Glasgow bank failed in 1878, the shareholders had to pay £2,750 for every £100 in stock they owned (Ellinger 1940) as there were no taxpayer bailouts for bankers in those days. The calls for limited liability from the share-owning middle classes were answered and banks assumed their modern form.

Scotland the Brave

Foreign readers may be unaware that, as the foregoing discussion of the extension of the Bank of England's monopoly implied, banks in Scotland and Northern Ireland issue their own banknotes. There are nearly £3 billion worth of Scottish banknotes in circulation (as well as half that much in Northern Irish banknotes). For odd historical reasons the issuing banks had to back their note issue with a deposit of 95 per cent of the value of notes outstanding, but only at weekends! Seriously. So during the week they can lend the money out and earn seigniorage. The Scottish banks currently earn good money this way so any change would lose Scottish banks some of the £65 million they now earn in interest and 'seigniorage' (income from selling their notes to other banks).

I have a particular interest in the history of Scottish banks because of the lessons from their period of 'free banking'. This does not, as you might think, mean that Scottish banks were once operated as charities but that they were free to compete in note issue. And the result, as most historians would confirm, was a period of incredible innovation when the more tightly regulated London and country banks failed more often than the less tightly regulated Scottish banks did (I know this is a flimsy précis of a complicated and interesting period, but I'm trying to make a bigger point). In fact, the famous writer Sir Walter Scott is commemorated on banknotes in Scotland precisely because he fought off the Bank of England's 1826 attempt to stop Scottish banks from issuing their own notes (*Economist* 2008).

Table 1. Scottish innovations in finance.

When?	What?
1695	Britain's first joint stock clearing bank, the Bank of Scotland, created by the Scottish parliament
1728	The first overdraft is granted by the Royal Bank of Scotland
1750	The British Linen Bank (Scottish, despite the name) starts to build the world's first branch network
1777	World's first multicoloured banknotes printed by the Royal Bank
1810	First savings bank established in Ruthwell
1826	Royal Bank of Scotland launches banknotes printed on both sides
1845	Westminster, despite Scottish protests, legislates against private note issue; since this date no major commercial banks have been formed in Scotland

In the era of independent free banking it was Scotland that had an enviable track record of innovation in the finance and banking sector. When the previous wave of innovation (paper money) swept through the economy, Scotland was far more successful than England in exploiting technological change to make the economy more efficient (and more stable). By 1850, in fact, when 90 per cent of all commercial transactions in France were still being settled in gold or silver (as were a third of those in England), 90 per cent of all commercial transactions in Scotland were being settled with paper (Ferguson 2001).

(Therefore, one cannot help but wonder if a future independent Scotland might once again become a hotbed of innovation when freed from the dead hand of the Old Lady of Threadneedle Street.)

Accounting for taste

In *A Christmas Carol* Charles Dickens wrote of something becoming as worthless as 'a US security': presumably a phrase that was recognizable to his readers when the novella was published in 1843.

To understand where the phrase originates you have to remember the state of the American economy in the 1830s: a time when – as Jason Goodwin puts it in his splendid *Greenback: The Almighty Dollar and the Invention of America* – 'America's money just grew and grew' because the volume of silver in circulation was climbing, land values were soaring and the Second Bank of the United States was printing dollars. Rising land prices and easy credit (heard this anywhere before?) led to the 'Panic of 1837' when Andrew Jackson shut down the Second Bank and commercial banks began demanding specie and refusing debased paper. This panic was followed by a five-year depression, with the failure of banks and then-record-high unemployment levels. Hence Dickens's disparaging phrase.

We Brits were not, of course, immune to boom and bust at the time. Here, as *Hard Times* Dickens was chewing his pencil, the railway boom was underway (see Christian Wolmar's fabulous *Fire and Steam* for a beautifully written history of this), leading to a colossal crash in 1866. It was caused (and here's a surprise) by the banking sector, but in that case it was because they had been lending money to railway companies who couldn't pay it back rather than to American homeowners who couldn't pay it back.

The British government then, as in 2008, had to respond. It suspended the Bank Act of 1844 to allow banks to pay out in paper money rather than gold, which kept them going, but they were not too big to fail and the famous Overend & Gurney went down. When it suspended payments after a run on 10 May 1866 (the last run on a British bank until the Northern Rock debacle) it not only ruined its own shareholders but caused the collapse of about 200 other companies (including other banks). The directors were, incidentally, charged with fraud, but they got off as the judge said that they were merely idiots, not criminals.

The railway companies at the time held the same commanding position in the world's largest economy as companies such as Apple and

Exxon do in the United States today, so the impact on UK plc was substantial. Bear in mind that the first railway service in the world started in 1830, running between Liverpool and Manchester, and less than two decades later (by 1849) the London and North Western Railway was already the biggest company in the world. When the directors of these gigantic enterprises went to see the prime minister in 1867 to ask for the nationalization of the railway companies to stop them from collapsing (with dread consequences for the whole of the British economy) because they couldn't pay back their loans or attract new capital, they didn't get the Gordon Brown approach of 2008: investment bank advisers, the suspension of competition law and much tea and sympathy. Benjamin Disraeli told them to get stuffed: he didn't see why the public should bail out badly run businesses, no matter how big they might be.

Needless to say, the economy didn't collapse. As you may have noticed, we still have trains and tracks. A new railway industry was born from the ruins, the services kept running and the economy kept growing. But there was another impact of great relevance to the story of money. The introduction of basic corporate accounting standards following the collapse of the railway companies was a significant benefit to Britain and aided the development of Victorian capitalism (Odlyzko 2011). You can't make an omelette, as the saying goes, without letting the bad eggs go to the wall. Just as the tulip crisis had led to regulated futures and options contracts, the railway crisis led to the creation of accounting standards. These standards determined what transactions were recorded in ledgers, how those ledgers were audited and what the state of the world represented in the ledgers meant. The standardization of profit and loss, assets and liabilities, credits and debits meant that the people could invest their money in far-flung enterprises of which they knew little.

Beginning money again

This chapter has naturally focused on England as it was the crucible of the Industrial Revolution. However, there are some other lessons to be learned from this period. While England was experimenting with banknotes and cheques, with capitalism and a gold standard, France was experimenting with revolution. England exported its revolution to the colonies and began a series of unplanned steps towards a new money. France, however, tried to reinvent money along with everything else and as a result delivered a fascinating case study in the relationship between money and trust, between the monarchy and the citizens, between the state and industry.

Rebecca Spang cautions against using the story of the attempted reinvention of money following the French Revolution as part of the 'transition to capitalism' (Spang 2015a), but as a non-historian, and with only the most limited knowledge of revolutionary France, it does seem to me that there is something for today in comparing the evolution of money in industrializing Britain with the evolution of money in revolutionary France. To me, it is a contrast between British mercantile pragmatism and flexibility in response to changing circumstances (you might want to label this 'muddling through' for short) to exploit bottom-up innovation, on the one hand, and French idealism and top-down change on the other.

Money in France was very different from money in England. In pre-revolutionary France it was the monarch's prerogative to set the exchange rate between the money of account (*livre*) and the money of reckoning (the coins, such as the ecus). In the last twenty-six years of Louis XIV's reign, this changed forty-three times (Spang 2015b). There was very little of this money out there in the real economy because pre-revolutionary France was, as pre-industrial England had been, a reputation economy. That is, there was virtually no cash in circulation. The great majority of the population engaged in commercial activities with well-known and trusted counterparties. For the great majority of the French population, buying and selling was done 'on tick'. That is, people would maintain a web of credit relationships for periodic reckoning. This is an economy based on trust, and once that trust is disturbed the substitute of money is required to oil the wheels of commerce. This is precisely what happened in France.

After the French Revolution, a lack of trust in the state quickly led to a shortage of credit in the marketplace and, therefore, to an immediate demand for a circulating medium of exchange. But from where? France did not have a central bank along the lines of the Bank of England. The failure of John Law's note-issuing Banque Royale in 1720 had turned the French away from banking, and the nearest thing to a central bank was the Caisse d'Escompte, which had been formed in 1776 but granted too many loans to the profligate state and over-issued its notes.

One of the first acts of France's new revolutionary government was to take over church lands and, on the basis of this security, to issue interest-bearing bonds with the redemption being a portion of the land itself. The interest and redemption were soon abandoned and the notes, the *assignats*, simply became state-issued inconvertible fiduciary notes. There followed what Glyn Davies calls 'the usual consequences': inflation, dual pricing (with note payers forced to give more than coin payers), hoarding and (Gresham's law again) the practical disappearance of coins and capital flight across international borders (Davies 1995c).

This was the first time that the French state had attempted to control the money supply (Spang 2015c). To be honest, it didn't end well. By October 1795, 100 Franc assignats could be traded for only 15 sous in coin and the Paris riots of the time opened the door for Napoleon. It wasn't until the Bank of France was founded in 1800 that the nation at last enjoyed the same kind of public institution that England, Holland and Sweden had had for more than a century.

There seems to me a useful comparison to be made between those revolutionary times and ours. If we expect the state to come up with some grand plan to reinvent a money *de nos jours*, we run the risk of it going hopelessly wrong. If we leave a regulatory space for the button makers to play in, they may well come up with a better idea.

A final point. Spang notes that when the assignats were put into circulation, people treated the new paper currency as the bills of exchange that they were familiar with. They did not value the anonymity of the currency, since they signed them and passed them on. Who had used a note attested to its validity, and the identity of the previous holders gave the notes value: an idea we will see reinterpreted from an artistic perspective in the chapter called *Reimagining Money*. Identity was the new money, so to speak. Fungibility is not all that.

PART II

THE PRESENT: MONEY THAT WE THINK WE UNDERSTAND

The judicious operations of banking, by substituting paper in the room of a great part of this gold and silver, enables the country to convert a great part of this dead stock into active and productive stock.

— Adam Smith (1723–90) in *An Inquiry into the Nature and Causes of the Wealth of Nations* (Volume I, Book II, Chapter II)

During Victorian times the combination of technology and regulation brought us to a vision of money and markets that we recognize. This vision is one of a central bank in control of nation state currency, money creation by fractional reserve banks and paper circulating in the place of commodities. (It is true that America did not yet have a central bank, but the die was cast.) We had banknotes and bank accounts, futures and options, savings and loans.

For the purposes of this discussion, then, we mark the present – the Money 2.0 era, the era of electronic money, the technological era of bits about atoms – as beginning in 1871 with the launch of Western Union's electronic funds transfer service. Money 2.0 ended, somewhat conveniently for this narrative, exactly a hundred years later, in 1971, when we entered the era of virtual money.

I call this era 'the present' because it accords with the mental models of money that are embedded in society. People believe, by and large, that money is anchored in something, even though they are not sure what that something might be, and this model dominates *thinking* about money even as the Money 2.0 era draws to a close and we examine the pressure for change, the mounting pressures for a seismic change to Money 3.0.

Chapter 5

Goodbye Pony Express

And commerce is the purpose of the far greater part of the communication which takes place between civilized nations. Such communication
has always been, and is peculiarly in the present age, one of the primary
sources of progress.
— John Stuart Mill (1806–73) in *Principles of Political Economy*
(ed. W. J. Ashley; Book III, Chapter XVII)

O N 3 APRIL 1860 a freight company started the Pony Express to
move mail between St Joseph, Missouri, and Sacramento, California.* The riders rode seventy-five miles at a stretch, changing horses every ten miles, so that the mail travelled the 1,900 miles
in ten days. It was a very ambitious start-up, intent on transforming
communications across a continent.

Speed was of the essence, so eventually everything was removed
from the horse except one revolver and a water sack to cut down
on the weight. There are documented emergency cases when a
rider rode two stages back to back, which meant more than twenty
hours on a galloping horse. The riders rode day and night, winter
and summer, receiving $25 per week in pay. (A comparable wage
for unskilled labour was about $1 per day for a twelve-hour day of
labour.)

---

*This story is wonderfully told in Glenn Bradley's 1913 book *The Story of the
Pony Express* (which is available in a 2010 facsimile edition published by Kessinger Publishing).

Despite its iconic status, and its lasting place in American history, the Pony Express was a commercial failure. It lasted only eighteen months: when the transcontinental telegraph was completed on 24 October 1861, the Pony Express was doomed. It closed *three days later* with a total loss of something like $200,000. Sending payments faster than a galloping horse was a genuine break with the past – a genuine revolution. The telegraph marked the beginning of the end for physical money.

Telegraph

The history of Western Union should be a focus for anyone interested in the confluence of finance and telecommunications: the 'electronification' of money. It began life as the New York and Mississippi Valley Printing Telegraph Company in 1851 and expanded by buying out competitors to try and build a national network, eventually acquiring some 500 companies. In 1856 the company changed its name to Western Union Telegraph Company, and it completed its transcontinental telegraph when the lines from each coast were famously joined at Salt Lake City after only 112 days of construction.

It is difficult today to imagine just how enormous the impact of that interconnection was. (Apart from anything else, it led to the introduction of standardized time zones and Western Union's clock circuit telegraph network, which was used to synchronize time across the United States and remained in service until the 1970s.)

Telegrams and telephones

By 1884 Western Union was a giant: it was one of only eleven stocks used to create the first Dow Jones Transportation Average in 1884, although I suppose you might argue that its decline began well before that when, in 1876, it turned down the opportunity to buy Bell's patents on the telephone for $100,000. Bell instead used these patents, which are often called the most valuable patents in history, to set up his own phone company: a company that was grossing a million dollars per annum well before the Dow Jones started. Yet at the time, Western Union management were making the right decision on the basis of the information available to them. As Clayton Christensen points out, it is very difficult for an incumbent to justify investment in new technology when it creates a different business model because it will always earn more in the short term from investing in its core business; competitors have asymmetric motivation (Christensen *et al.* 2005). And naturally, if the incumbent asks its customers what they want, they will direct the investment in the same direction.

Were the management wrong? It was twenty-five years before the telephone made serious inroads into Western Union's business, a business that was still growing at that time despite the cost of telegrams falling continuously (Christensen *et al.* 2005). When the company began, a telegram cost $20 (a vast sum for the times). By 1868 that had fallen to $1.04, and by 1898 it was 30 cents. When telegrams hit peak volume in 1929, the company carried 200 million messages. In its final year a decade ago it carried only 20,000 and generated only half a million dollars (see 'STOP – Telegram era over, Western Union says' from 2006: http://nbcnews.to/2mioF2U).

Follow the money

The telegram business has gone away but Western Union has not. How did this come to be? It was the unexpected consequences of the interplay between technology and money. By 1858 around one in eight of the telegrams sent on the major New York to New Orleans route were in code: commercial organizations had simultaneously realized the value of the new network and the need for security. Governments tried to ban the use of encryption on the telegraph network, as governments generally do, but eventually gave up after the formation of the International Telegraph Union in 1865.

A few years later, Western Union developed a proprietary standard for the transfer of sums of up to $6,000 in fifteen designated major cities, and of up to $100 throughout the rest of United States. It worked using a system of secure code books and passwords, and was a great success. They had invented EFT, which went on to be their main business!

As an aside, I cannot resist pointing out that Western Union has another special place in the history of modern financial services. In 1914 it issued a consumer charge card, so-called metal money, for making calls and having them charged to an account. The idea of metal 'charge plates' was not new even then, as they had been in widespread use by department stores, but the idea of a mass market cash replacement in a particular sector was certainly a milepost on our road.

Paper

Throughout this period, paper money replaced specie almost universally in the industrializing world. The pound sterling and the mighty dollar were universal currencies, linked by the gold standard, and global trade was at all-time highs. And the greenback is still, today, a universally acceptable means of exchange. As a technology, paper money worked pretty well, provided that the level of counterfeiting was tolerable – an observation that provides the opportunity for me to tell one of the most interesting stories of counterfeiting in the history of the world.

Unexpected consequences

The 2007 Oscar for best foreign film went to *The Counterfeiters*, directed by Stefan Ruzowitzky. It is the true story of a plot to destroy the Allied economies during World War II and is based on the memoir of Adolf Burger, a Jewish Slovak typographer who was imprisoned in 1942 for forging baptismal certificates to save Jews from deportation. He was sent to a camp to work on 'Operation Bernhard'.

Operation Bernhard was the Nazi plan to devastate the British and American economies by flooding them with counterfeit banknotes. They took 143 Jews from a variety of trades – printers and engravers plus at least one convicted master counterfeiter, Salomon Smolianoff – and moved them from a variety of death camps to the special unit ('Block 19') at Sachsenhausen. There they set about forging first the British and then the American currency. And they succeeded. They were able to make sterling notes that fooled the Bank of England and then, almost at the end of the war, fake dollars.

As the Allied armies converged on Berlin, the contents of Block 19, including printers' plates and counterfeit bills, were jammed into crates and chucked into Lake Toplitz in Austria. These crates were subsequently retrieved by treasure hunters searching for Nazi gold and looted art, which is how come some of the notes were preserved for collectors (indeed, I have two of the original counterfeit notes in front of me as I write).

The Nazis were therefore never able to put their plot into operation. The original idea, conceived at the very start of hostilities, was to drop the worthless banknotes over England, thus causing economic instability, inflation and recession. Remember, in 1939 the German people had very recent memory of worthless paper currency devastating the economy, so to them this must have seemed like a weapon of mass destruction. In total, the prisoners forged around £132 million, which is about four billion quid at today's prices.

Figure 11. A genuine fake banknote from Sachsenhausen.

Now, printing four billion quid's worth of worthless paper money not backed by anything might sound like a reasonable way to destabilize the economy, but I don't think it would have worked. Following the recent financial crisis, under what is now known as 'quantitative easing'

(QE) rather than 'counterfeiting', the Bank of England printed more than two hundred billion imaginary pounds (i.e. fifty times as much as the Nazis) and rather than crash the economy, they stabilized it. Many other central banks have also done this on a large scale. And yes, I know, QE isn't actually printing. It takes the form of asset purchases, mainly from non-bank financial companies, which serve to increase the amount of money in circulation. It achieves this by adding to bank balances (i.e. those of the companies that the assets are purchased from) because, as we will discuss in Part III, money is actually created by commercial banks, not central banks (McLeay *et al.* 2014).

It is impossible not to observe that some people think that Hitler's roll-out method (i.e. dropping the money from planes) would have had a more positive impact on economic growth than the method used by many central banks (i.e. giving the money to banks who, by and large, kept it). So is quantitative easing a sound government policy or a secret plot to destroy our economy? Were the Khan's successors printing real or counterfeit money? That depends on your perspective. I will leave the topic by highlighting the final supreme irony of Hitler's attempt to ruin sterling: Laurence Malkin points out that after the war the Jewish underground passed on thousands of the counterfeit banknotes to help Holocaust survivors fleeing to the British Mandate for Palestine and purchasing war matériel for the nascent Israeli army (Malkin 2008).

Chapter 6

Consumer technology

> The currency as we manage it is a wonderful thing. It performs its office
> when we issue it. It pays and clothes troops and provides victuals and
> ammunition; and when we are obliged to issue a quantity excessive, it
> pays itself off by depreciation.
> — Benjamin Franklin (1706–90) in a letter to Samuel Cooper (1779)

A T THE SAME time as the structures of post-Bretton Woods money
took hold, new technology began to revolutionize the experiences of consumers in the mass market. The development of
the payment card and the ATM changed the way that consumers saw
(perhaps even felt about) money, setting in train a fundamental change
in the very idea of currency. As banking automation proceeded in parallel with these new technologies, the notion of cashlessness brought on
by technology began to form and grow. (We now know, looking back,
that we would have to wait for the future – the world of the mobile
phone and smart chips – before cashlessness became a realistic goal.)

The evolution of the payment card is, in particular, important for
the study of future money because it involved technological, business,
social and regulatory change.

The card

When the first modern card network (Diners Club) was launched in
1949, the idea that there would be an essentially free and ubiquitous

network connecting all consumers with all merchants and all banks was unimaginable* so it made complete sense to invent just such a network: by telephone and post, in the first instance, so that merchants would phone the network for authorization and then send in their slips for payment.

Figure 12. Cards are part of the fabric of everyday life.

If you want to see how payment cards worked in those early days, the days before magnetic stripes or the Internet, check out the old Danny Kaye movie *The Man from the Diners' Club* (written by William Blatty, who went on to write *The Exorcist*). There was a wonderful report about the world première of this film in the *Hartford Courant* (23 October 1962):

> The Board of Selectmen unanimously adopted an ordinance Monday night to prohibit the use of money and place the entire town on credit for a day next March 13. Columbia Pictures 'The Man from the Diners' Club' will have its world premier at the Strand Theater here that day. On the day of the premier, all transactions by local merchants will be by Diners' Club cards only. The ordinance says it will be 'unlawful for any person to pay cash for any article or goods purchased and it shall be unlawful for any merchant to accept cash for any article or goods

---

* Although not unimaginable to science fiction authors: see Robert Heinlein's *Beyond This Horizon*, for example.

sold.' Diners' Club cards will be issued to the entire population of the town for the premiere day with junior cards for children. The ordinance states 'any merchant convicted of a violation of this ordinance shall be punished by forfeiture of his vendor's license and any other person convicted of a violation thereof shall be punished by confinement in the town stockade for not more than a day.'

The mayor, a Mr John E. Lynch, was reported as saying:

I am especially pleased to participate in this progressive experiment in the use of credit which may prove to the business world that the future method of transacting business will be through such a device as a single credit card.

I was so fascinated by this story of what is, as far as I know, the first movie to feature a payment card as a plot device that I ordered a copy. Sadly, it's not a very good movie (although it was quite fun seeing a young Telly Savalas hamming it up as a gangster). The plot is irrelevant, but I couldn't help noticing that at several points in the film characters stopped the action so that they could explain how a Diners Club card worked. Someone would say 'now I'm going to phone Diners Club to check that this card is valid' and someone else would say 'Hey, the Diners Club card comes with a booklet showing you all the places you can use it', or an incredulous supporting player would gasp when told that you could use a Diners Club card to pay for an airline ticket. I assumed that Diners Club had sponsored the movie or provided some commercial support to introduce the idea of a payment card to a wider audience.*

Credit where credit is due

Diners Club was a charge card. Customers paid the bill in full at the end of the month, as they did with the American Express card when it was launched. The credit card came soon after. On 18 September 1958 (there should be a national 'Payments Day' holiday on this date) Bank of America

---

*Although when I spoke to the world's leading authority on this film, Lana Swartz from the University of Virginia, she told me that there is no evidence of direct commercial support.

officially launched its first 60,000 credit cards in Fresno, an unremarkable town in California. They did this by simply delivering credit cards to the adult inhabitants, an action labelled the 'Fresno drop'.

If you want a good introduction to the history of the credit card, from the Fresno drop right up to the Internet, I'd recommend Joe Nocera's *A Piece of the Action* (Simon & Schuster, 1994), which I read many years ago and still pick up from time to time. There is no need to repeat Joe's work here, but I do want to highlight the fact that the trajectory of credit cards was not a simple, straight, onwards-and-upwards path. For the first decade or so, it was far from clear whether the credit card would continue to exist as a product at all, and as late as 1970 there were people predicting that banks would abandon the concept completely. In September of that year, the third issue of the Nilson Report (now familiar to those of us in the business as a respected and long-standing source of news for the payments industry) said that the 'heyday of bank card profits may be over as officials begin to wonder if there will ever be such a thing as "profit"' (Nocera 1994). One problem, it noted, was that too many customers paid on time!

In the United Kingdom credit cards began when Derek Wilde of Barclays travelled to San Francisco in 1965 to strike a deal to licence the BankAmericard software. In 1966 Barclays used it to launch Barclaycard out of an old boot factory in Northampton. It took more than five years for the new card to reach 1.5 million cardholders and 75,000 merchants and finally turn in a profit, but when it did so the profit was sufficient to stimulate their main competitors (National Westminster, Midland and Lloyds) to band together and launch the rival Access card in 1972 (Lascelles 2016).

Technology played a key role in creating this profitable industry, and not just because you needed computers to manage the credit risk crucial to profitability and for the automation of the credit card accounts. Dee Hock, the visionary founder of the interbank organization that became Visa, writes in his history of the industry that at the end of the 1960s fraud was spiralling out of control and threatening to kill the industry stone dead. Blank cards were stolen from warehouses, personalized cards were stolen from the mail and organized crime was on the scene (Hock 2005). Shortly afterwards, however, technology changed the customer experience and prompted a significant reduction in fraud at the same time. The introduction of the magnetic stripe and the online authorization system transformed risk management and cut costs dramatically.

I cannot resist pointing out here that it was the London transit system that pioneered the use of magnetic stripes on the back of cardboard cards in a mass market product. It did this many years earlier, with the first transaction at Stamford Brook station on 5 January 1964 (Day and Reed 2001), well before BankAmericard introduced their first bank-issued magnetic stripe card in 1972 in conjunction with the deployment of the BASE I electronic authorization system in 1973. So as I said a decade ago, by my 'I have seen the future, and it is the London mass transit system' theory of payments, we should look at what Transport for London has been doing to see what banks will be doing with payments in the near future, and that was, of course, going to contactless cards!

Regulation combined with technology to cause the credit card business to explode after its near death at the beginning of the 1970s. In the United States, the banks had expanded the infrastructure for a nationwide credit card payment system through the precursors to Visa (created in 1976) and MasterCard (created in 1979) and convinced merchants nationwide to accept their cards. State usury laws prevented card issuers from reaping all the benefits of a nationwide system (Ellis 1998). The differences in state laws imposed a costly legal burden on issuers and issuers did not always find it profitable to extend credit lending in states where usury ceilings were low. At that time, the United States had strict usury laws that limited bank lending to 10 per cent, but South Dakota took steps to deregulate, prompting the Supreme Court to rule in 1978 (in its famous 'Marquette decision') that interest rates could be exported across state borders via credit cards, whereupon Citi (and other banks) shifted their credit cards operations away from New York to take advantage.

It was this regulatory decision along with the technological change that reshaped the industry. After the low-profit late 1970s and the loss-making early 1980s, credit cards were profitable and the business exploded. In the United Kingdom, regulators opted for a light touch and allowed Barclaycard to grow. In both countries credit cards became a mass-market phenomenon, leading to increased competition, which in turn drove financial innovations and additional products and services ranging from frequent flyer miles and cash rebates to credit towards future purchases and a wide variety of 'cobranding' in all sorts of industries.

A note about card fraud

Dee Hock's earlier comment on card fraud is very interesting because the co-evolution of cards and fraud helps us to learn a great deal about putting new money technology in place. In his excellent autobiography *Tough Guy* (which ends with his prison conversion to Judaism!), Mafia criminal Louis Ferrante gives a poetic description of card fraud in the years before mobile phones and laser beams. Louis's enterprising confederates in the New York mob had discovered that you didn't need to be able to forge cards terribly well to enter the counterfeiting business, provided you had collaborators.

> For years I made big wood with Sonny's 'dupes', phony credit cards with real numbers. He sold them to me for a hundred bucks a piece. Sonny had salespeople in retail stores on the take, boosting charge card receipts... I'd visit a jeweller who was in on the scam and buy a Rolex. If the watch retailed for five grand, I'd tell him to hit the card for ten. I'd leave with the watch. He'd made money. Both of us happy.

What the wise guys, as I believe they are known, really wanted though, rather than Rolex watches and the like, was cash. Card fraud was a means to that end:

> If I knew a guy who sold stuff I didn't want, like Paulie Flowers, I'd work out a cash split. I'd show up and tell him 'hit my card for four grand, keep two and give me two when you get paid'. He'd tell the card company he'd delivered arrangements to a wedding, and send them a phony bill of sale, and that was that.

Things have changed since then. That kind of card fraud was a sort of cottage industry, almost quaint. Today the fraudsters have followed the banks and the rest of the business world and globalized. It is no longer about getting a Rolex and a few thousand to spend, it is about investment and return on investment.* Card fraud is part of this, and that's a big problem. From being a minor branch of mafia robbery, it has become easy money for funding drug dealing, trafficking and even terrorism. This explains why, even though the business case for the transition away from magnetic stripes was (and still is, in the United States!) marginal from the bank point of view, governments were keen to see it go ahead.

For the payments industry, card fraud is a cost of doing business: a few basis points. In the United Kingdom, that is more than half a billion quid a year (the figure is still rising), which isn't that much compared with total card spending, so it's not surprising that it may not be the banks' absolute top priority at a time when charge-offs (unrecoverable debts) are running at many times the rate of chargebacks. A few basis points of turnover is a tiny fraction of the money spent on cards but a big income for organized crime. So even though the crime is tolerated by the payments industry, it shouldn't be.** Tolerating crime that we can tolerate because it doesn't stop us from doing business is a bad policy.

So where are we now, just as a baseline for new technology to improve on in Part III? Well, if you look at recent figures you can see the picture worsening. Back in 2012 global card volumes were around $21 trillion of which $11 billion was fraudulent, meaning fraud accounted for in the region of 5.2 basis points (Nilson Report 2013). The most recent estimates I have seen (from March 2016) indicate that while global card volumes are rising at about 15 per cent per year, fraud continues to outpace it at 20 per cent, meaning it will reach more than $35 billion in 2020. And remember that these figures are the direct losses: they do not include the money spent on reissuing cards and so on.

(I feel the need to point out, as an aside, how the late decision of the United States to switch to chip technology shows up in these figures.

---

* I enjoyed Moises Naim's book *Illicit: How Smugglers, Traffickers and Copycats are Hijacking the Global Economy* (2010) about the emergence of cross-border, enterprise-scale organized crime.

** As payments expert Scott Loftesness said on Twitter when we were discussing this, we need to remember the 'broken window' theory of policing.

US fraud is about 13 basis points; fraud everywhere else in the world is about 4 basis points. The United States accounts for about half of all card fraud in the world but only a fifth of the card volume.)

Card fraud is rising, and (unsurprisingly) it is worst in the places where cards were never designed to be used: in card-not-present transactions (i.e. remote transactions over the Internet, via telephone, etc.). Note, though, that while new schemes that have been invented since the Internet do better, they are not immune to fraud. This is because the problem of payment fraud is not just a problem of card technology: it is an instance of a more general identity and authentication problem that impacts everything from card fraud to cheque fraud (which, according to the American Bankers Association, still amounts to more than $2 billion per year in the United States) to remittance fraud. Naturally, this is something we will return to later. If the digital money of the future is to work, then it needs to build on the secure digital identity and authentication infrastructure of the future. Enough said.

The road to electronic money

After World War II, the invention of computing changed banking just as much as it changed every other industry. Well, perhaps not quite as much. By 1956 Britain's *New Scientist* magazine was complaining that 'the telegraph, television and facsimile telegraphy are not exactly novelties, but transactions in banking still have to wait upon the post' (Calder 1956).

Now remember: at the time that was written the United Kingdom was a world leader in computing. Indeed, the world's first general-purpose computer set to work for commercial purposes was the Lyons Electronic Office, which started work on the payroll for J. Lyons and Company (a chain of tea houses) in 1954.

A subcommittee on 'electronics' had been created in 1955 by the Committee of London Clearing Bankers but, again according to *New Scientist*, the initial results were disappointing (*New Scientist* 1961). This was blamed on the banks' inability to rethink anything, with the article stating that the banks 'elected to do their own thinking, and the teams engaged on automation projects [were], in most of the banks, composed entirely of bank officials who have taken courses in data processing'; it goes on to jibe that the slow progress 'can scarcely be through lack of funds' before suggesting that British banks may as well just give up and do exactly what the American Bankers Association did: that is, go for automation based on cheque sorting, magnetic ink and so forth. Even then, there was a problem with siloes, as the computers 'for ordinary bookkeeping, using information supplied on punched paper tape' were not connected with the 'sorting machines' that read the cheques.

Nevertheless, computers and networks began to spread even within banking, and by the mid 1960s the sector began to reorganize itself around electronic payments.

National infrastructure

Now, obviously, in developed countries banks had long since given up carrying around bags of gold to settle with each other periodically and had instead moved to net settlement through clearing systems of one form or another. For example, the New York Clearing House began netting in this way back in 1853. After 1914 the net settlement was accomplished, as it still is today, by debits and credits at the Federal Reserve Bank of New York. Such high-value interbank payments are absolutely crucial to modern economies.

The Bank of England's role as a settlement agent emerged in the middle of the nineteenth century with the provision of settlement accounts for the commercial banking sector. Since 1996 these accounts have been held within the Bank's Real Time Gross Settlement (RTGS) system, which provides for real-time posting, with finality and irrevocability, of debit and credit entries to participants accounts (see the Bank's guide online at http://bit.ly/2miUEzL). This system, which is an element of vital national infrastructure, is used for several purposes.

- It is used settle for the Clearing House Automated Payment System (CHAPS) in real time.

- It is also used for real-time settlement of the payment system embedded within the CREST securities settlement system.
- It is used to settle several times per day on a deferred net basis for the Faster Payments Service (FPS).
- And it is also used to settle on a deferred net basis for a variety of other retail payment systems (BACS, Cheque & Credit, LINK and Visa).

So, crucially, the RTGS system is used by CHAPS. This is real-time final settlement to any limit in 'Bank of England money'. If I send you a billion quid through CHAPS, then you have the billion quid and that's that. The current system settles almost a third of the United Kingdom's annual GDP (about £500 billion) every single day.

The American RTGS system is Fedwire, a service of the Federal Reserve Banks that is available to all banks that have an account at the Federal Reserve (i.e. all nationally chartered banks plus state banks that want to participate). In 1918 the banks established a proprietary telecommunications system to process funds transfers, connecting all twelve Reserve Banks, the Federal Reserve Board and the US Treasury by telegraph. Treasury securities became transferable by telegraph in the 1920s. The system remained largely telegraphic until the early 1970s.

The separation of paper settlements and electronic settlements in the United States also began in 1970, when the New York Clearing House began to automate. It created a system called the Clearing House Interbank Payment System (CHIPS) that used RTGS to provide net settlement between its member banks.

Automated clearing houses

The idea of automated clearing houses (ACHs) for retail payments has its origin in the automation of cheque processing (Benson and Loftesness 2012). In the United Kingdom, the ACH is called the Bankers' Automated Clearing Services (BACS). The United Kingdom, like most other countries, has only one of these, but the United States has two large-scale ACHs. These are the bank-owned non-profit National Automated Clearing House Association (NACHA) and the Electronic Payment Network (EPN) owned by The Clearing House.

ACHs have largely been associated with bill payment, cheque replacement, salary payments and so on. However, if you look at recent figures from NACHA, you can see an explosion in account-to-account (P2P) payments, which, I think, is related to growth in mobile app-instructed transfers.

Table 2. US ACH transactions (autumn 2015).

Transaction type	Volume (m)	Change
IAT (cross border)	17.8	Up 27%
WEB debit (bills)	987.5	Up 13%
WEB credit (P2P)	14.2	Up more than 700%
BOC, ARC, POP (checks)	484.7	Down another 7%
TEL (phone)	114.3	Up 15%
PPD debit (recurring)	886.8	Up 4%
PPD credit (payroll)	1,450	Up 4%

As you can see in the table, all categories of ACH transfer are growing in the United States except for check replacement, the volume of which continues to fall (including at POS), as you might expect. I expect this trend to be even more marked in Europe, where the arrival of PSD2 means that retailer direct access to payment accounts will be one of the defining trends of the next era of payment evolution.

Now, Visa and MasterCard are rather good at what they do, so it would take something special to be better at it than them. It might, in some observers' calculations, be better to focus on delivering products into new channels where Visa and MasterCard must work harder, such as mobile and online. Creating a direct-to-account service, with appropriate security and consumer protection, delivered through access to open banking would mean an important new 'push platform' for product and service innovation in the payment space. I imagine that in Europe, as in the United States and elsewhere, the use of ACHs and instant payment networks will grow the electronic payments pie at the expense of conventional card networks.

International expansion

By the 1970s banks around the world were using the slow and insecure telex network to send payment instructions around the world, and it was clear that a shift to modern computers and networks was needed. In 1973 a couple of hundred banks came together to create the Society for Worldwide Interbank Financial Telecommunication (SWIFT). Today, most international interbank messages use the SWIFT network to send payment instructions that are then settled through correspondent accounts. So, I tell Barclays to send $100 of mine to the Citi account of my colleague in New York. Barclays sends the message through the SWIFT network and debits my account, crediting the account that Citi has at Barclays. Meanwhile, Citi debits the Barclays account that they hold with Citi and then credits my colleague's account. Some of the money is lost in friction, but you get the picture.

Where did the technologies take us?

Here's a snapshot of where the road to electronic money has taken us so far (from the annual Cap Gemini World Payments Report: see www.worldpaymentsreport.com). In 2015 global non-cash transaction volumes grew around the globe. In mature markets they grew by around 6 per cent to account for around three-quarters of all payments, and in developing markets they grew at twice that rate to account for around a quarter of all payments. Card payments are still growing, cheques are vanishing and EFT continues to grow. The advent of 'instant payments' will surely boost that latter category in the future. As transactions move online, the pressure on cash increases – but so does the pressure on cards. The 'alternative' (i.e. non-card) payment mechanisms now account for more than half of online payments, so we should prob-ably find a new word for them. If you look at the top ten electronic commerce markets (as shown in figure 13), you will see that there are very different means of exchange in play from Russia (where cash on delivery still dominates) to China (where non-banks are running away with things) to the United States (where cards rule the roost).

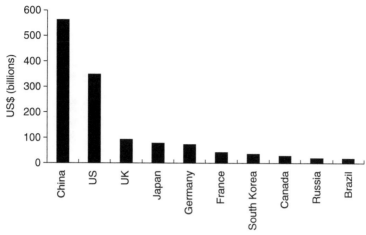

Figure 13. Top ten electronic commerce markets.
(*Source*: Payments Cards & Mobile, February 2017.)

In developing countries cash continues to dominate retail payments by both value and volume; in developed countries the rule of thumb is that cash accounts for two-thirds of the volume and one-third of the value. But, as you can see in the appendix to this book, in some countries cash is already on the way out – and a good thing that is too.

Chapter 7

Moving to mobile

Machine intelligence will make us far smarter [because] our smart phones are basically supercomputers.

> — Eric Schmidt, Google's executive chairman, at
> the World Economic Forum in Davos in 2015

CARDS TRANSFORMED THE payments world but they did not, as was once thought, spell the end for cash. We can now see, with the perspective of decades of use, that it was a later invention that brought about the reinvention of money. Not computers, not the Internet, not digital technology in general. It is the specific technology of the mobile phone that will bring us monetary revolution.

Mobile payments are mainstream. In the United Kingdom, which has a very well-developed contactless infrastructure, the use of contactless payments is now mainstream in London, meaning that I can leave home without a wallet and use my phone all day.* I can pay for parking at the train station using an app, buy my coffee using Apple Pay, buy lunch using Apple Pay or apps, pay on the bus using an app, and so on.

This is only the beginning. The use of apps is growing. Much of the discussion around the 'xPays' (e.g. Android Pay, Chase Pay, Samsung Pay, Walmart Pay and so on) has focused on the 'tap and pay' simplicity of the mobile phone using contactless technology. However, there are

---

* With the annoying exception of South West Trains, whose ticket machines do not accept contactless payments and who provide no in-app alternative.

lots of reasons for thinking that this will be a sideshow rather than the main event. The introduction of new security infrastructure ('token-ization') means that in-app payments ('app and pay') can now be more secure than chip and PIN payments, and since I rather imagine that most retailers would prefer no POS at all to enhanced POS, there will be pressure from them to shift. As far as they see it, tills and chip and PIN machines and cash drawers are a waste of good retail space: move that stuff onto mobile phones and they'll be more than happy. Given the experiences that we already see around us, from Uber to Airbnb and KFC, I think that in-app payments will become the norm: the most frictionless way to pay. Once again, this is hardly a wild prediction, given the number of organizations in the United States that have already implemented Apple Pay inside their apps. As Google and Samsung and others shift their offerings into the same space, I predict that it will become natural to pay with your supermarket app, your fuel app and your fast-food app (collecting your rewards as you go) rather than use something from your bank.

Figure 14. Global mobile: paying contactlessly for a taxi ride in Australia using my UK mobile phone.

Let us be clear about the dynamic here. In the developing world these new kinds of mobile-phone-based payment schemes are not (as some bankers seem to think) simply poor substitutes forced on desperate people as a stopgap until 'proper' bank-based payments such as prepaid open scheme cards arrive on the scene. These mobile schemes match the requirements of most of the people, in most of the world, most of the time. They are their own new locus of innovation, distinct from the developed world's structures, customs and assumptions.

On to the key impact of mobile. We're at the inflexion point where, as long predicted, you will go back to the house if you forget your phone but not if you forget your wallet. This inflexion point is crucial in the story of technology and money because it marks the end of the physicality. We now understand that the payment card was never going to get rid of cash. The payment card is not the future of money. With payment cards you could pay retailers. With mobile phones, people can pay each other. And that changes everything.

In the developed world we are moving to mobile for some reasons, and in the developing world we are moving in that direction for other reasons. But we are all moving to mobile, and that brings the future of money closer.

The M-Pesa story

No treatise on the future of money is complete without a discussion of the M-Pesa mobile money transfer scheme in Kenya. It will be a business school case study for years to come and I am sure that it will in time be seen as what futurologists call a 'weak signal for change' to a new monetary order. Indeed, the economist Tim Harford featured it in his 2016 BBC World Service series 50 Things That Made the Modern Economy (available at http://bbc.in/2fjzkYf).

M-Pesa launched in Kenya in 2007 and subsequently spread to Tanzania and Afghanistan in 2008, South Africa in 2010, India in 2011, Romania in 2014 and Albania in 2015. M-Pesa is so important that its origins and trajectory need to be recorded and reported from many perspectives. In their definitive history Money, Real Quick – The Story of M-Pesa (Guardian Shorts, 2012), Tonny Omwansa and

Nicholas Sullivan tell its story, which I shall précis here to make a couple of points.

Figure 15. M-Pesa uses inexpensive feature
phones to deliver financial services.

The first hero of the story (in my eyes, anyway) is Nick Hughes. Nick was then Head of Social Enterprise at Vodafone, which owned 40 per cent of Kenya's Safaricom. Safaricom was the market leader in Kenya, with just over half the market. Nick had had the idea of using mobile phones to make the distribution of microfinance loans in Africa more efficient and he submitted a proposal to the UK Department for International Development for matching funding. This was granted back in 2003, and M-Pesa was born.*

The second hero of the story is Susie Lonie, also from Vodafone. Susie had been working on mobile commerce in the United Kingdom, and in 2005 she was sent to Nairobi to get the M-Pesa pilot up and running. She combined first-class project management skills with real vision, and together with Nick steered the system from a pilot that could so easily have run out of control (such was the popularity of the system once it launched) to the launch of a genuinely new national payments scheme. (I should say, incidentally, that it isn't only me who sees Nick and Susie as heroes. In 2010, *The Economist* gave them its Social and Economic Innovation award.)

---

* It was at this point that Nick brought in Consult Hyperion to help to develop the idea, but modesty prevents me from mentioning this.

Once Nick and Susie had got the pilot up and running, the very forward-looking CEO of Safaricom, Michael Joseph, realized that something big was going on and drove the team on to scale. Within a year they had two million subscribers and were handling $1.5 million per day, at which point he turned his attention to developing the agent network. Safaricom already had agents, of course, because they used them to sell airtime, but Michael realized that they needed to increase the size of the network substantially, and quickly. I won't distract the reader with more detail here, but I strongly recommend anyone who is interested in the topic to read about how this was done and about the issues that needed to be managed: agent incentives, float management, trading and so forth. Suffice to say that becoming an M-Pesa agent became an attractive proposition.

When the system went live it was immediately apparent that the market was using it in ways that had not been part of the original business model. In particular, businesses began to use it. They started to deposit cash (as a kind of 'night safe') as well as settling transactions and paying wages. Now there are some 600 businesses in Kenya that accept payments through M-Pesa. These include the national airline, the power utilities and insurance companies.

In summary, a non-bank payment system founded on new technology rather than legacy infrastructure has changed people's lives in ways that could not have been envisaged by the people who created it.

The scheme, which allows people to deposit and withdraw cash from accounts associated with their mobile phone numbers, has been an incredible success, with more than two-thirds of the adult population using it and tens of thousands of agents allowing consumers to pay cash into the system or take cash out of it. To put these numbers in context, note that it took banks in Kenya a century to create a mere 1,000 bank branches, 1,500 ATMs and 100,000 credit card customers.

Lessons from M-Pesa

What general lessons can we draw from M-Pesa's rise? One lesson is about the regulatory environment that allowed M-Pesa to flourish and about how, despite banks' reservations about the scheme, once it was successful banks were able to use it to offer financial services to a new customer base. Omwansa and Sullivan indeed note that 'commercial banks have finally decided to expand their borders beyond branches by hiring agents [but] only after they tried, and failed, to shut down M-Pesa'. This is why, for me, the most interesting part of the story came after M-Pesa reached five million subscribers (more than all forty-three of Kenya's commercial banks combined) back in 2008. At that time the acting finance minister said he was not sure that M-Pesa would 'end up well'. No one was sure who was supposed to be regulating M-Pesa, but the minister asked the central bank to study the scheme with the result being that the permanent secretary in the Ministry of Finance, Joseph Kinuya, declared the service 'safe and reliable'. He also said 'there is nothing wrong with competition'.

From the beginning the commercial banks had offered new services over the M-Pesa network, thereby demonstrating that mobile money could deliver financial inclusion. As the banks began to offer more services, and became part of the M-Pesa ecosystem as savings accounts and super agents, it seems to me that the whole financial sector was invigorated. Dynamic partnerships (such as the one with Equity Bank that led to M-Kesho savings accounts) delivered products that simply would not have existed in a 'traditional' bank environment. These included pensions, micro insurance, 'layaway' and more. In essence, as Omwansa and Sullivan say, a new financial sector emerged.

Another lesson I draw is that I simply do not believe that a bank-led solution would have triggered the innovation revolution that M-Pesa clearly did. A key element in its success is that it was born in telco culture, and conceived as an infrastructure for others to build on. Mark Pickens, a microfinance specialist at the Consultative Group to Assist the Poor, which is part of the World Bank, makes a point about the 'adjacent industries' stimulated by M-Pesa and this seems to have led to a high-tech boom in 'Swahili Silicon Valley' around iHub in Nairobi. Cashless schools, pay-for-use water, e-health and an incredible range of applications have been made possible by the ready availability of a mass market payment system for the twenty-first century. As the CEO of Kenya Commercial Bank is quoted as saying in the book, in response to being asked if M-Pesa is a threat to banks: 'if you don't respond it's a threat, but if you embrace it, then it's an opportunity'. I see this as a template for payment system evolution in Europe and hopefully in the United States as well.

As a final lesson I cannot help but point to the relationship between identity and money. One of the most unexpected impacts of M-Pesa was the use of M-Pesa transaction histories as substitutes for conventional credit ratings. Remember that many M-Pesa agents are merchants, so it is natural for them to extend credit in this way. In other words, M-Pesa became a means for previously excluded people to demonstrate identity and reputation.

And on a final semi-technical note, I can see a future in which the regulator insists on interoperability between mobile money schemes and regulates the interchange rates, but some players want more than this, and in this they adumbrate skirmishes that are about to break out in developed markets. In chapter 7 of their book, Omwansa and Sullivan refer to Safaricom's control of the SIM and tensions arising from this because banks want (but don't have) access to it. I can remember from the early days of the project that there was considerable debate about how to implement the service for consumers. In the end they opted for hardware-based security. This meant writing new 'SIM Toolkit' software and reissuing Safaricom SIMs to customers who wanted to use mobile payments. Safaricom decided to make the investment required to go down this high-security route rather than use SMS or USSD, hoping that it would act as an anti-churn factor in a SIM-based market. This was at the time a brave decision, but one that has been repaid many times over. Good for them. I cannot see how regulators could realistically force operators to open up the SIM for more SIM Toolkit applications. But, as in the case of smartphone applications in developed countries, it might be realistic to ask operators to agree on a standard, SIM-based identity management infrastructure and then provide open, transparent and non-discriminatory access to it. That, though, is another story.

Implications for cashlessness

In Kenya there are only two payment choices for most people: cash or M-Pesa. A raft of economic activity is now floating on the M-Pesa river of money, supporting businesses that simply could not exist in a cash-only economy, so it is always interesting to try and understand why. It is clear that in understanding the social, cultural and economic factors around electronic money, a 'rational calculative approach' is not adequate to understand people's decision making (something I learned back in the days of Mondex). One clear message from studying these factors in Kenya is that different groups will have different reasons for wanting to shift from cash to digital alternatives (Iazzolino and Wasike 2015).

The non-rational, non-calculative approach helps to explain the dynamic in Kenya, where mobile money is replacing cash but cards are not. Central Bank of Kenya statistics show a decline in the use of credit and debit cards, despite the fact that an increasing number of Kenyans hold them. There are more than ten million debit cards in Kenya (and around 160,000 credit cards) but only 4 per cent of Kenyans use credit and debit cards for shopping.

The study referred to above talks about the embedding of 'financial devices' in social structures, remarking that 'how cash, payment cards and mobile money are used and what they stand for are entwined issues', using the case study of *chama* gatherings, where people want to be seen pooling money in a public act.

Mobile innovation and regulation

India is a useful and illustrative case study of the relationship between payments, mobile technology and innovation. The Indian emerging payments environment and what the Reserve Bank of India called its 'calibrated' approach to mobile payments, beginning with very strict regulation back in 2009, failed to unleash the latent demand from Indian consumers or the inherent enterprise and creativity of Indian businesses. Figures from the World Bank's Consultative Group to Assist the Poor show that while India has a fifth of the world's unbanked population and nearly a billion mobile phone connections, less than a third of 1 per cent of Indian adults uses mobile money services.

That is not to say that nothing happened in India, but it is still some way from fulfilling its potential in mobile payments. A couple of years ago it was clear to many people that India was missing out because of this and that something would have to be done to allow the multiple benefits of mobile payments to spread within the country. Mobile payments have a key role to play in financial inclusion and this is vitally important to India, so the lack of progress was becoming a social and political issue. Back in 2013 there was an article in the *New York Times* titled 'Mobile payment startups face reluctant Indian consumers' (Bergen 2013) that I suggested at the time should really have been titled 'Mobile payment startups face reluctant Indian regulators'! The sticking point in India was never a lack of consumer demand.

The initial Indian approach towards national financial inclusion was to use 'business correspondents' (or BCs). The idea was that banks were to use third-party non-bank BC agents to deliver services. One interesting BC case study is Eko India Financial Services (Realini and Mehta 2015). The most widely used Eko service is domestic remittance, which is, as far as I am concerned, a payment application and not really a banking application at all. So while India may have relatively few bank accounts but a lot of mobile phones, it is not in my view a natural corollary to imagine that getting people to open bank accounts and then access those bank accounts using those mobile phones is a way forward. This isn't just my opinion: the figures show that it is not the optimum route to inclusion. More than half of the 160 million bank accounts created during the Indian government's most recent account-opening drive have never been used, and at cost of $3–$4 to open and maintain that is a lot of wasted money. Having said that, as you will see later, in the appendix, the Indian government's recent actions to boost non-cash payments seem to be having an effect.

Most consumers, most of the time, need payments not banking.

Unbanked is not the problem

This observation leads me to make a more general point. Calling people 'unbanked' misstates the basic inclusion problem. And, as an obvious corollary, forcing people to use banks is not the solution. They should be able to store their money in more useful and more cost-effective places! I was therefore very happy to see the steady relaxation of the Indian mobile payment regulations that allowed alternative paths to inclusion to flourish. This culminated in 2015 with the decision to create a new category of financial institution (similar to the 'Payment Institution' approach adopted in Europe) and issue licences to these new 'Payment Banks'. The Reserve Bank of India granted the first eleven licences in this new category to a variety of fintech, tech and telecoms companies and consortia. Among the successful bidders were the mobile operators Vodafone M-Pesa and Bharti Airtel, the technology companies Fino PayTech and Tech Mahindra, as well as the Department of Posts. These Payment Banks can

- accept deposits from individual customers, with a maximum limit of Rs 1 lakh (around €1,300);
- issue debit and ATM cards for transactions, but not credit cards; and
- allow transactions through Internet and leverage technology to offer low-cost banking solutions.

Importantly, a key to overall systemic risk evaluation is that a payments bank cannot undertake any lending activity. This makes it possible to expand the systemically less risky payments business while keeping the systemically risky core banking credit activities under tight control. Once again, we see payments separating from banking.

Cardmageddon

Magnetic stripes and automated authorization, chip cards and 3D security have all made card payments more efficient, but the basic concept hasn't changed. So, certain persons (e.g. merchants) say, why not? Through mobile phones we now have a network that connects all the consumers and all the merchants and all the banks, so why don't we just use that? Why bother with Visa and MasterCard? Provided the consumer has some 'token' to identify the relevant bank account, why can't they just give this token to the merchant and have the merchant go directly to the bank account to get their money?

One day soon, my Waitrose app will obtain tokens from my V.me wallet, my MasterPass wallet, my PingIt app, my Zapp app and any other wallets it can find on my phone through a standard discovery process and a standard API. Then, when I check out at Waitrose my app will pop up and take care of business. Maybe I will have configured my MasterPass wallet, which is where my John Lewis MasterCard will be stored, to allow the Waitrose app to charge £100 without additional authorization. This will completely change the experience of POS for most people. At some point in time, when plastic cards are less than half of all of the non-cash transactions made at retail POS (otherwise known as 'cardmaggedon day'), the complexity of introducing new currencies will fall away.

The new point-of-sale

Electronic money at POS needs identification and authentication in place and secured to an appropriate degree to make things work properly. We need to identify the source of the funds for the transaction and we need to authenticate the consumer's right to those funds. So, typically in the United Kingdom, the customer presents a debit card that identifies the source of the funds and then enters a personal identification number (PIN) to demonstrate their right to use those funds. While the two functions of identification and authentication are often implemented using the same device and the same underlying technology, they are conceptually different, so I just want to touch on trends in each area to establish the broad shape of the evolutionary curve around POS before we move on.

Identification typically takes place through the presentation of some credential, such as the chip on a plastic card or some cryptographic jiggery-pokery inside a mobile phone or a hat, a watch, a badge or whatever else works. Now, I strongly suspect that in the longer term identification will inevitably move over to biometrics. When I walk into Tesco, Tesco will know it is me from my face or my body odour or my voice or some other physical characteristic. I have to say that, in common with many other people, I am slightly nervous about this because I do not think society has in place the social, legal or regulatory infrastructure for biometrics just yet. Personally, I prefer to see identification through a cryptographically secured but revocable token.

As a further aside – and one that is not really the point of this discussion – the connection between the revocable token that is to be used for payment and the relationship between the retailer and the consumer (I'm talking about loyalty schemes and that kind of thing) also needs to be considered if we are to create a workable electronic money solution for this mass market. For example, if the revocable token were to generate a different cryptographic identification on each use (which would be one obvious way of protecting the privacy of shoppers), then it would not be possible for the retailer to link it to a loyalty scheme and they would therefore need some other identification token to do this. However, it may be greatly to the advantage of both the retailer and the consumer to build a long-term relationship on an identifier, so these factors need to be considered. An example of this interplay can be found in the current evolution of the EMV specifications. The international card schemes introduced tokenization, as described in Part II, as a solution to problems around card fraud, but of course many retailers' systems used the card identifier as the basis for relationship management. The tokenization specifications therefore had to be revised to include a field known as a PAR (payment account reference) that remains unique across tokens.

The Talmudic perspective on authentication

As identification moves to smart devices, these devices need smart authentication to go with them. The issue of signatures and the general use of them to authenticate customers for credit card transactions in the United States has long been a source of amusement and anecdote, but it serves to help to explore where authentication is going. I am as guilty as everybody else is for using the US retail purchasing experience to poke fun at the infrastructure there (with some justification since, as many people know, the United States is responsible for about a fifth of the world's card transactions but half of the world's card fraud). I've also used that experience to illustrate some more general points about identity and authentication. My good friend Brett King did the same when he made a general point about authentication mechanisms for the twenty-first century (King 2014), noting that in a recent UN/ICAO commissioned survey on the use of signatures in passports, a number of countries (including the United Kingdom) recommended phasing out the long-held practice because it was no longer deemed of practical use.

In an interview about this topic for an episode of NPR's *Planet Money* (episode 564, broadcast on 29 August 2014), the Colombia law professor Ronald Mann notes that card signatures are all about distributing liabilities for fraud transactions and calls them 'eccentric relics', a phrase I love and use often. The show also interviewed a Talmudic scholar on the topic. The Talmud is the written version of the Jewish oral law (the *Mishnah*) and the rabbinic commentary on it that was completed in its current form in the fifth century BCE (the *Gemara*). It is admirably clear about the use of signatures. The purpose of the signature is to identify the person. The scholar made a very interesting point about this when he was talking about the signatures that are attached to the Jewish marriage contract, the *Ketubah*, pointing out that it is the signatures of the witnesses (not the couple themselves) that have the critical function in dispute resolution. The signatures are used to track down the witnesses so that they can attest as to the ceremony taking place and as to who the other participants were. The show narrator made a good point about this, which is that it might make more sense for the coffee shop to get the signature of the person behind you in the line than yours, since yours is essentially ceremonial whereas the one of the person behind you has that Talmudic forensic function.

I bring this up to observe that when it comes to making a retail transaction, my signature is utterly unimportant. This is why transactions work perfectly well when I either do not give a signature (for contactless transactions up to £30 in the United Kingdom, for example, or for no-signature swipe transactions in the United States) or give a completely pointless signature as I do for almost all US transactions, either just scribbling an irrelevant line or carefully printing Sergio Leonel 'Kun' Aguero Del Castillo (when I can make it fit).

Figure 16. Signatures remain the principal authentication mechanism in some parts of the world.

But now consider a more generalized version of this experience when the future retail transaction is a witnessed exchange of data between my computer (for the sake of argument, let's say my mobile phone) and the store's computer (for the sake of argument, let's say their tablet). Not only is there no need for me to sign this transaction, there is no need for me to enter a PIN either, since the phone already knows that I am its rightful owner because I've already used the pass-code or a fingerprint or whatever to unlock it. And it would be pointless if the clerk gave their signature to the transaction since what my mobile phone wants is the digital signature that it can validate to know that it is talking to a real and accredited store and that the payment has been properly recorded and acknowledged.

The Talmudic scholar also mentioned in passing that according to the commentaries on the text, the wise men from twenty-five centuries ago also decided that all transactions deserved the same protection. It doesn't matter whether it's a penny or a thousand pounds, the transaction should still be witnessed in such a way as to provide the appropriate levels of protection to the participants. The Talmud says that every purchase is a big purchase. So goodbye to electronic cash and goodbye to chip and PIN, and hello to biometric authentication and secure elements. We have here the prospect of a common payment experience in store, on the web and in-app: you click 'pay' and your phone asks you to confirm and you put your finger on the home button. For everything: the cup of coffee and the pair of shoes and the plane ticket. It turns out that once again we can go back to the future in the design of our next retail payments system.

The push for push

Let me quickly define 'recognition'. In the context of economic exchange, recognition is the combination of 'good enough' identification and 'good enough' authentication. What I mean by 'good enough' is that the risks associated with a transaction are acceptable to the counterparties. For a sandwich, recognition might be a nickname and possession of a phone. For a pair of shoes, recognition might be a store loyalty card, a credit card and a PIN. For a car, recognition might be a passport, a phone and a voice biometric. (Although I cannot resist noting here that I bought my wife's current car with chip and PIN and the last coffee I bought in Las Vegas necessitated the production of a passport to accompany a card swipe).

Once we can recognize all the counterparties in a transaction, we can minimize the transaction costs and reduce the exchange to minimal form. In commercial exchanges this means a shift to push payments, where money is pushed from one payment account to another. No credit, no authorization, no settlement. The money goes from my account at Barclays to Pret A Manger's account at NatWest and I get my sandwich. End of.

Since push payments minimize the overall costs, there is pressure to implement them all around the world; the advance of 'instant payment' interconnections between banks is well under way, with the shift to mobile being one of the main reasons for this. A simple (and possibly overused) example will serve to illustrate how a mobile-centric model in a world of instant payments changes things. Right now, my gym* either has my card on file or my bank account details for direct debiting. Either way they pull money from my account each month. Most of the time this works fine, but when it doesn't (because of errors or fraud or failures) it costs time and money to repair. A decade from now, my phone, watch, hat, earrings and key fob will all contain cryptographically unforgeable tokens generated for them by my bank, and when it is time to pay the monthly gym fee they will use the token to instruct the bank to send the money from my account to theirs. I will soon get bored with authorizing the individual transactions, naturally, and so I will give my watch permission to respond positively until I instruct otherwise. Now, the money is being pushed from me to the gym. Instantly and securely.

And when I don't want to go to the gym any more, I will tell my watch not to pay any more. No mandates, no instructions, no personal details for hackers to steal from the gym or from the watch. The defences that are now being deployed in the world of mobile phones – that tokenized infrastructure that sits behind Apple Pay and Android Pay and Samsung Pay, and soon every other pay – adumbrate a generalized tokenization that will deliver similar security and convenience benefits throughout the whole payments ecosystem.

---

* This is, of course, an entirely hypothetical case study.

Chapter 8

The case against cash

Cash is the enemy of the poor.
— Ignacio Mas of the Bill & Melinda Gates Foundation (2012)

T O REITERATE ONE element of the 'present' mentality, the post-war technological developments discussed in the previous chapters meant that people began to think seriously about cashlessness and began to connect ideas about new forms of money to new technological possibilities. While we are still in our present mindset, then – before we begin to think about the impact of the newest technologies, the technologies of the edge – I think we should pause to take a long look at cashlessness. Should the future include a cashless society? Should we allow technological pressure to nudge that rump of physical cash over the cliff? Why? What's wrong with cash?

It used to be said that the cashless society is as likely as the paperless office or paperless bathroom. But the statistics show that paper use in offices peaked a decade ago and I first used a paperless bathroom years ago (in South Korea), so perhaps the cashless society is not only due, but overdue.

Baseline: the cost of payments

How much does it cost to make a payment? The European Central Bank (ECB) carried out its first comprehensive cross-country analysis of the aggregated costs of making payments when purchasing goods and services back in 2012. The survey was conducted in cooperation with the central banks of Denmark, Estonia, Finland, Greece, Hungary, Ireland, Italy, Latvia, the Netherlands, Portugal, Romania, Spain and Sweden. The ECB analysed the social and private costs of making retail payments in these thirteen European countries and discovered that they are substantial, amounting to around €45 billion, or almost 1 per cent of the countries' combined GDP. If extrapolated to cover the twenty-seven member states of the European Union, these costs would be around €130 billion (Schmeidel *et al.* 2012).

Based on a representative sample, the study also found that cash payments account for nearly half of the total costs. As the most commonly used payment instrument, cash has, on average, the lowest social costs per transaction, at €0.42, closely followed by debit cards, with a cost to society of €0.70 per transaction. Cheques are the most expensive form of payment, with unit costs of €3.55. However, in some countries cash does not always have the lowest unit cost: in five of the countries covered the costs were lower for debit cards. Such rankings depend on characteristics specific to each country's payment system, on the market size and its development, and on payment behaviour.

The ECB also looked at *private* and *social* costs. Private costs are those incurred by individual participants in the payments chain, including items such as transportation of cash, management of electronic transactions, acquisition of new customers, credit risk analysis, provision of terminals, fraud prevention and fees for other participants. Social costs are defined as the aggregate costs to society, excluding fees and tariffs, for participants in the payment chain. About half of these total costs are incurred by banks and interbank infrastructure providers, with retailers bearing the other half.

Cash in society

Back in 2015 I saw the Chief Cashier of the Bank of England give an interesting speech about the trajectory of cash (Cleland 2015). This is important to the Bank of England because the note-issuing

department of the bank is the most profitable nationalized industry in history, and demand for their product continues to grow, as
shown in figure 17.

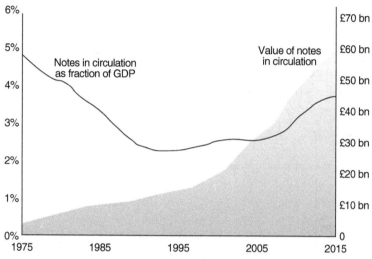

Figure 17. Value of Bank of England notes in circulation.
(*Source*: Bank of England, October 2015.)

The Chief Cashier said that aggregate demand for Bank of England
notes has grown quickly, increasing by around three-quarters over the
past decade, and has outpaced the growth in GDP since the 1990s.
Today there are nearly three-and-a-half billion notes in circulation, with
a total value of more than £60 billion. She went on to say:

> Demand for cash as a medium of exchange appears broadly stable,
> its use as a store of value appears to have grown... We estimate that
> around 20% to 30% of total UK cash was in, what we refer to as, the
> 'transactional cycle' – cash held by banks, consumers, and retailers for
> the purposes of facilitating everyday transactions.

The Chief Cashier essentially said that their latest figures show that
only about a quarter of the cash that they put into circulation is for
transactional purposes (i.e. used): the rest of it is either shipped overseas (i.e. exported), which we will put to one side for the moment; kept
outside of the banking system (i.e. hoarded); or used to support the

shadow economy (i.e. stashed). In other words, it is not in circulation at all but stuffed under mattresses.

If you look at the trend growth of that cash 'in circulation' over the last few years, it has accelerated well ahead of trend GDP growth as well as past trend ATM withdrawal growth (figure 18). And we also know that the use of cash in retailing has continued to fall steadily, so the 'cash gap' between the small amount of cash that is used to support the needs of commerce and the large amounts of cash that are used for other purposes has been growing.

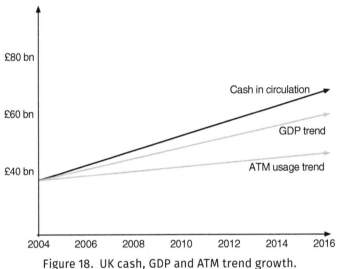

Figure 18. UK cash, GDP and ATM trend growth.

The Bank of England's *Quarterly Bulletin*, in presenting the figures that the Chief Cashier referred to, asks a straightforward question (Cleland 2015): 'If the majority of Bank of England notes are not being used for everyday transactions in the domestic economy, what are they being used for?'

Well, let us look at the categories set out by the Chief Cashier. The first, cash that is *used*, is easy. As we will explore shortly, the driver of change in this category is technology but the impact is weak. In other words, new technology does reduce the amount of cash in circulation, but very slowly.

Moving on to the next category, I know it's a rather simplistic ana-lysis, but if the amount of cash that is being *hoarded* has been growing, then that would tend to indicate that people have lost confidence in formal financial services or are happy to have loss, theft and inflation eat away their store of value while forgoing the safety and security of bank deposits irrespective of the value of the interest paid. The Bank believes that 'a small number of individuals hoard large amounts of cash' and so might account for a lot of the notes.*

If, on the other hand, the amount of cash that is being *stashed* has been growing, then the Bank of England is facilitating an increasing 'cash gap' that the rest of us are paying for. In this context cash is a mechanism for greatly reducing the cost of criminality while it remains a penalty on the poor, who must shoulder an unfair proportion of the cost of cash. In this case we should expect to see a strategy to change this obviously suboptimal element of policy.

The amount of cash that is being *exported* is hard to calculate, although the Bank itself does comment that the £50 note (which makes up a fifth of the cash out there by value) is 'primarily demanded by foreign exchange wholesalers abroad'. I suppose some of this may be transactional use for tourists and business people coming to the UK, and I suppose some of it may be hoarded, but surely the strong suspicion must be that these notes are going into stashes.

The Bank notes that 'given the untraceable nature of cash' they cannot tell where cash is going. That is true, and it is unlikely to change short of adopting a policy of having ATMs record the serial numbers of notes that they dispense and having cash recycling centres record the serial numbers of notes coming in to rectify this lack of data. The Bank does, however, look at some proxies to help it establish the rough proportions used and hoarded, stashed and exported. It says that it thinks that around 25 per cent is used and around 25 per cent is hoarded, with the rest being stashed and exported. If most of the exported cash is stashed, as I suspect, then heading towards half of the cash out there is for, not to put too fine a point on it, criminals.

Given that aggregate demand continues to increase, which of the categories is responsible for that growth (we know it's not the cash

---

* Rather famously, British comedian Ken Dodd had £336,000 in suitcases in his attic.

that is being used). The Bank says that 'no single source of demand is likely to have been behind the sustained growth', but I'm not so sure, because I think stashes have grown at the expense of hoards.

Stashes and hoards

Professor Charles Goodhart (London School of Economics) and Jonathan Ashworth (UK economist at Morgan Stanley) have studied the subject in some detail. They note that the ratio of currency to GDP in the United Kingdom has been rising (as you will recall from figure 18) and argue that the rapid growth in the shadow economy has been a key cause. In their detailed examination of the statistics, they make a clear distinction between the 'black economy' (e.g. drug dealing and money laundering) and the 'grey economy': activities that are legal but unreported in order to evade taxation. When your builder offers you a discount for cash and you accept, you are participating in the grey economy. When your builder offers you crystal meth and you pay him, you are participating in the black economy. They define a total 'shadow economy' as the sum of the black and grey economies.

They consider the financial crisis as one explanation of the growth in cash held but reject it. Looking at the detailed figures shows that there was a jump in cash held outside of banks around the time of the Northern Rock affair, but as public confidence in the banks was restored fairly quickly, and the impact of low interest rates on hoarding behaviour seems pretty marginal, there must be some other explanation for why the amount of cash out there kept rising.

Two rather obvious factors that do seem to support the shape of the sterling cash curve are the increase in VAT to 20 per cent and the continuing rise in self-employment, both of which serve to reinforce the contribution of cash to the shadow economy. The Bank say that there is 'limited research to confirm the extent of cash held for use in the shadow economy', but Goodhart and Ashworth make a reasonable estimate that the shadow economy in the United Kingdom could have expanded by around 3 per cent of UK GDP since the beginning of the current financial crisis.

According to Tax Justice UK, that expansion means that there were £100 billion in sales that were not declared to UK tax authorities, which translates to a tax loss of £40 billion in 2011/12 – and that will rise to more than £47 billion this year. The International Monetary Fund (IMF) has noted that Her Majesty's Revenue and Customs (HMRC) is not good at estimating losses outside the declared tax system, which is why their latest estimates for the tax gap are low, at £33 billion for 2011/12. Yet while we all read about Starbucks and Google and other large corporates engaging in (entirely legal) tax avoidance, the figures that HMRC does have indicate that half of all tax evasion is down to SMEs and a further quarter is down to individuals. There are an awful lot of people not paying tax and simple calculations will show that the tax gap that can be attributed to cash is vastly greater than the seigniorage earned by the Bank on the note issue. Cash makes the government (i.e. us) considerably worse off.

The cash gap

Goodhart and Ashworth refer to an older paper from the LSE Financial Markets Group that asked more directly whether cash remains necessary to facilitate bad behaviour (Drehmann and Goodhart 2000). This paper looks in detail at the substitution of cash at retail POS and shows that while ATMs and POS terminals have an impact on the demand for small notes, overall – and I think this is a really interesting and important point to bear in mind – the central conclusion was, in their words, that 'on our evidence, the effects of modern payment technologies on the demand for cash are not that strong', adumbrating the Bank of England's comments on the slow reduction in cash use in the face of technological change.

Once again, just to reinforce what this means, there is a double problem here. The first problem is that the Bank of England is producing cash to support shady activity (reducing tax revenues) and the second is that shady activity may also be bad for growth. Shadowy firms find it hard to borrow, which limits their productivity. (According to Francesco Pappada of the Einaudi Institute of Economics and Finance, many small firms in Greece deliberately avoid taking out loans because it involves being more transparent.) And unproductive firms pay low wages (*Economist* 2014a).

Goodhart and Ashworth's work (which estimates that the UK economy is significantly bigger than official figures suggest) seems to me to explain both the growing cash gap in the United Kingdom and some other strange economic behaviour around the labour market.*

Cash costs

One of Europe's leading experts on the competition between cash and electronic payments is Leo van Hove from the Free University of Brussels. He used the situation in the Netherlands to illustrate the dynamics. The Dutch central bank's baseline scenario has cash use falling to 20 per cent of retail transactions in 2015, yielding savings in the hundreds of millions of euros, and they have been looking at two potential measures to increase cash replacement over this baseline. The first is simply to keep the number of ATMs down at the 2005 level, thus making cash relatively less convenient. The second is to increase the number of electronic POS terminals capable of accepting electronic payments. (As I hope to demonstrate, this latter measure is inevitable, irrespective of central bank direction, because of the rise of the mobile phone.)

An alternative set of measures, as van Hove suggests, might be based on a different assumption: that is, that cross-subsidizing cash is not a welfare-maximizing strategy and that society should switch to cost-based pricing and leave the rest to the market (van Hove 2006). This strategy would see debit card transactions triple or quadruple while cash transactions would fall by a third (in value). This approach would make Belgium about €200 million better off and the Netherlands about €150 million better off. Note that cards account for only 7 per cent of retail payments under £10 in the United Kingdom, so a similar impact might be expected here as well: moving more small payments to debit cards saves money for society as a whole.

---

* In a talk about electronic money that he gave in 2014, Charles Goodhart was kind enough to refer to some of my thinking around 'privacy money' as a way forward.

Scaling up, the European countries van Hove studies would save about 0.14 per cent of GDP overall (i.e. about a third of the total social cost). So if customers who wanted to use cash were made to pay the full price for it, the electronic alternatives would become more attractive and the net welfare would increase, to the benefit of all.

Laura Rinaldi from the Centre for Economic Studies at Leuven University carried out some research that confirmed that customers see cash as being 'almost free'. She concluded that proper cost-based pricing would shift debit cards from being 4 per cent of retail transactions in Europe to a quarter: a change that would add 19 basis points to the European economy. Rinaldi's research further concluded that in these circumstances the European economy would grow by an additional 9 basis points because moving to electronic money would shrink the cash-based 'shadow economy'. I'm sure she's right. When the Proton 'electronic purse' (e-purse) was launched in Belgium a decade ago, I recall a number of people at the time saying that one of the reasons for the poor usage figures was the size of the country's informal economy.

Time to scrap metal

There's a thing that economists call 'the big problem of small change'. In essence, there's a problem because it's hard to make a living out of producing small change, so no one does it (Sargent and Velde 2002). The state therefore has to do it, delivering the token money that is supported by law. But as inflation erodes the value of that small change, it becomes increasingly unprofitable to provide it and the state has to bear the cost in the interests of the economy as a whole. This is why you get apparently bizarre behaviour such as the United States Mint producing nickels that cost eight cents and that people throw in the trash rather than carry around with them. If this was your business, you'd get out of it.

Is it still in the interests of the overall economy to produce these stupid small coins? I have no idea why the Royal Mint are messing about wasting our money on making 1p and 2p coins that nobody uses any more. It's about time we recognized low-value coins for what they are: scrap metal.

If you want proof that our coins are indeed scrap metal, then instead of taking my intemperate ranting at face value you should, as the man says, follow the money. In this case it leads to China, which has featured in a number of related stories around scrap coins. For example, in 2013 Denmark held two Chinese men for a number of weeks after they tried to exchange a massive hoard of scrap Danish coins that were mistaken for counterfeit money (Agence France-Presse 2013).

I thought it was a pretty unusual incident and I mentally filed it away to use as a conference anecdote at some point in the future, but when I spotted another similar case I began to suspect an interesting underlying story (BBC 2013). In 2013 two Chinese tourists were held in France on suspicion of forgery after trying to settle their hotel bill with €1 coins. Police were called in after a hotel owner in Paris became suspicious about the two men, and 3,700 €1 coins were then found in their room. But the coins were not counterfeit and the men said they had got the money from scrapyard dealers in China, who often find forgotten euros in cars sent from Europe.

This tallies with the Danish story. A sufficiently large number of coins from Europe end up as scrap that it makes it a worthwhile enterprise (in China) to collect up these coins and ship them back here to use!

Coins are still counterfeited, however, and on an industrial scale. The Italian police discovered counterfeit coinage worth more than €500,000 from a Chinese mint in a container ship docked in Naples in 2014 (Pantaleone 2014). This is to be expected, really: if container-loads of euros are coming back to Europe from China, then it's inevitable that this trade will attract counterfeiters looking to make a rather slow buck out of the business.

I suggest we make a virtue out of necessity. Since the Chinese gang responsible can presumably produce these coins at a lower cost than collecting them as scrap metal (otherwise they wouldn't make them, they'd just collect them), why don't we just stop producing coins above face value and sending them for scrap and instead let the Chinese counterfeits circulate in their place? Think about it. It costs the United States Mint 1.5 cents to make a penny that no one cares is real or not. So why bother? If Chinese criminals can produce one for half a cent, ship it to the United States in a container and make a profit of 0.2 cents on it, why not let them?

Exchange without banks

One interesting building block for our emerging narrative is the role of institutions in general and, specifically, the role of banks. It is not surprising that the payments system naturally evolved to emphasize transfers of claims on banks (such as cheques) as an alternative to cash payment. However, the term 'naturally' in this instance does not mean 'inevitably' (Roberds 1997). Not only is there a theory that says that economic life can continue without retail banks, there are practical examples of it happening.

One often-discussed example (indeed, I discussed it my previous book) comes from Ireland in the decade from 1966 to 1976. In that time there were three major 'all out' bank strikes in Ireland, which shut the retail banks for a year in total. The way the Irish economy functioned under such duress is both interesting and illustrative (Murphy 1978).

When the strikes hit, around four-fifths of the money supply disappeared and the public were left with the notes and coins in their pockets and nothing else. Since people could not go to the bank and draw out more money, they developed their own currency substitutes: while some people began to use sterling, it was the cheque that kept the economy going. People began to accept cheques directly from each other, and these cheques began to circulate. Antoin Murphy points out that one of the key reasons why this 'personalized credit system', which must have been very similar to that operating in Mesopotamia five millennia ago, could substitute for cash was the local nature of the circulation. The people exchanging cheques and IOUs knew each other well, and if they did not, they could soon find the necessary information to assess each other's creditworthiness. Ireland had 11,000 pubs and 12,000 shops at the time, and they became substitutes for the banks. Indeed, their information was likely to be much better than that held by a bank manager or by bank staff (Cockburn 2015), and because of that the credit risk was minimized. The owners of shops and pubs knew their customers very well and were therefore perfectly capable of deciding whether to accept cheques (or just IOUs) from those customers. And since the customers also knew each other very well, they too could make sensible decisions about which paper to accept.

What I draw from this example is that with 'local' transactions, everything can work perfectly well with no currency and no banks. A generation ago Ireland's economy was built up from such local trans-actions, so people could self-organize their own money supply. But, as I think we all understand, in the modern economy 'local' means something entirely different. While none of us know how this is going to pan out, there is clearly a redefinition of locality underway, and it has social networking, virtual worlds and disconnection technologies as inputs. One of my son's localities is World of Warcraft: if Zopa were to offer loans in WoW gold, my son could perform the same function as an Irish publican in the example above and provide an assessment of creditworthiness for avatars he knows.

Chapter 9

Why keep cash?

Money is like muck, not good unless it be spread.
— Francis Bacon (1561–1626) in his *Essays, Civil and Moral*
(Number XV: Of Sedition and Troubles)

THERE ARE, OF course, many arguments for keeping cash despite the post-war techno-utopian fantasies of cashlessness – a cash-lessness that with the wisdom of hindsight we know could not have been achieved with the fiat currencies and technologies of that era. The key arguments in favour of retaining cash were set out neatly by David Keohane in a piece for *FT Alphaville* (Keohane 2015). I have used his categorization here, setting out the five categories of conservatism, demographics, seigniorage, security and privacy and exploring each of them in turn.

Conservatism

Keohane says that abolishing currency will constitute a noticeable change to many people's lives, and change often tends to be resisted. Cash is still used in the great majority of global consumer transactions. But let me reiterate that in the advanced economies at least (and in many emerging markets), there is an ever-growing range of electronic payment and settlement vehicles, with cash pretty much becoming a redundant medium of exchange and means of payment for legitimate, legal transactions (see, for example, Bolt 2006). Among legitimate payments, cash is mostly used for smaller retail payments, which is why the share of cash in transactions by value is usually much smaller than by volume. For instance, in the United States, cash accounts for 46 per cent of consumer transactions by volume but only 23 per cent by value (Bargnall *et al.* 2014).

The use of cash is steadily declining, yes, but we might expect a strong negative reaction to its disappearance simply because of the natural conservatism about money. This needs to be recognized in any planning for a cashless society.

Demographics

Cash use remains high among the poor and some older people, even in developed economies. I agree with Keohane, though, when he says that this should at most mean we keep some coins and low-value notes. There is no need to print $100 bills or €500 notes for these purposes. Addressing that big problem of small change again, I think we should look to the future and find alternative ways to obtain inclusion. We need alternatives to cash to reach everyone, whether in the formal or informal economy, and (and this will have implications when we discuss privacy later) without moral censure. Douglas McWilliams entertainingly set this out in his Gresham College lecture on the Italian black economy (McWilliams 2014), explaining how Italy decided to revise its GDP calculations back in 1987 in order to obtain membership of what is now the G8 by including estimates for its 'black economy' in the figures. When these estimates were added Italy's GDP surpassed the United Kingdom's and Italy was asked to make a greater contribution to the European Union. Oops! Anyway, to restore fair contributions, some years later EU statisticians revised their methodologies to treat the black economy equally in all EU countries and things like software and drug dealing and prostitution were added to the figures in 1991, which in turn boosted the UK economy significantly.

Diane Coyle explores this statistical revision in her book *GDP: A Brief but Affectionate History*, saying that 'the largely cash-based informal economy of moonlighting, avoiding taxes and regulations, but creating work and output, has been placed inside the production boundary'

(Coyle 2014). So it is measured, but the people in that economy are not contributing their fair share to the national piggy bank. We (by which I mean me and my colleagues in the payments industry) don't spend much time thinking about the black economy, but it's an untapped market for electronic payments. Why? Well, yes, on the one hand there is a tax penalty to switching to electronic payments, but, on the other, dealing in cash is not always the optimum transactional solution.

This is because people who live in the margins get screwed by cash, even if that cash is electronic. One hardy soul who was attempting to live on Bitcoin alone reports on a visit to a strip club that accepted the cryptocurrency (Hill 2014), where a dancer explained how she had been tipped in Japanese and Pakistani currency in the past and had no idea what it was worth until she went to a money exchanger to cash it in. (The latter wasn't even worth changing for dollars.) I was fascinated by this story about the weakness of cash in relation to Bitcoin and it reminded me of something I'd seen on the BBC about the relationship between cash and – and I hope readers of a gentle disposition won't be offended by this phrase – 'sex workers'.

A non-governmental organization in Kolkata has started a pro-gramme to help sex workers recognize fake currency given to them by clients. In all the impassioned rants against cash I have made at industry gatherings, it had never occurred to me that one of its fail-ings was that people would use strange currencies and counterfeits to defraud strippers and prostitutes. Another count is therefore added to the prosecution charge sheet. It transpires that prostitution is illegal in India (where there are some three million prostitutes) so sex workers cannot complain to police if they are paid with fake notes. In a country where counterfeits are widespread, it is obviously the marginalized groups trapped in the cash economy who are the big losers; they might very well be winners, then, when they are moved out of that economy (see the discussion about India in the appendix).

What's my point? Cash has a strong hand when it comes to demo-graphics but we can still trump it if we need to provide payment sys-tems that deliver privacy (not anonymity) so that we can provide better alternatives to cash for people who live in the margins. They deserve better than cash.

Seigniorage

Cashlessness would mean central banks and governments losing seigniorage revenue. This is true, and the amounts of money involved could be non-trivial unless there was offsetting through a significant increase in the demand for the other components of the monetary base – a point I will cover in more detail in Part III. For instance, required reserves that pay less than the interest rate on non-monetary financial instruments would be a source of seigniorage, and if excess reserves have some material non-pecuniary convenience yield, the central bank could even make profits on excess reserves that it held.

The resources that can be appropriated through the issuance of central bank liabilities (including currency) that pay less than the market yield on otherwise-similar non-central bank liabilities can be an important source of state revenue, either for the central bank or for its beneficial owner, typically the Ministry of Finance or the Treasury, or for both. For example, over the course of 2014 the stock of euro banknotes and coins increased by €61 billion (0.6 per cent of GDP). For the Federal Reserve, the increase in the stock of coins and notes was $87 billion (0.5 per cent of GDP). Even at the current historically low interest rates, the income obtained is valuable.

Incidentally, given some of the discussion around the use of high-value banknotes for illegal activities, it is interesting to note (see table 3) that the United States earns far more in the seigniorage on its $100 bill than other countries earn from their highest-value note because such a high proportion of US currency is held in stashes and hoards outside of the country.

Table 3. Seigniorage from large notes. (*Source*: Sands (2016).)

Country	Biggest banknote	Seigniorage ($ billion)	% GDP (basis points)
UK	£50	0.1	1
Eurozone	€500	1.9	2
US	$100	23.6	14
Japan	¥1,000	2.0	5
Switzerland	SFr 1,000	0.1	2

Privacy

The abolition of currency would inevitably be associated with a loss of privacy and create risks of excessive intrusion by the government (and other would-be inspectors). Charles Goodhart indeed refers to the proposal to abolish currency as 'shockingly illiberal'. But this cost must be seen against the cost that the anonymity of currency presents to society. As I think we have established (with support from the Bank of England, Deutsche Bank and others!), the underground economy and the criminal community are among the heaviest users of cash because the value of anonymity that cash provides is likely to be highest for them. Evidence consistent with this hypothesis includes the fact that high-denomination notes account for a rather large share of total currency outstanding. The net benefit to society from giving up the anonymity of currency holdings is likely to be positive (including for tax compliance).

Is anonymity essential?

We can use clever cryptography to make electronic cash anonymous. But should we? It is one thing to note that anonymity is one of the factors that may make it difficult for digital currency to substitute for physical currency (Cohen 2006a), but it is quite another to say that electronic money must therefore be anonymous. Indeed, my experiences in the early days of e-cash – the age of Mondex, VisaCash, DigiCash, CyberCoin and all the others – lead me to a different conclusion. When I first began working around these schemes, I assumed that anonymity was a key requirement for cash replacement. For one thing, that's what customers said they wanted in market research, but after a time I began to realize that I was misunderstanding the customers' desire for anonymity. For the most part, it was not a real requirement at all, but a kind of comfort factor introduced into the portfolio of cash-like features, and neither the consumers, nor the banks, nor the retailers, nor anyone else valued anonymity at all. If you put it in a tick box, some people would tick it, but that's because they had not thought about it. Once they had thought about it, their interest in anonymity plummeted. The consumer's view of anonymity is essentially negative, because they see the practical day-to-day issues as more important. If I lose my digital money, I want the bank to find it for me; if I use my digital money to buy something, I want the merchant to give me loyalty points; and so on and so forth. And if you ask me to pay extra to be anonymous... no chance.

There are two issues here. The first is the issue of anonymity itself, and whether it is a necessary, or even desirable, characteristic of the means of exchange. I don't think it is, and I don't therefore see it as essential to the design of future digital money systems. The second is the issue of the implementation of those systems: whether it is feasible (spoiler: it is) to implement a digital money system that can deliver the requisite degree of anonymity. The reason I can say this so confidently is because, again, I think that the well-understood structure of pseudonymity is the appropriate implementation. It is more than a decade since Kim Cameron published his seminal 'seven laws of identity' that included the key principle of *minimal disclosure* (Cameron 2005): that is, that we want systems that disclose the least possible amount of identifying information to enable a transaction. If we design money along these lines, we inevitably find ourselves in a world of pseudonymous transactions, where (say) the bank knows who you are but the counterparty doesn't, since it is not necessary for them to know who you are to complete the transaction. As shown in figure 19, it is entirely possible to implement anonymous, pseudonymous and non-anonymous transactions in the same infrastructure, and there are good reasons for wanting to do so.

Barclays certifies wintermute!barclays.co.uk is David G. W. Birch	nym	
Barclays knows 101101101100010101010101 as wintermute!barclays.co.uk	Vodafone knows 11010101111010101111101011 as neuromancer!vodafone.com	pseudonym
This money belongs to 101101101100010101010101	This money belongs to 11010101111010101111101011	This money belongs to 01010011001101111101010101 anonym

Figure 19. Anonyms, pseudonyms and nyms.

We must, though, ask ourselves what we want. To use the post-modern visualization of Umberto Eco, we shouldn't be creating virtual money, but *hypermoney*: not an electronic version of money as it is, but an electronic version of money as it should be. I'm not advocating the construction of fantasy money that disconnects from the real world – Eco warns of the dangers of feeling 'homesick for Disneyland' (Eco 1986) – but more of an inclusive approach. We should be able to at least categorize the requirements of the various stakeholders (I do not propose to do that here!) to get a better idea of what digital money ought to be aiming for, rather than raise the bar no higher than an electronic simulation of the plastic simulation of the paper simulation of money that we have now.

My feeling is that, as we develop these ideas later in the book, we will return to that middle layer in figure 19 because it provides the means to deliver both privacy and security in future transactions.

Security

Switching to exclusively electronic payments may create new security and operational risks. At times, payment systems – or other critical elements of infrastructure needed for transactions, bookkeeping or appraisal purposes – may be unavailable or malfunctioning. It is true that anything that can be programmed can probably be hacked: there is no cast-iron guarantee that a system will be secure for ever (look at the notable case of SWIFT and the Bank of Bangladesh for a good illustration of this). But technological progress is accelerating and it seems to me that blockchains and clouds and biometrics and so on should further reduce the incidence of outages and malfunctions over time. I do not propose to divert further into security here: suffice to say that if it were not possible to provide some reasonable security around digital financial services, banks would already be bankrupt!

Chapter 10

Thinking about the cashless economy

> Everyone thinks cash is simple and so easy and so fast and so secure. It's none of those things. It's really expensive to move it, to store it, secure it, inspect it, shred it, redesign it, resupply it and round and round we go.
>
> — David Wolman, author of *The End of Money*, quoted by CBS News (2012)

L ET US SUPPOSE that we accept the case against cash and plan to overcome the barriers to cashlessness set out in the previous chapter. We can then ask ourselves what issues we need to consider in planning the transition to a future that is going to include some form of electronic money as a replacement for physical money. At the 1997 World Economic Forum in Davos there was a discussion about electronic cash that attempted to cover all of the relevant topics (Kobrin 1997). Two decades on I still think it provides a useful starting point so I've updated that list of issues and brought them together in a structure that I think rather helpfully identifies nine key issues and four policy areas (as shown in figure 20 on the next page) to examine.

To build up a picture of the cashless economy we need to begin by looking at all of the issues set out here to build our understanding of the cashless economy and what it means for regulators, governments and national (and supranational) institutions. Let us therefore work through those issues individually.

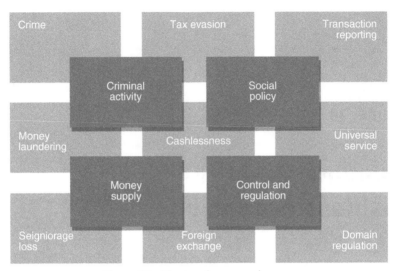

Figure 20. Electronic money issues.

Crime

Citi's chief economist Willem Buiter has noted the odd conspiracy between finance ministries, central banks and organized crime (Buiter 2009):

> Large denomination bank notes are an especially scandalous subsidy to criminal activity and to the grey and black economies. There is no economic justification for $50 and $100 bank notes, let alone for the €200 and €500 bank notes issued by the ECB.

The euro example is particularly noteworthy. Two-thirds of the euros in circulation are in the form of these €100, €200 and €500 notes, which I have never seen. ATMs only give you €20 and €50 notes and I would imagine that many retailers would be reluctant to accept €200 or €500. Indeed, as noted monetary scholar Andy Warhol once said, 'if you try to use a $100 bill in the supermarket, they call the manager'. It's wrong to even talk about these notes as being 'in circulation', since they are not: €95 billion worth are stuffed under mattresses in eastern Europe (Wiesmann 2009). It is interesting to reflect on Buiter's position that it is only the high-denomination notes that should be abolished. He says that as a 'concession to the poor' we should keep a limited number of low-denomination notes and coins in circulation, but this doesn't seem right to me. Cash isn't a concession to the poor: it forces them to pay higher transaction costs than their better-off neighbours. And if the amount of cash falls, then the cost of the whole infrastructure of ATMs and cash registers, armoured vans and night safes will fall on the poor, thus further raising their transaction costs.

It is clear, then, that cash plays a major role in facilitating crime, so cashlessness ought to tackle crime in useful ways: at least by making it more expensive, even if it is unable to eliminate it. But what if – rather than traditional money-related crimes such as fraud and counterfeiting – the primary problem created by electronic money will be in its use to support other kinds of crime? This may well be the case, but possibly not in 'conventional' ways. I don't think that electronic money will make that much of a difference to drug dealers, for example. For my retirement plan I need to find something unique to the virtual, which is why I was sufficiently interested in the novel concept of assassination markets to write about them. I was excited to find that an enterprising chap by the name of Kuwabatake Sanjuro had taken advantage of the invention of Bitcoin to set one up (Greenberg 2013).

In case you are wondering what an assassination market is, it is a prediction market where any party can place a bet (using anonymous electronic money, and pseudonymous remailers) on the date of death of a given individual and collect a payoff if they 'guess' the date accurately. This would incentivize the assassination of specific individuals because the assassin, knowing when the action would take place, could profit by making an accurate bet on the time of the subject's death.

Here's how the market works. Someone runs a public book on the anticipated death dates of public figures. If I hate a pop star or politician, I place a bet on when they will die. When the person dies, whoever had the closest guess wins all of the money, less a cut for the house. Let's say I bet £5 that a specific person is going to die on April Fool's Day 2024. Other people hate this person too and they put down bets as well. The more hated the person is, the more bets there will be.

April Fool's Day comes around. There's a million pounds in bets riding on this particular person. I pay a hit man £500,000 to murder the person. I win the bet, so I get the million quid and give half to the hit man. I don't have to prove that I was responsible for the assassination to get the money: I'm just the lucky winner. If someone else had bet on 31 March and murdered the person themselves the day before, then it would only have cost me a fiver, and I would have regarded that as a fiver well spent.

This is rather an old idea (which, incidentally, is artistically reinterpreted in the chapter 15). The first name it brings to my mind is that of Jim Bell, who back in 1995 wrote an essay on 'assassination politics' that brought the idea into the popular imagination (well, amongst a nerd subgroup). I suppose it was inevitable that the arrival of Bitcoin would stimulate experiments in this area, although I would have thought that Bitcoin was a poor choice for this sort of thing because, whatever the newspapers might think, Bitcoin is not terribly anonymous, as we will discuss in Chapter 13. Bitcoin transactions are public and you can track them until the end of time. Kuwabatake Sanjuro's market is therefore unlikely to destabilize our democratic system, although it might lead to a few arrests for incitement to murder. If it *were* likely to destabilize our democratic system, the FBI would simply set up their own assassination market and put a few quid on Kuwabatake Sanjuro. (Come to that, how do we know that Kuwabatake Sanjuro isn't the FBI anyway?)

Transaction reporting

If non-fiat electronic money did become the primary means of payment, then it would be nearly impossible to effect national economic management. How would the government know whether GDP growth was good or bad if it had no way of knowing what GDP was? In this category, e-cash is really a symptom of fundamental change: as the developed economies have become information economies, the problem of trying to measure, assess and control those economies has sharpened. Economists already wonder about existing measures. Figures that may have understated actual growth and productivity gains over the past few years could have sent the wrong signals to both policy makers and financial markets. In what economist Diane Coyle called the 'weightless economy' (Coyle 1997a) the task of measuring and managing economic activity may well move beyond the bounds of what is possible through traditional structures, and electronic money could contribute to (but not create) a real problem for governments: the lack of intermediaries for reporting on monetary flows.

The idea of a weightless economy, with no physical means of exchange, is now taken for granted but I'm not sure that the implications are. The point is that if there is no physical means of exchange, then there are no entry barriers to alternative stores of value becoming means of exchange. If, in the weightless economy, frequent flier miles and IBM stock became as liquid as dollar bills, then it's not clear how that economy could be managed. How are these transactions to be accounted (absent a win–win–win shared ledger)? And if they cannot be accounted, how are they to be managed?

Since the government cannot simply measure all the money flows in the economy and use that actual data instead of ancient statistical estimates that often need to be revised, it has, in essence, no idea what is going on. This was observed most famously, as Diane Coyle has noted, when Denis Healey went cap in hand to the IMF because Britain was in recession – only to discover, when the figures were later updated, that it hadn't been. This led me to reflect on the old Robert Heinlein science fiction novel *Beyond This Horizon*, in which cash is extinct and all payments run through computers and all the computers are connected to the government computer so the government can twiddle the knobs and dials to keep the economy on course. One might imagine certain other benefits to this electronic economy as well, such as tax collection, to which we turn next.

Tax evasion

The tax gap identified earlier is significant, even for relatively law-abiding countries such as the United Kingdom. If a few tens of billions are being lost here, imagine the size of that tax gap in Greece or Russia – or the European Union.

In 2010 when the EU was studying the feasibility of alternative methods for improving VAT collection (a good example, because VAT evasion is colossal), they estimated the 'VAT gap' (due to VAT fraud, insolvencies, mistakes and VAT avoidance schemes) to be around 7 per cent of GDP,* and more than 10 per cent of the total VAT liability in the EU-27. In other words, more than €100 billion is lost.

When I gave a talk on this topic at the Crossing Borders conference in the Hague in 2013, a chap in the audience told me that he owned fourteen properties in the Netherlands, some houses and some apartments, and that he always paid his builders in cash. He said that the 'white price' for building work in the Netherlands is approaching twice the 'black price' because the builders use cash not only to evade VAT but also to pay their staff and suppliers in cash, thus avoiding income and corporate taxes as well. I joked with him saying that €200 and €500 notes were never used for legitimate transactions and he replied, entirely seriously, that he had never used a €100 note in a legitimate transaction either!

No wonder the taxes I pay as a middle England wage slave are so high when half the population is on the fiddle. An old acquaintance of mine – who used to work for the police, by the way – happened to mention to me that he was having some work done on his driveway. The contractors had quoted him two grand for the work but offered him a £400 discount for cash. When I bumped into him in the town centre he had just been to the bank and had £1,600 on him. I said that I thought he should be prosecuted for conspiracy to defraud Her Majesty's Revenue and Customs but he said that he shouldn't, because he had no knowledge of whether the contractors would declare the income or not, and the fact the payment was in cash did not constitute prima facie evidence of their intention to evade tax. I replied with the time-honoured legal phrase: 'pull the other one, it's got bells on'.

Electronic money isn't all about the stick, though, it can be about the carrot as well. It permits innovations to reward law-abiding businesses.

---

* This is taken from the executive summary of the *Study on the Feasibility of Alternative Methods for Improving and Simplifying the Collection of VAT through the Means of Modern Technologies and/or Financial Intermediaries* (20 September 2010; available at http://bit.ly/2m3UWPo).

VAT, for example, could be automatically levied – and reimbursed – in real time on transactions between liable bank accounts. Countries that struggle with tax collection could go a long way towards solving their problems by restricting the use of cash. Greece, in particular, could make lemonade out of lemons, using its current capital controls to push the country's cash culture into new habits (*Financial Times* 2015).

Not only would electronic money cut my tax bill, it would stop the ridiculous cross-subsidy from the lawful to the lawless that plagues our moral fibre. But my point is that if the black economy were turned white, UK GDP would grow by 20 per cent or so. And if you think I'm joking, let me mention that there is work already underway to look at estimating the illegal drugs trade and prostitution as components of GDP, in compliance with EU rules. Prostitution in Britain is set to be valued at around £3 billion a year, while the drug dealing sector is set to be valued at £7 billion! How much better it would be for the Chancellor of the Exchequer to have accurate figures for all of the economy in his dashboard each morning rather than estimates, and to have tax receipts coming in where and when they were due.

Money laundering and terrorist financing

Huge quantities of cash already flow across borders: electronic money is not going to invent this problem (although it may make it easier to shift money across borders at the retail level). Even without the widespread use of electronic money at the retail level, the cost and complexity of measures to target money laundering are steadily increasing. Years ago, during the first wave of electronic money experiments, the Financial Action Task Force report on *Money Laundering Typologies* (10 February 1999) said that 'no case of laundering has been detected in [the electronic money] sector', and more recent reports on Bitcoin have said the same.

Criminal proceedings that need to be laundered are usually represented by cash. A recent study that tried to answer the question of how much of the cash deposited via official financial institutions can be traced back to criminal activities looked at the case of Italy (Ardizzi *et al.* 2013).

It used a model of cash in-flows on current accounts and proxy money laundering with two indicators for the diffusion of criminal activities related to both illegal trafficking and extortion. The study controlled for structural (legal) motivations to deposit cash, as well as the need to conceal proceeds from tax evasion. Using data from ninety-one Italian provinces observed over the period 2005–8, the study found that the average total size of money laundering is around 7 per cent of GDP: three-quarters from illegal trafficking and a quarter from extortion. (Interestingly, the incidence of 'dirty money' coming from illegal trafficking is higher in the centre/north of the country than in the south, while the inverse is true for money laundering coming from extortion.)

That's Italy. Yet the British government's own October 2015 national risk assessment of money laundering and terrorist financing rates cash as *high* risk, electronic money as medium risk and digital currency (which, according to section 9.24, includes Bitcoin) as *low* risk. We shouldn't regulate digital currency as cash because it's cash that is the big problem and the anti-money-laundering (AML) regulations around cash reflect our helplessness concerning cash transfers. Since cash cannot be tracked around the economy, we (society) have put in place a whole bunch of complicated and expensive rules about accounting for cash when it enters the financial system. But suppose there wasn't any cash. Suppose there was only Bitcoin. In that case, you wouldn't need AML regulations because you would be able to follow every coin around the blockchain. A simple rule that required banks to investigate any coins that had originated in anonymous wallets (or mixers) would be sufficient.

Under the current AML regime, poor people like me are annoyed and inconvenienced about an account that will hold something in the region of five or six grand maximum, whereas rich people who want to ship huge amounts of anonymous cash around the world find it no problem at all, as evidenced by the report of a British businessman who summoned an HSBC banker to his London office and demanded that he authorize a £2.25 million payment to be handed over to him in Swiss francs in Switzerland. The head of the Swiss bank gave the go-ahead (Leigh *et al.* 2015). We find a similar theme in the story of the theft of £400,000 in cash from a twelve-car convoy taking the entourage of a

Saudi prince to Le Bourget airport. Now, if you or I were to carry more than €4,700 into or out of France, we would have to declare it to customs. However, at Le Bourget, as *The Times* puts it, such controls are not 'strictly' applied (Bremner 2014). 'Not strictly applied' means, here, not applied at all, I imagine, so rich people can fly as much cash as they like in and out of France in their private planes. For those without private planes, the cross-border payments infrastructure is less facilitating.

All of which makes me wonder what the point of these rules is. The stringent money-laundering regulations have limited impact on criminal activities. Yet tracking illicit money flows requires considerable bureaucracy and enforcing the regulations costs an estimated $7 billion in the United States, and probably far more (Kenny 2015). These costs are huge and getting bigger; they are out of control from the point of view of the banks and there seems no prospect of reining them in. And yet the controls implemented at vast expense seem to be of limited value at best. In the best of cases, AML efforts are likely to do no more than raise the cost of transactions. A system that misses all but a fraction of a percent of criminal financial flows is almost guaranteed to miss terrorism finance in particular, which involves very small sums.

There might be a better way

In a blockchain world, instead of using AML rules that impose costs and a high entry barrier (which is nothing more than a mild inconvenience to criminals but a serious charge on the poor and a barrier to innovation), the flow of value would be policed by apps and smart contracts. Merging compliance and auditing into real-time monitoring would transform the nature of AML activities. Many levels of bureaucracy might be rendered obsolete both in banks and at regulators because of the ambient accountability* that comes with the blockchain.

Regulatory requirements in the case of cash are designed bearing in mind its 'invisibility' and intractability, while in the case of a blockchain the opposite is true. Although Bitcoin, for example, is often described as 'electronic cash', consider the crucial difference (crucial for AML

---

* This is a term borrowed from architecture: see Zinnbauer (2012).

purposes at least) that when you hold a £10 note in your hand you have absolutely no idea where it might have been before: maybe it comes from an illegal drug hoard or maybe it comes from a charity tin – you don't know. With blockchain assets, on the other hand, you could know exactly the provenance – the entire history of ownership – and anyone, including regulators, can observe the market in real time.

On 18 November 2014, in his first major speech on taking office, the European Commissioner for Financial Stability, Financial Services and Capital Markets, Jonathan Hill, talked about innovation in digital money and virtual currencies (among other things), saying that 'when considering electronic financial services, we need to strike the appropriate balance between guarding against fraud, hackers and money laundering and maintaining ease of use for customers'.

He is right about this, of course, but I wonder what the benchmark for determining what is 'appropriate' is? I don't think we should cripple the development of digital money by applying benchmarks that are so stringent, so rigorous, so absurd that they stop progress completely. We should be building digital money systems that are better than cash, certainly, but to pick up on one of the commissioner's specific points we should not be applying utterly inappropriate, expensive and pointless AML rules, especially when Europe as a whole is doing nothing about cash.

In addition, money-laundering regulations are putting impossible demands on systems designed to serve the poor, requiring, for instance, know-your-customer (KYC) procedures like taking copies of ID documents for anyone receiving an international payout. One cannot help but wonder what the point is of stringent KYC/AML/ATF (for anti-terrorist financing) controls over people sending part of their meagre pay packets back to Somalia from the United Kingdom, or to the Democratic Republic of the Congo from South Africa, when rich people with private planes can import and export unlimited amounts of untraceable cash.*

---

* Somalia, incidentally, is a fascinating case study in monetary evolution since it has had no currency for a generation, and more than a third of the population have mobile money accounts whereas less than a tenth have bank accounts. Almost all the currency in circulation is counterfeit.

The impact of such controls, as far as I can see, is twofold: firstly, criminals and terrorists use cash so we can't monitor their activities; and secondly, the costs of sending money are higher than they would otherwise be. Those costs are significant. The Overseas Development Institute reckons that Africa pays a 'remittance supertax' of nearly $2 billion a year due to the higher-than-average cost of sending money to the continent (Blas 2014). Average remittance fees for sending money to Africa are around 12 per cent (as opposed to the global average of 8 per cent and the UN target of 5 per cent). And remember, these fees fall on people sending money home to their families.

Now, it's not as if the powers that be do not know about this problem. The international body that is charged with reviewing such things is the Financial Action Task Force and in their February 2013 paper on 'Anti-money laundering and terrorist financing measures and financial inclusion' they themselves point out that overly prescriptive legislation can cause payment organizations to be so risk averse that millions of people are excluded from global remittances. And, as Consult Hyperion has noted in its work for the UK government in this area, payments organizations are wary of offering services even when they think they comply with such overly prescriptive legislation because of their worries about future turns of events.

Surely there is something fundamentally wrong with a set of legislative arrangements that mean that the rich can ship money around freely but the poor must pay 12 per cent to transfer tiny amounts? The current system cannot be 'appropriate' whichever way you look at it. Electronic money shouldn't be subject to the same AML rules as physical money: it should be subject to better ones.

Universal service

Regulating money in the mass market means regulating payment systems so that they are inclusive. However, there are several fundamental problems with regulating the payment market (Wang 2010).

- There is a lack of transparency, so regulators find it hard to determine precisely what bank, merchant and scheme costs actually are.

- The private costs do not reflect the social costs, which – and I strongly agree with the author here – should be the regulators' top priority.
- Regulators focus on exogenous factors because the endogenous factors are opaque to them. In other words, reducing the profit on transactions may reduce the incentives for stakeholders (e.g. banks) to introduce new products and services or to invest in R&D.

Neither the banks nor the merchants nor the regulators know what is coming next, and the experiences of regulators who have meddled with the price of payments (in Europe, Australia and the United States) have confirmed the ineffectual nature of this kind of transfer of private costs between market participants.

Given these problems, what should be regulated? Well, if we focus on minimizing the social cost of payment systems as a key reason for delivering electronic money as a universal service, we might reasonably expect social benefits. The social cost of cash (that is, the resources that society as a whole consumes to use cash) has been difficult to estimate in the past, but recent, detailed central bank studies in Belgium and the Netherlands have shown that that cost in developed markets with high card penetration is around 0.5 per cent of GDP (0.48 per cent in the Netherlands and 0.58 per cent in Belgium, in fact).

In relation to the universal service arguments, note that the marginal costs are noticeably different, with the marginal cost of cash being about four times the marginal cost of electronic money (van Hove 2006). Cross-subsidizing cash is not, therefore, a welfare-maximizing strategy, and society should switch to cost-based pricing and leave the rest to the market. This strategy would see debit card transactions triple or quadruple in value while cash transactions would fall by a third. A Belgian study estimates that this approach would make Belgium and the Netherlands about €200 million and €150 million better off, respectively. Scaling up, the European countries they study would as a whole save about 0.14 per cent of GDP (i.e. about a third of the total social cost).

So if we get rid of cash, we save everybody money and everyone's life is made more convenient. Well, if everyone is using electronic money, that's true. What we do not want is for electronic money to become the demarcation line in a two-tier society. We do not want electronic money to become the hallmark of the included while physical money becomes the hallmark of the excluded. But what about those people who cannot or will not move to electronic money. There are, essentially, three options:

- people should be allowed to continue to use notes and coins at their own expense or
- people should be allowed to continue but at someone else's expense or
- people should not be allowed to continue to use physical cash.

While the first two options might intuitively seem to fit with people's conservative nature, and while certain lobby groups (for the aged, the poor and so forth) might prefer the subsidized approach, it could be that taking the apparently extreme step of dumping notes and coins altogether is the only realistic future (there is an analogy here with the turning off of the analogue TV spectrum). This option implies the use of some form of regulation or, at least, firm government policy to open up the benefits to society as a whole.

To be clear, it need not be retail banks that offer universal service. We might reasonably expect financial services organizations, mobile operators, retailers, Internet giants and others to provide services, including this issuing of electronic money itself. One might envisage regulated institutions being compelled to offer a kind of 'universal account' that is nothing more than a prepaid account and a smartphone app: no cheque book, no debit or credit cards, no statements and so on. This would be much cheaper to operate than the 'basic bank accounts' that regulators seem rather fond of. The minimal cost of operating such an account could either be covered by explicit subsidy or it could be paid for from money saved elsewhere: automation of social benefits payments, for example, is one area where considerable savings could be envisaged (Salter and Wood 2013).

Disaster

An important aspect of a universal service is resilience. Recent Japanese experiences with major disasters provides useful input to discussions about electronic money as a cash replacement. After the magnitude 9 Tōhoku earthquake and tsunami in 2011, there were some temporary problems with the card networks because of the disruption but it's important to note that this did not impact all cards because Japan has quite a rich and diverse retail payment ecosystem. I saw Nobuhiko Sugiura, Associate Dean of Chuo University Business School, give a good talk about the current situation at the 2011 E-Money, Cards and Payments conference in Moscow. He said that e-money usage in Japan is growing rapidly but is still a small fraction of total consumer spending (¥1 trillion out of a total of ¥300 trillion, with a 300 per cent increase in the last three years). A third of the population uses e-money, and half of those people (i.e. one-sixth of the population) use it in their phones. It's a competitive market, centred on non-banks because Japanese banks have no real interest in handling small payments because of the cost. The non-banks, to reinforce a theme we will return to later, have different business models, not based on transaction fees. The railways, for example, don't expect to earn anything from their e-money: its purpose for them is simply to reduce their costs. By comparison, con-venience stores want to issue e-money to reduce their cash float. The bottom line is that the use of cash at POS in Japan is 'already falling' because of electronic money.

After the earthquake and tsunami, the offline electronic purse systems (such as Edy and nanaco) carried on working so long as there was power and the backup battery systems or generators were work-ing, so you could still pop round to 7-Eleven and buy your staples. In fact, it was the people who kept their money in cash who suffered greatly: lots of people in Japan – especially older people – keep their life savings in cash in their homes. This is all well and good until a tsu-nami destroys your home and washes your money out to sea (Schneier 2011).

People wanted cash after the tragedy and the demands on ATM net-works surged. But did they really need it? In this kind of catastrophe, where the online POS network goes down but the ATM network stays up and the ATMs remain stocked with notes, you could see why people would go and withdraw cash. But suppose there were no ATMs?

Imagine that there was a magnitude 9 earthquake and a tsunami in Woking* and when I go round to Waitrose to buy some bottled water and rice my John Lewis MasterCard proves useless because the acquiring network is down and the ATM proves useless because the ATM has no power. The store manager at Waitrose can leave the food to rot on the shelves or he can accept a signed IOU. He could accept zero sales because of flaws in the electronic payments system or he could develop a rational fall-back strategy. I discussed this in *Identity Is the New Money*, with reference back to the already discussed case study of the Irish bank strike.

The idea that we must, ultimately, rely on cash because there may be a nuclear war seems out of date. Here's a quote from an NPR *Planet Money* podcast on 'Paper or plastic':

> I'm a retail manager. Please, please, please, for the love of god, let cash die already. It's expensive to store, sort, count, and transport. It goes missing. It falls apart. It sticks together. It slows down the checkout process.

This plea by itself would merit comment here, but what particularly fascinated me was the manager's subsequent comment about power and fall-back. In that shop I imagine that the POS terminals are hand-held devices with rechargeable batteries, so the manager reports that power failure does not stop his shop from accepting cards although it does prevent the shop's cash registers from operating in a secure and *auditable* (my italics) fashion.

And if the POS terminals run out of juice after a few hours, then I'm sure the store manager could just use a Square or an iZettle and get on with things. Note, however, the manager's emphasis on the final point: auditable. Getting rid of notes and coins and replacing them with electronic payments has implications for retailers beyond the basic cost savings of cash handling.

---

* This is, admittedly, unlikely, since our last natural disaster was an ice age 11,700 years ago.

Seigniorage loss

It seems to me that there is something a little wrong in charging central banks with maintaining efficient, effective and stable payment systems when not only do they have a dog in the fight, they have a particularly naughty dog in the fight. If a central bank's income derives from cash, it can hardly be expected to take an independent view of cash as one of a number of alternative payment options in the economy, can it? Or, to put it another way, if we are to replace physical money with electronic money, should it then be provided by the central bank as a public good? If it isn't, shouldn't private issuers compensate the government for lack of income?

If notes and coins are replaced by electronic money, and if that money is not issued by the central bank, then we have to tackle this issue. As noted earlier, central banks stand to lose should electronic money begin to replace notes and coins. Notes and coins represent non-interest-bearing central bank liabilities, and their replacement would lead to a corresponding decline in asset holdings and interest earned on those assets (the seigniorage) as commercial banks would take the 'float' from the central bank. The Bank for International Settlements has calculated that the Bank of England would lose half of its seigniorage profit even if electronic money only replaced coins and low-value notes. The picture in the United States is different, but the situation there is unusual in that around two-thirds of the dollar bills in circulation are outside the country, earning fantastic profits from the wads of $100 bills stuffed under mattresses in Latin America, Russia and elsewhere. (The US Treasury received $77 billion in profits from the Federal Reserve in 2011.)

So, money for nothing, as they say. In essence this is a stealth tax on the people who use cash. But it's significant government revenue. If you look at the United Kingdom, the seigniorage income to the Treasury peaked at £2.4 billion just before the financial crisis. I suppose it might be fairly argued that it's a pretty reasonable stealth tax as it falls largely on drug dealers and money launderers, but it also falls on the poor: a matter that deserves more consideration. In the current year seigniorage will be in the region of only £500 million or so.

You can see the problem with this not being zero, though: if alternatives to cash that are better for the economy (because they are cheaper, for example) come along, then it means that the central bank, and therefore the government, will lose revenues unless they decide to issue the electronic money themselves – this will be one of the options we explore in chapter 14.

It seems to me, then, that the advent of electronic money and the reduction in cash in circulation, or M0 (except for criminal purposes), mean a revenue gap opening up. Governments therefore have two choices: they can reduce expenditure and become more efficient and effective users of tax revenues, or they can find alternative sources of tax income. Since the former is a fantasy, the latter is inevitable. As is often the case, M-Pesa helps us to make these issues concrete. M-Pesa is widely used, but it clearly isn't part of Kenyan M0 since the ultimate liability for the M-Pesa balances rests with the commercial banks where the float is deposited (M-Pesa has a 100 per cent reserve). The fact that it isn't part of M0 is a potential problem, however, from the government's point of view. If M-Pesa keeps growing and M0 keeps shrinking, this deprives the state of seigniorage revenue. This has indeed happened, and the Kenyan government decided to compensate with a special tax on mobile money operators (a 10 per cent duty on transaction fees for all mobile money transfer services provided by cellular phone providers, banks, money transfer agencies and other financial service providers was introduced in a 2012 Finance Act there).

The predictable impact of this was that Safaricom (Kenya's largest taxpayer) put up its M-Pesa fees by 10 per cent. So just as the unbanked trapped in a cash economy pay the stealth tax on notes and coins, so too are they paying the not-so-stealthy tax for the replacement. I'm not sure that's what we want.

Foreign exchange

It's not clear to me why people think that a global currency would improve the global economic outlook any more than creating a new

European currency has helped the European economic outlook, but from time to time there are calls for new currencies for different parts of the globe: there is talk of an African currency, a Gulf currency and even a wholly new world currency.

At the G20 summit in 2009, for example, Nursultan Nazarbayev, the president of Kazakhstan, called for every member of the United Nations to adopt the 'acmetal'. He said the name of his proposed currency was an amalgamation of the Greek work 'acme', meaning 'the best', and 'capital', and he was confident that the new currency would be a success. Indeed, he said that the world would soon be talking of 'acmetalism' instead of 'capitalism' and that Kazakhstan could play a vital role in the implementation of the new money (Blomfield 2009). The newspapers of the time reported Nobel Laureate Professor Robert Mundell (an intellectual architect of the euro) as saying: 'I must say that I agree with President Nazarbayev on his statement and many of the things he said in his plan, the project he made for the world currency, and I believe I'm right on track with what he's saying'.

President Nazarbayev was not the only world leader to experiment with new forms of money in response to the financial crisis. In Venezuela, as in Greece and other countries, community currencies were explored. An example was the cimarrón there. The circular cardboard tokens (with a picture of a runaway slave on them) were supported by President Chavez with the aim of tackling poverty and establishing new economies.

These types of currency tend to be used to mediate barter in 'prosumer' markets, where you can't get the currency to buy things without producing things. Imagine something along these lines at Internet scale: currencies that are specific to markets, that you can't obtain without bringing things to the market. Interesting, not in the sense of Mr Chavez's national socialism but in the sense of reputation currencies, a favourite topic of mine.

The point here is that while we tend to think of central banks and retail banks as the issuers of money, and we tend to think in our 'present' mindset of a single global currency standard, neither of these are necessary to the future. We may have digital currencies that grow bottom up as much as they may be imposed top down, and they may come from governments, companies, communities or elsewhere.

Domain regulation

With electronic money still in its infancy, relatively speaking, early regulation may not only be inappropriate, it may be downright harmful. Nevertheless, some kind of regulatory structure is both inevitable and desirable. New thinking is required. The regulatory model originally adopted by the Bank for International Settlements expert group was based on three distinct domains: the clearing and settlement domain, the operating domain (where electronic value is issued and acquired) and the retail domain. At that time, it was thought that perhaps a European approach could have been developed, with appropriate regulation in each of these domains (Lelieveldt 1997). To some extent this has happened. I am most certainly not a lawyer, but it seems to me that the impact of the European Payment Services Directives has been to begin to separate the regulation of the payment services in the operating and retail domains from the regulation of banking services. The second Payment Services Directive ('PSD2') and the continuing implementation of the Single European Payments Area (SEPA) should bring considerable efficiency gains (Wandhofer 2016).

In the United Kingdom, regulators have gone further and started to open up the clearing and settlement domain as well, in order to increase competition. The 'new access model' to allow wider access to the instant payments infrastructure is already being implemented.

Where should regulation be focused? When banks in the United States last issued private notes, the most serious risk to the holders of those 'free banking era' banknotes, and hence the greatest source of discounting, was not fraud risk but credit risk. The credit risk was, of course, that notes would not be honoured at full value because of either the insolvency or the illiquidity of the issuing institution. This suggested that electronic regulation should be about the 'credit status' of the issuer rather than anything else (Roberds 1998) and I have yet to see any compelling evidence to shift this perspective. We should be rigorous about systemic credit risk but more relaxed about payments.

Managing the cashless economy

In recent times it is economists who have put the concept of cashlessness back on the agenda. First, back in May 2014, Willem Buiter (global chief economist at Citigroup, former chief economist of the European Bank for Reconstruction and Development and a former external member of the Bank of England's Monetary Policy Committee; Buiter suggested early on in the financial crisis that negative interest rates be put on the table as a tool for central banks (Buiter 2009)) said that we should:

> Abolish currency. This is easy and would have many other benefits. The main drawbacks would be the loss of seigniorage income to the central bank... Advanced industrial countries can move to electronic and bank-account-based means of payment and media of exchange without like problem.

Shortly afterwards, *The Times* reported that even conservative Japan might be about to start 'mulling the most radical monetary policy of all – the abolition of cash' because several MPs in the ruling Liberal Democratic Party believed that the abolition of cash, though politically radioactive, might be technically feasible.

I strongly agree that the concept is at last technologically feasible because of key technological advances such as mobile payments. Look again at what is going on in Africa as discussed earlier in relation to M-Pesa in Chapter 7. People who aren't allowed to hold dollar bank accounts hold dollar-denominated mobile top-up vouchers instead. Before Ugandans had an effective electronic payment system they used M-Pesa from Kenya to execute local transactions in Kenyan shillings! Congolese without access to any banking network were using mobile money instead (and may never ever want or need a bank account as a result). In India, Nigeria and elsewhere the banks managed to put a regulatory finger in the dyke for a while but the pressure is building and money is already leaking away from conventional institutions and networks into newer, mobile-centric, customer-facing organizations. The dam will, at some point, burst. How will governments be able to 'manage' the money supply when it is being zipped across borders by mobile phones: global handset hyper-hawala?*

At the very first Digital Money Forum I organized way back in 1997, the late Glyn Davies (author of the magnificent *History of Money*) said that every technology revolution in money has led to less centralized control (Davies 1997). That's a good thing, but it also explains why the conservative nature of governments and regulators comes to the fore in questions concerning money. If anyone anywhere in the world can transact in any currency, then the weak will go to the wall very very quickly. Gresham's law on a global scale.

Money is a field in which conservatism – preserving the status quo – is very definitely a bad thing. Caution is not the best course of action. Why? Because the current system is a bad system. It is a legacy of the pre-information age: a combination of future technology and present thinking. It is not working and it works least well in the developing world, where the International Finance Corporation estimate that the cost of financial transactions could be reduced by as much as 80 per cent through reform of inefficient systems. It is time to think about a transformed cashless economy, not a chromewashed version of the present.

---

* Hawala is an informal value transfer system using a huge network of money brokers, primarily located in the Middle East, North Africa, the Horn of Africa and the Indian subcontinent, operating outside the banking system.

Chapter 11

After the gold rush

In truth, the gold standard is already a barbarous relic.
— John Maynard Keynes in *A Tract on Monetary Reform* (1924)

THE CULMINATION OF the 'present' era was the post-Bretton Woods world of international institutions (the World Bank, the International Monetary Fund), the newfangled computer, electronic communications, the gold window, national currency and central banks. In the great sweep of the history and future of money, this will prove to be a very brief interlude.

The end of the gold era

There are many excellent works on what we might term 'the classical gold standard' and I do not plan to add to them, so I will fast forward our story to its demise. Despite the fuss about it, the global gold standard only lasted for a century and it collapsed before World War II. Britain had created the standard in its modern form in 1821 and left it in 1931 because of the Invergordon Mutiny, which was an industrial action by around a thousand sailors in the British Navy that took place on 15–16 September 1931. For two days navy ships at Invergordon were on strike (one of the few military strikes in British history). This mutiny caused a panic on the London Stock Exchange and a run on the pound, bringing Britain's economic troubles to a head and finally forcing it off the gold standard for good on 21 September 1931. The United States left on 5 June 1933.

As World War II drew to a close, the Allied nations decided to create a new international monetary system. Delegates from many nations came together in July 1944 in Bretton Woods, New Hampshire, and after three weeks of discussions drew up the Bretton Woods Agreement, which created the International Monetary Fund and the International Bank for Reconstruction and Development (now part of the World Bank). The goal from the beginning was to come up with some international infrastructure to use instead of the gold standard. The position of John Maynard Keynes, probably the world's most famous economist at the time, was that the gold standard was a non-starter (Conway 2014a). His view was that it had worked only briefly in the late nineteenth century, and even then only because of a sequence of happy accidents. It failed because when countries found themselves with a balance of payments deficit, the painful adjustment was 'compulsory for the debtor and voluntary for the creditor'.*

Thus, the Bretton Woods delegates decided to replace the old gold standard with a new system based on the US dollar, with that dollar backed by gold. Under the terms of the agreement the United States would sell gold at $35 per ounce to any foreigner who wanted it.

Straightforward. However, the Bretton Woods system that came into being towards the end of the 1950s was a very different arrangement from the one Keynes and the other delegates had devised in 1944. The World Bank had been designed in large part to finance European recovery but in the event the Marshall Plan aid was twenty times greater than any of the bank's loans. The IMF was designed to regulate a system of convertible currencies but the prospect of such a scheme had been punctured by the British crisis immediately following World War II. (The United Kingdom, weighed down by its wartime debts, soon distinguished itself as 'the most persistent troublemaker within the international monetary system'.)

_____

* Keynes's aim was to devise a scheme that made this adjustment equal: where those countries that have built up large surpluses by exporting their goods around the world will be just as responsible for reducing the imbalance as the debtor countries that imported goods from them.

As the world's reserve currency, the dollar became even more central to the system. The dollar was very literally as good as gold but, since the United States developed a massive current account deficit, there were lots of foreigners with dollars and lots of those foreigners wanted actual gold. In fact they wanted gold a lot, so they would also borrow dollars and use them to buy gold. In 1963 the United States imposed a tax on foreigners borrowing dollars. As a result of this a new market grew up in London. People who had lots of dollars (i.e. people who exported lots of stuff to the United States) could lend those dollars to other people in London, thereby avoiding the new tax. Thus was created the 'eurodollar market'.

From the 1950s onward, as foreign competitors churned out goods, America's share of world economic output fell from a third to a quarter. The growing trade deficit and the ballooning budget deficit (the cost of the Vietnam War) meant that by 1969 inflation was above 6 per cent and the eurodollar market was so large ($15 billion) that American banks were able to evade the Federal Reserve's efforts to restrict the American monetary supply. This market continued to grow long after the end of convertibility, incidentally, and by 1994 the 'eurodollar contract' that gave the purchaser the obligation to borrow $1 million in London in three months' time was the most heavily traded financial instrument in the world (Mayer 1998b).

The drain on the American reserves simply could not continue. In 1971, when Richard Nixon made the famous decision to end the convertibility of the US dollar into gold, we entered the world of fiat currency, floating exchange rates, computers, global telecommunications and global trading. In March 1973 the European countries that were still tied to the US dollar announced that they would sever the link, bringing the Bretton Woods system to an end. In 1973, then, one economic era ended and another began (Conway 2014b). We arrived at the point where the Bank of England backs its notes not with gold bars but with fixed-interest instruments bought from the British government (and remits the interest earned to the Treasury).

At this point all the world's national and supranational currencies became 'pure manifestations of sovereignty conjured by governments' (Steil 2007b), and the majority of these currencies were unwanted. That is, they are currencies that people may well use in the marketplace but they do not choose to hold them as a store of value. Governments can force their citizens and subjects to hold fiat currency by requiring its use for state transactions (e.g. tax) but they have no such control over foreigners. In a world in which people will only willingly hold a handful of fiat currencies (US dollars, sterling, euros, Swiss francs and so on) in lieu of gold, the mythology tying money to sovereignty is, as Steil says, 'costly and sometimes dangerous'. He goes on to say:

> Monetary nationalism is simply incompatible with globalization. It has always been, even if this has only become apparent since the 1970s, when all the world's governments rendered their currencies intrinsically worthless.

I strongly agree with Steil's view that the era of floating exchange rates between nation-state-based fiat currencies is a historical 'blip' that won't be part of the future of money (Steil 2007a). I think a reactionary reset to digital gold is unlikely, though, because of the wider spectrum of alternatives that will be enabled through new technology. I hope to persuade you of this in Part III.

PART III
THE FUTURE: MONEY THAT UNDERSTANDS US

The economics of the future are somewhat different. You see, money doesn't exist in the twenty-fourth century.

— Patrick Stewart (as Captain Jean-Luc Picard)
in *Star Trek: First Contact* (1996)

The future of money started back in 1971, and the mental model of money that we have now is out of date. We are in a world of fiat currencies and those fiat currencies are 'pure manifestations of sovereignty conjured by governments' (Steil 2007b) – or, as I said in the introduction, they are just bits. But there's more going on than this dematerialization. We no longer need governments to create money, we no longer need banks to move money, and we no longer need cash to make money real. We think we do, but that's because our mental model is rooted in that present version of money. As former governor of the Bank of England Mervyn King has written, both money and banking are particular historical institutions that developed before modern capitalism and *owe a great deal to the technology of an earlier age* (King 2016b, my italics). In my book *Identity Is the New Money* I wrote in similar vein that there is a mismatch between that mentality and a new, post-industrial economy with a different technological basis for money and that in a generation or so there will be a completely new set of monetary arrangements in place.

Whether you think of it as money with a memory or programmable money or smart money or whatever, understanding the money of the future means a new mental model.

Chapter 12

Seeds of the future

The value of the dollar is social, as it is created by society.
— Ralph Waldo Emerson in *The Conduct of Life* (1860)

ONEY IS NOTHING more than bits; we will have a cashless economy and all money will be digital money. What does this mean for the future? I will begin by observing that talk of 'digital money' can be confusing. Almost all money has existed only in computers for some time, so we need to clarify before we move on. My working definitions are as set out in table 4.

Until now digital money has been conservative: nothing more than an electronic emulation of the physical currency it is replacing. We have had plenty of innovations in payment technology, but these must not be confused with the basic construction of a monetary system (Schlichter 2011), something that I expect will change in the next generation. While payment technology may be changing more rapidly than before, the monetary system has been drifting, freed from its mundane anchors. It is time for someone to seize the wheel!

As cash disappears the potential not only for cash substitutes but for cash alternatives grows. The tectonic plates of money are about to buckle and fracture through the combination of technological push and societal (and regulatory) pull. A generation back, Michael Klein (then chief economist of the Royal Dutch/Shell group of companies) pointed out that monetary regimes have tended to change around once every generation (Klein 2000), and that time-frame has stuck with me. It made me think that those changes were never going to stop with Nixon's closing of the gold window. It is time for another regime change.

We need not panic about it. We've been here several times before. We British are used to it. Around four hundred years ago things were going horribly wrong with money in Britain. If you had asked people about the future of money at that time, they would have imagined better-quality coins. What in fact happened was monetary revolution and a new paradigm. A generation later Britain had a central bank, paper money (although the smallest banknote, £5, was worth a month's pay for a professional (Levinson 2009)), a gold standard, current accounts and overdrafts.

Table 4. What do we mean by digital money?

Money of the past	Money of the future
Physical money Money that exists, at least in part, in a physical means of exchange	*Electronic money* Money that has no physical medium of exchange
Cash Money that can be passed from person to person	*Electronic cash* Electronic money that can be passed from person to person
Mundane currency Physical money that is a unit of account	*Virtual currency* Electronic money that is a unit of account but only in a virtual world
Analogue currency Physical money that is a unit of account	*Digital currency* Electronic money that is a unit of account in mundane and virtual transactions
Fiat currency Analogue currency whose value is maintained by the reputation of the issuer	*Crypto currency* Money without an issuer: a currency whose value is maintained by cryptography

We are at a similar point now, with a mismatch between the mentality and the institutions of paper money in the industrial age and a new, post-industrial economy with a different technological basis for money. In a generation or so there will be a completely new set of monetary arrangements in place. Just as that machine-made, uniform, mechanized coinage introduced by Isaac Newton in 1696 better matched the commerce of the Industrial Revolution, so we can expect some form of digital money to better match the commerce of the information age (Birch 2001).

Mentally, we're still in the present. But can we look around in the present to find the distributed building blocks of the future? I think we can, and they are not just about money and they are not just about technology. We observed earlier that the digital money of the future needs a digital identity for the future. I would add here that our 'past' identity paradigm is being replaced just as our 'past' money paradigm is. They are co-evolving and we need to divert here to explore this relationship.

Identity is evolving

A new understanding of identity is essential and ultimately inevitable, but what that understanding is depends on the complex co-evolution of technology and paradigms. It is very difficult to predict how these will co-evolve even a few years ahead. Technologists (like myself) tend to overestimate the speed of adoption of new technologies but underestimate the long-term impact on society. In other words, it will take longer than people like me expect for new forms of identity to reshape mass markets but when they do, the impact on society will be far greater than just making it easier to log on to the *Daily Telegraph* website. Once you begin to look more than a few years ahead, in fact, the social changes wrought by new technology become hard to imagine.

This has always been the case. For example, on 3 April 1988 the *Los Angeles Times Magazine* published a description of life in 2013. It contained all sorts of bizarre views of life in Los Angeles today, including such unimaginable fantasies as supersonic jet travel and people smoking cigarettes. But it's a fun read, and in the true spirit of palaeo-futurism I encourage you not to laugh at what the writers got wrong but to reflect on why they got it wrong. For example, what is wrong with the following picture from the magazine story?

> Bill is trying to locate his wife to tell her about the dinner guests. Unable to reach her either at home or the office...

It has been at least a decade since my wife called me either at home or at the office or, indeed, anywhere else. If she wants to talk to me, she calls *me*, she doesn't call a place where I might be. The mobile phone didn't just change the payphone business, it changed the communications paradigm: the common mental model that we share as the basis for thinking about communications.

Uneven

The Canadian novelist William Gibson – author of the wonderful *Neuromancer* (the seminal work of fiction for the new economy) and the man who coined the term 'cyberspace' – famously observed that 'the future is already here, it's just unevenly distributed'.

He means that the technologies that will shape society in our lifetimes already exist, it's just that we might not have noticed them yet. One of the key elements missing from that 1988 vision of 2013 was the mobile phone, despite it having existed for a decade. I'm sure that some of the people writing that magazine piece had a mobile phone, they just hadn't realized where mobile phones were going.

Talking about the problem of forecasting across a generation, the futurologist Richard Watson identifies a central problem: that the kind of digital bubbles people are living in lead to a kind of Balkanization of the future (Watson 2011). One must look out of the corner of one's eye to see how technology is being used in ways that might disrupt existing business models, and that is difficult. This leads me to think, in the spirit of William Gibson, that just as those magazine writers didn't see that the decade-old technology of mobile phones would change the communications paradigm, there must be a decade-old technology that is going to be pervasive two decades from now, leading not just to disruption in old businesses and the creation of new ones but to a fundamental shift in mental models.

Social identity is the new paradigm

I think that that technology might be 'social identity'. I specifically do *not* say social media. Yes, social media includes a variety of incredible new technologies and yes we can use them for all sorts of exciting new purposes, but it is what they are doing to identity that will be disruptive in business, commerce and government. Facebook, LinkedIn, Twitter, Tumblr and the rest are already demonstrating just how our identity paradigm is changing. Identity is becoming a concept built on networks, rather than index cards in a filing cabinet.

We already use these social networking identities, albeit in primitive ways, to log in and browse around on the web. We could find ourselves using them for 'serious' business soon. Why shouldn't I be able to log in to the Benefits Agency using my Facebook identity? This might be very convenient for me and it might also be very convenient for the Benefits Agency, but right now the Benefits Agency couldn't really be sure it was me because it has no way of identifying the 'legal me' online, and neither has Facebook.

But that is changing as identification and authentication technologies continue to develop. Suppose these social identities were made a little more secure. We can begin to imagine how more sophisticated and secure forms of identity might begin to change this equation. Perhaps I use my bank account to log in to Facebook, so now Facebook can be sure I am 'Dave Birch', then I can use my Facebook account to log in and sign on for unemployment benefit. This would take us into a different kind of online world: a different online experience where privacy becomes an active, rather than passive, part of life.

The author John Lanchester captured this dynamic very well when he observed that we are more connected in more ways to more people than we have ever been at any point in human history, noting that 'this is changing everything, and it would be deeply strange if it didn't change money too' (Lanchester 2016). It is clear to me that identity is changing profoundly, and that money is changing equally profoundly, and because of the same technological change. The two trends are converging so that all we need for transacting will be the reputations attached to our identities. The technological change that I am talking about here, and I am hardly the only observer to focus on this, centres on the evolution of social networks and mobile phones. They will enable the building of an identity infrastructure that can enhance both privacy and security: there is no trade-off.

Identity and reputation and money

What will link changing identities with changing money as these trends converge? In a word, trust. In a world based on trust it will be reputation rather than regulation that will animate trust in economic exchange (Birch 2000). The 'social graph' – the network of our social identities – will be the nexus of commerce, administration and interaction.

In our distant past we were just as defined by our social graph as we are now (Lessin 2013). There were no identity cards or credit reference agencies or transactional histories of any kind. In the absence of such credentials, you were your reputation. Managing and maintaining these reputations among a small social group of an extended family or a clan was not a scalable solution as civilization progressed and moved on to growing trade as the source of prosperity. In the interconnected future, however, there is every reason to suspect that the social graph will resume its pre-eminent position since, as I will explore, it is the most trustworthy, reliable aspect of a persona. This is where the link with money begins to take shape.

Far-fetched? I don't think so. In 1696 there was no cash in England with the result that 'no trade is managed but by trust' (Levinson 2009). With trust, you don't need cash, as demonstrated by the example of the Irish bank strikes (see page 121). The economy did not collapse in the absence of cash (which soon ran out), as personal cheques and IOUs provided the circulating means of exchange. There were, at the time, some 12,000 retail shops and (perhaps more importantly) some 11,000 public houses that provided transaction services. As Antoin Murphy's seminal work on this reports (Murphy 1978):

> It appears that the managers of these retail outlets and public houses had a high degree of information about their customers – one does not after all serve drink to someone for years without discovering something of his liquid resources.

Identities and credentials are easy to create and destroy. Reputations are much harder to subvert since they depend not on what anyone thinks but on what *everyone* thinks. Reputations are a sound basis for interaction. People make judgments based on other people's reputations, and behave better out of concern for their own (Dyson 2001). There would have been precious little chance of pretending to be someone else at the local pub in Ireland in the 1970s, and as a consequence the social graph could provide the necessary infrastructure: the landlords knew whose IOUs were good and whose were not and did not need money to substitute for their memories.

There you go bringing class into it again

Remember that *Los Angeles Times Magazine* prediction about 2013? It included a trip to the ATM to draw out cash:

> After parking the van, Alma stops for some cash at the bank-teller machine in the lobby of her building. She punches in her ID number and then puts her thumb on the screen. After several tries, the machine finally recognizes her fingerprint and gives her two $20 bills with bar codes that verify the money has been issued to her.

The last time I went to the United States I paid for everything using cards and my mobile phone (Starbucks, LevelUp and Google Wallet). And yet a Gizmodo article from 2012 (http://bit.ly/2nsczb2), discussing the near future, makes the following claim:

> There's some debate about whether plastic credit and debit cards will be totally replaced by mobile payment systems in the next few years. However, there's no doubt that, in 2030, my son will carry a wallet with cash in it, because we'll still be using paper and metal money well into the future.

That leads me to speculate that there might be a social class element to the money transactions roadmap. Perhaps in another quarter of a century the middle classes will have abandoned cash and it will exist only to serve the poor and excluded. That is a plausible scenario but I do not think we will see it. The device formerly known as the mobile phone is a way to accept payments as well as make them, and this is what will do for cash.

The UK media reaction to the suggestion that cheque clearing might be abandoned in a decade is illustrative. 'How will I pay my cleaning lady?' was the typical insurmountable hurdle to change identified in the pages of the *Daily Telegraph*. This strikes me as exactly analogous to the mid 1980s comments about mobile phones that went along the lines of 'well if I want to make a phone call when I'm out, I can always use a payphone'. (Just for the record, I pay my cleaner using my bank's mobile app and the money is sent via interbank systems with immediate availability of funds.)

People thought plastic cards would one day replace cash but this never happened because, while it was very easy to issue cards to everybody, it was not possible to give everyone terminals to accept cards. The mobile phone has profoundly altered this dynamic because it can replace both the plastic card and the terminal for accepting plastic cards. It is this latter point that is truly disruptive.

Tally sticks turned the mechanism for deferred payment into a store of value. The cheque turned the store of value into a means of exchange. The gold standard created a stable unit of account. None of these implementations is a law of nature. They depend on technology push and societal pull.

Today, I think we are in the same position as the medieval court experimenting with tally sticks or industrializing England paralysed by pre-industrial means of exchange. We have a paradigm mismatch that explains the midlife crisis: money feels out of place, unconnected, uncomprehending. We're using the mentality of coins and the institutions of paper to try and deliver the money for a new economy. It is time for the debate on redesign that Christine Desan called for.

Chapter 13

Counting on cryptography

A purely peer-to-peer version of electronic cash would allow online payments to be sent directly from one party to another without going through a financial institution.

— 'Satoshi Nakamoto' (2008)

AVING SAID EARLIER that the iconic technology of money is the plastic card, right now the iconic money of the future seems to be cryptocurrency. Spurred on by the widespread interest in Bitcoin, there are many people looking at the concept and wondering whether cryptocurrency – money that depends on cryptography rather than the belief of a community – might be a feature in the emerging money landscape. There are, of course, cryptocurrencies other than Bitcoin and cryptocurrencies that are yet to be invented (Birch 2015), but if we use Bitcoin as the case study then it seems the jury is out. Stefan Brands, a leading cryptographer and one of the pioneers of digital currency, describes Bitcoin as 'clever' and is loath to denigrate it, but he believes that, fundamentally, it is structured like 'a pyramid scheme' that rewards early adopters (Wallace 2011) – a charge also levelled by other observers of the financial markets (Robinson 2014).

Whether this is true or not, there is no clear evidence that Bitcoin (despite the media attention) is being used at all. While the public debate around Bitcoin has, from the earliest time, focused on the supposed anonymity of the payment system and therefore its use for black market purchases (Greenberg 2011), detailed analysis of data from the Bitcoin system by the Federal Reserve has shown that it has barely been used at all for payments for goods and services (let alone for guns and drugs), and further that the pattern of circulation of Bitcoins and the dynamics of the exchange rate are consistent with low usage of Bitcoin for retail transactions (Badev and Chen 2014). Despite the widespread interest, Bitcoins do not seem to be gaining much traction in the 'real world' of payments.

Wait? Bitcoin?

Bitcoin is a decentralized, peer-to-peer means of exchange. If you have a Bitcoin, which is just a string of numbers, you can send that Bitcoin (or a subdivision of it) to anyone else. (If you want to understand how Bitcoin works, a good place to start is the original paper on the topic: 'Bitcoin: a peer-to-peer electronic cash system' by 'Satoshi Nakamoto'.) I'm no expert on cryptography but there's no reason I know of to question the basic idea: use a computationally difficult challenge to create strings of bits that it's hard to make but easy to copy, then use digital signatures for transactions. I get my Bitcoin (a string of bits) and then to transfer them to you I add a digital signature and send them to you. Every time we do a transaction, we tell (essentially) everybody else that the bits now belong to you. The closest analogy to this – one that I used in my previous book – is the stone currency of the island of Yap in the South Pacific, as described by Milton Friedman (Friedman 1991). The huge stones that represented money never went anywhere, people just remembered who they belonged to.

Why would people use Bitcoin? There seem to be three key reasons: one is that they want a cheap, irreversible online means of exchange (cash for the twenty-first century); another is that they want an anonymous and fungible means of exchange (coins for the twenty-first century); and yet another is that they want to use a non-government currency because they don't trust governments to manage money properly (a store of value for the twenty-first century).

Now, having been involved in a previous attempt to create a global, decentralized, peer-to-peer means of exchange that addressed the first two of these issues, Mondex, I'm naturally interested to see how Bitcoin develops. I'm frankly sympathetic to many of its goals, because I too believe that a 'frictionless' means of exchange for the online world would stimulate a new era of trade, and therefore prosperity. In an essentially frictionless system, where the transfer of value is simply the transfer of bits, the key problem to overcome is that of 'double spending'. In other words, if I send you some value (bits), how do you know that I haven't already sent that value (i.e. a copy of those bits) to someone else? Two different solutions to this problem were explored in the 1990s.

- The usual solution was, and still is, to have a central register.
- The Mondex solution was to use tamper-resistant hardware (smartcard chips) to store the balances.

The Bitcoin solution is to distribute the transaction record across the network (every node knows every transaction). When you send a Bitcoin it takes a few minutes before your payee can spend it again because the network needs to be updated. This all works if consensus can be coordinated (otherwise the nodes wouldn't know the order of the transactions). Bitcoin uses some clever mathematical jiggery-pokery called 'proof of work' to make it exceedingly difficult to subvert the consensus.

Which solution is best? The combination of central register plus tamper-resistant hardware, so that low-value payments can be handled quickly (e.g. M-Pesa), looks pretty good, especially if it can be extended to work offline in some environments. However, the combination of some form of shared ledger with tamper-resistant hardware for strong authentication may be the best way forward.

As discussed in chapter 9, I think that what the public want is privacy, not anonymity. If I lose my wallet, I want my money back. This is why I carry prepaid cards when I travel, rather than carrying cash. I recently went through the very process of getting my money back because I gave my son a prepaid euro card to use on a school trip in Spain and he lost it when there was still €70 left on the card. No one else could use that card (they wouldn't know the PIN and it has no name on it so they couldn't pass AVS online) and I got the money back. Personally, I think this is closer to the kind of cash that makes sense in the new economy. It's economically infeasible (although not computationally infeasible) to track and research every payment, but when something goes wrong it can be restored. And if I did use the card for some illegal purpose, the police could get a warrant and the card issuer would of course point them to me.

I'm not sure that I want to live in a society where unconditional anonymity exists for money. I don't want the bad guys to be able to operate with impunity. But neither do I want every little transaction I make trawled by corporates, the media, the government. The solution must be money with privacy built in, so that privacy is the default and it takes legal process to uncover transaction details.

Steaming ahead

When the Mallard set the world speed record for a locomotive in 1938 it was powered by a steam engine. But it was a very different kind of steam engine to the Thomas Newcomen 'atmospheric engine' that went into commercial use two centuries before, in 1712. Cryptocurrency might well be the future of money, but that doesn't mean that Bitcoin is.

There is one big difference though: Bitcoin is open, whereas the steam engine was encumbered by the patent system that retarded its development. The lesson of history is unequivocal and well studied, and that lesson is that the rigorous enforcement of patents around the steam engine slowed innovation to a crawl. Bolton and Watt came up with the critical invention that transformed the inefficient steam engine used to pump water into an efficient engine that could power an industrial revolution: the separate condenser. They patented it in 1777 and until that patent expired in 1808 there was virtually no innovation in steam engine design and the efficiency of working engines barely changed. The result was an average performance improvement of less than 4 per cent per annum. Once their patent expired, the rate of growth more than doubled, to 8.5 per cent per annum, and the multiplying effect of exponential growth meant that the performance exploded to the point where you could put an engine on wheels and use it to carry passengers.

Not only did Watt use patents to hold back competition, his own efforts to invent a better engine were sabotaged by the same structures since he couldn't use the more efficient Pickard system (for converting rotary motion) until James Pickard's patent expired in 1794 (Nuvolari 2004).

The point of this diversion is that Bitcoin is like pumping water out of mines and the Bitcoin blockchain is like the Newcomen engine that was invented for that single purpose. It is hopelessly inefficient but it does that one thing (pumping water in the case of the steam engine; censorship resistance in the case of Bitcoin) well enough to be adopted. However, someone will come along and invent better shared ledger technologies (of which the Bitcoin blockchain is only one kind, remember) and create entirely new businesses as a by-product. What is more, because they will be unencumbered by patents (unless the US Patent Office is daft enough to grant patents for trivial and obvious uses of shared ledgers), the progress will be rapid.

It seems to me, therefore, that while cryptocurrencies may well become mainstream (something I will discuss later in this book), it does not follow that Bitcoin will.

Is Bitcoin money?

The IMF itself suggests that history and economic theory broadly seem to support a monetary regime with public provision of currency over a competitive private system. While noting that there are examples of currency being provided by private banks, for example, without high over-production, it also notes that the inflation performance of public money has been (in their words) mixed (He *et al.* 2016).

They conclude that currencies such as Bitcoin do not, at present, fulfil the economic roles associated with money. Firstly, Bitcoin is not a reliable store of value because of its volatility – although I could personally be persuaded that, over time, volatility could decrease to a point where it could become an acceptable store of value. Secondly, it has very restricted use as a medium of exchange, and my interpretation of the widely available usage figures is that it remains primarily a tool for speculation (there is very little retail use, and it is not clear to me that it will grow). And thirdly, it does not seem to be used as an independent unit of account against which other currencies might be measured. Taken together these points suggest that Bitcoin is better understood in economic terms as a peculiar kind of digital commodity rather than as money.

Looking to regulators for guidance results in confusing advice. Charles Evans attributes the problem with classifying Bitcoin to its multiple facets and the way each looks to different constituencies (Evans 2015). As he notes, specific regulators oversee specific subsets of regulated activities and view Bitcoin in terms of a pre-existing category over which they have authority rather than opt for a laissez-faire approach until we (i.e. society) work out what to do and then set the right regulatory framework. There is no holistic view or logical regulatory position on cryptocurrency (which is what the IMF means by 'virtual currency'). Evans goes on to make an interesting comment that I think illustrates a very fundamental point about the interplay between technology and money, identifying a line of thought that the historical functions of money – medium of exchange, store of value, unit of account and measure of value – can be separated and that each function can be performed by different means.

This defines my thinking too. One of the first things I ever wrote for a client on the topic of electronic money, a couple of decades ago, included the observation that technology would allow us to separate these functions from one another and implement each in a different way – another example of the 'back to the future' dynamic of a more interconnected world. While we might therefore find it odd to use London Loot as a medium of exchange and Islamic e-Gold as a store of value and US dollars as a mechanism for deferred payment, our phones will not. To return to Mervyn King's point about money being a 'particular historical institution' (King 2016b), there is no reason why money should continue to work the way it does in response to continuing technological change, and no reasonable person would expect it to.

Is Bitcoin the future of money?

If Bitcoin is not money now, might it be the future of money? I think not: Bitcoin is not the future of money, and the future of money is not Bitcoin. Why the interest then? A reasonable conjecture is that the interest in Bitcoin points to a latent demand for change and, usefully, generates and focuses debate about current monetary structures (Jansen 2013). Much of the interest isn't, therefore, specifically in Bitcoin, to my mind, but rather in the feasibility of an alternative to the state-issued, interest-bearing fiat currency money system that has been in place for the last forty years. If that interest helps to facilitate debate about what society wants from money in the future, that is very helpful, but it does not imply that Bitcoin satisfies whatever requirements might emerge from that process.

The post-industrial economy needs a new kind of money, not one devised by representatives of the status quo, and it won't be the single galactic currency of science fiction imagination (we can't even make a single currency work between Germany and Greece, let alone between Ganymede and Gamma Centauri) but thousands, even millions, of currencies.

Crypto-alternatives

Not only will there be cryptocurrencies beyond Bitcoin and not only will they be better – more powerful and more efficient – there will also be a great many of them as the cost of launching a digital currency falls. Without launching into a treatise on cryptocurrencies, I think it would be useful to take a quick look at a couple of the newer cryptocurrencies on the block (pun intended) to give a sense of the spectrum of possibilities.

Ethereum

Ethereum is comparable to Bitcoin, in that it uses a blockchain, but it was designed to provide a better platform for shared ledger applications. One of the most interesting users of such applications was the Distributed Autonomous Organization (DAO). The general concept of a distributed autonomous organization goes back a few years, having roots in organizational decentralization theories that have been turbocharged (as William Mougayar puts it) by cryptocurrency technologies and trust-based automation (Mougayar 2016), but the DAO in question was created as a new kind of business: an investor-directed investment fund. In June 2016 it delivered a valuable case study when a software vulnerability enabled an attacker to move something like a third of the funds into a subsidiary.

The subsequent debate about what to do was fascinating. On the one hand there were advocates of the 'code is law' school of thought who felt that the investors should take their medicine, and on the other there were advocates of the 'pragmatic' school of thought who felt that the transactions should be reversed. Since you can't go back and edit a blockchain (which is sort of the point of it), this is achieved by 'forking' to create a new blockchain. This was done but a significant minority of miners felt that this was the wrong decision so they continued with the original blockchain as Ethereum Classic.

At the time of writing, the 'market cap' of Ethereum is significantly higher than that of Ethereum Classic.

Ripple

After Bitcoin and Ethereum, the third biggest cryptocurrency is Ripple, which unlike those first two has its roots in local exchange trading systems (Peck 2013). It is a protocol for value exchange that uses a shared ledger but it does not use a Bitcoin-like blockchain, preferring another kind of what is known as a 'Byzantine fault-tolerant consensus-forming process'. Ripple signs every transaction that parties submit to the network with a digital signature. Each user selects a list, called a 'unique node list', comprising other users that it trusts as what are known as 'validating nodes'. Each validating node independently verifies every proposed transaction within its network to determine if it is valid. A transaction is valid if the correct signature appears on the transaction, i.e. the signature of the funds' owner, and if the parties have enough funds to make the transaction. If a node believes that the transaction is valid, it 'votes' for it to be included in the updated ledger. If a super-majority (in this case, 80 per cent) of nodes do not vote for the transaction, the system rejects the transaction and it is not reflected in the next updated ledger (Rosner and Kang 2016).

Interestingly, the Ripple consensus algorithm has a great deal of flexibility in the 'permissioning' process, giving transaction architects the option of allowing entirely permissionless access (to create a public ledger, similar to Bitcoin's) or allowing participants to extend trust to new partners and revoke the trust of existing partners. Participants can therefore choose which other participants they want to include in their 'consensus quorum' (Kelleher 2015).

Rather than target consumers, Ripple targets banks, positioning itself as an efficient intermediary for payments, remittances and cross-border exchanges. It makes payments using its native cryptocurrency, 'the ripple' (XRP), by having users make digitally signed updates to its ledger and leaves the users to determine which other users they do or not trust for the purposes of consensus.

Zcash

As I write, at the end of 2016, the newest kid on the block is Zcash: a cryptocurrency with the added special sauce of genuine anonymity, rather than the pseudonymity that got some people into trouble when they used the Satoshi system for various nefarious purposes. The claim of Zcash's founders is that it is true electronic cash because it shares the characteristics of cash, such as fungibility.

Zcash has two types of electronic purse that are used to store the electronic cash: *transparent* and *shielded*. The transparent wallets and the amounts that are sent to and from them show up on the blockchain just as they would in Bitcoin. But if a user opts to use a shielded wallet, it will be obscured on the public ledger. And if both the sender and the receiver of funds have opted for shielding, then the amount sent will be encrypted as well.

Transactions remain confidential unless the counterparties reveal their purses by 'selective weakening' of the cryptographic protection. Now, while I am sceptical about whether confidential transactions will get much traction in the mass market, that does not mean that the creators do not have a point. An electronic cash system that is going to offer some form of privacy must be built on an anonymous infrastructure. You can't do it the other way around. And yet…a truly anonymous infrastructure provides ample opportunities for mischief and some of this mischief might be of significant harm to society as a whole. What will happen?

Trying to think this through, it seems to me that there is something of a paradox here in our mental transaction models. We believe that our own transactions should be anonymous because we are good people, but we want other people's transactions to be tracked, traced and monitored because they might be criminals. Obviously, we don't want child pornographers and terrorists to have access to anonymous electronic cash but we do want freedom fighters and oppressed minorities to have access to electronic cash.

So how might this paradox be resolved? As I suggested on page 127, one option might be that society assumes that anonymous cash will be used primarily by criminals and possession of it will be taken to be prima facie evidence of criminality. People, companies and governments will not use the underlying anonymous currency but instead use the privacy-enhancing kinds of money built on top of it.

The idea that counterparties can choose whether a transaction is visible or not is interesting and under-explored. Whether Zcash succeeds or not, and I have no relevant knowledge to help me to decide one way or the other, the general principle strikes me as unlikely to vanish and it makes consideration of the institutions and structures that are needed in the presence of anonymous electronic money all the more pressing.

Digital fiat

Whichever cryptocurrencies succeed or fail, I don't think there will ever be a 'Britcoin'. Central bank digital currency is about balances and an appropriately private protocol for moving value between accounts. My prediction is that this is likely to look more like the bastard child of Ripple and M-Pesa than a blockchain cryptocurrency with a one-to-one reserve in sterling. Does this kind of digital fiat currency make sense? I think it does, and so does the Bank of England, which says in its study of the issues that (Barrdear and Kumhof 2016):

> We study the macroeconomic consequences of issuing central bank digital currency (CBDC) – a universally accessible and interest-bearing

central bank liability, implemented via distributed ledgers, that competes with bank deposits as medium of exchange. In a DSGE model calibrated to match the pre-crisis United States, we find that CBDC issuance of 30% of GDP, against government bonds, could permanently raise GDP by as much as 3%, due to reductions in real interest rates, distortionary taxes, and monetary transaction costs. Countercyclical CBDC price or quantity rules, as a second monetary policy instrument, could substantially improve the central bank's ability to stabilise the business cycle.

I find the observations of the authors compelling (although my knowledge of relevant economic theory is limited) and I have come to similar conclusions from the technological direction. Since the observations of the Bank of England from an economic perspective correlate so closely with my observations from the technological perspective, I think the concept must have some validity. I will now make a few observations about the impending changes.

A monetary regime with central-bank-issued national digital currency (i.e. digital fiat) has never existed anywhere, a major reason for this being that the *technology* to make it feasible and resilient has not, until now, been available.

The monetary aspects of *private* digital currencies (a competing currency with an exogenous predetermined money supply) are *undesirable* from the perspective of policymakers. Also, the phrase 'digital currency' is perhaps a regrettable one as it may invite a number of misunderstandings among casual readers.

Digital fiat means a central bank granting universal, electronic, 24/7, national-currency-denominated and interest-bearing access to its balance sheet. The Bank of England says that it envisages the majority of transaction balances continuing to be held as deposits with commercial banks and observes (as I did above) that digital currency has nothing to do with shared ledgers, distributed ledgers or blockchains.

The cheapest alternative for running such a system would clearly be a fully centralized architecture (M-Pesa in Kenya is the obvious example), but as the Bank notes this will come with increased resiliency risks that are likely to be deemed unacceptable. However, options that are distributed but permissioned would provide an improvement in the efficiency of settlement and serve to improve resiliency relative to the status quo, both of which would represent a *reduction in cost* to the real economy (hence my earlier observation about the desirability of a shared ledger implementation).

The key feature of such a system is that the entire history of transactions is available to all verifiers, and potentially to the public at large, in real time. It would therefore provide vastly more *data* to policymakers, including the ability to observe the response of the economy to some kinds of policy change almost immediately.

There is, in my opinion, no sane argument against digital fiat. Let's get on with it. And let's have no limit on the number of different currencies that the banking system's ledger might hold.

Here comes the blockchain

What might that ledger look like? The emerging consensus, at least in the finance sector, seems to be that the technology behind Bitcoin, the blockchain, will disrupt the sector (Raymaekers 2015), although many commentators are not at all clear how (or, indeed, why). Melanie Swan posits that even if all of the infrastructure developed by the blockchain industry were to disappear, its legacy could persist (Swan 2015). This is because the blockchain has provided new larger-scale ideas about how to organize financial services and, as Swan and other observers have noted, there is a very strong case for decentralized models. She is surely right to say that 'decentralisation is an idea whose time is come', and to identify the Internet as a new cultural technology that admits techniques such as shared ledgers. The blockchain is, as I have mentioned, only one kind of such a shared ledger, and the Bitcoin blockchain works in a very specific way. This may not be the best way to organize shared ledgers for disruptive innovation and it may not, in my opinion, point towards where the disruptive influence of shared ledger technology will deliver its biggest benefits to society.

Shared ledgers

Interest in shared ledger technology has been rekindled as interest in the blockchain has grown. The blockchain is the specific distributed shared ledger technology that underpins Bitcoin (Wood and Buchanan 2015), and it can be seen as a consensus database that everybody can copy and access but, by clever design, not subvert: a permanent record of transactions that no one can go back and change. The key characteristics of this blockchain that make it a special kind of shared ledger – and that are particularly appealing to developers and to its proponents – are that it is distributed, decentralized, public or transparent, time-stamped, persistent and verifiable (DuPont and Maurer 2015). However, the blockchain is just one kind of shared ledger. Let us put the blockchain to one side for a moment and build up a view of shared ledger technology that will both locate the blockchain in the right context and inform interaction between technologists and financial services imagineers.

A shared ledger is a view of the current state of a marketplace, and all the transactions that led to that current state. Technological advances in networks and storage mean that it has now become possible for all market participants to be able to store copies of all transactions and to resolve, in a reasonable time, discrepancies between the different copies. Since the copies are held by multiple market participants, there must be a mechanism for determining which copies are true in the event of discrepancies that might be caused by errors or fraud. This is known as a 'consensus mechanism' and it varies by type of ledger.

A simple way to see how shared ledgers might work in practice is to start by considering the basic building blocks of the shared ledger. I have set these out in four layers in table 5. This sets out the communication, consensus, content and contract layers, each of which leads to a different key driver for the use of a shared ledger rather than a database.

Table 5. Shared ledger layers: the '4Cs'.

Layer	Function	Why
Contract	How can we animate the immutable record?	Innovation
Consensus	How do we agree an immutable record of those transactions?	Integrity
Content	What is in the transactions?	Flexibility
Communications	How are transactions propagated to appropriate entities?	Robustness

I think it might help to give a short case study of what these different layers mean in practice. I will use the example of the Bank of England to do this because its Deputy Governor for Markets and Banking, Minouche Shafik, gave a speech concerning the review of payment systems early in 2016 that mentioned shared ledger technology (Shafik 2016), saying that

> instead of settlement occurring across the books of a single central authority (such as a central bank, clearing house or custodian), strong cryptographic and verification algorithms allow everyone in a [ledger] to have a copy of the ledger and give distributed authority for managing and updating that ledger to a much wider group of agents.

But why would the Bank of England want to do this? Why would the market participants? Shafik was talking in the context of the United Kingdom's Real Time Gross Settlement (RTGS) system, as described earlier. A couple of years ago this vital piece of national infrastructure had a bit of a hiccough and went down. The situation was so serious that Mark Carney, the governor of the Bank of England, launched an independent review into what was the worst disruption of Britain's banking payment system in seven years (the breakdown meant that the CHAPS payment system was down for more than nine hours; the bank was forced to start processing the most important payments manually).

Now you can begin to see why a sensible, conservative and practical institution like the Bank of England might be thinking about shared ledger technologies. It doesn't need a blockchain or Bitcoin, proof of work or mining. What does it want? Well, if you go back to the four layers shown in table 5 you can see that the Bank's interest makes sense at every layer.

Robustness

Suppose that every bank had an RTGS gateway but that there was no actual RTGS system, just a ledger, as the deputy governor mentioned? Each gateway would have a full copy of the ledger (the Bank of England would have a copy too!) holding the participants' balances with each other. There's no RTGS to go down now.

Innovation

The banks might decide to hold balances in new assets, so that final settlement might be in something other than central bank money. This might be what Mervyn King, the former governor of the Bank of England, was alluding to when he remarked that we may not use money in the future (King 2016c). I once had the great good fortune to have lunch with Otmar Issing, who was a member of the board of the Deutsche Bundesbank and subsequently a member of the executive board of the ECB as its first chief economist.* In a speech at the turn of the millennium, he said 'it is conceivable that at some point in the future the settlement might take place without regular recourse to central bank reserves' (Issing 2000). I took this to mean that because of technological and economic change, settlement could be in corporate paper, energy, Islamic e-Dinars, water, land, gold or London Lucre, all of them appearing as content on this kind of ledger. Using claims on future products and services, companies might net out central bank money altogether.

Integrity

A very fast consensus protocol can be used to ensure the near-immediate verification of the integrity of the copies held by each participant so that counterparty risk would be down at the same level as it is today using the centralized system. This integrity is especially for delivery versus payment settlement, as is used for CREST. The integrity of the ledger would, in this case, represent finality of payment (and the reduction of counterparty risk) because of the legal status conferred on the RTGS shared ledger technology by the Bank of England.

Flexibility

It may well be that the members of the RTGS shared ledger technology might want to add shared ledger applications (or SLAPPs) to run on

---

* I don't think I've ever met in person anyone who knows more about money.

their consensus computer (I dislike the misleading term 'contracts' for these*), creating new kinds of financial application and, indeed, new kinds of financial market. Current centralized systems (such as the RTGS system) are inflexible and difficult to change, whereas SLAPPs give markets tools to build customized self-enforceable agreements across the sector and the ability to manage new kinds of assets introduced at the content layer. In a SLAPPs world, business rules could be invented and implemented with relative ease.

The Bank of England is right to be exploring this new technology and I certainly think that it has something to offer. But that does not mean that the Bank is going to start using Bitcoin as a settlement system or that Bitcoins will replace sterling!

---

* But '4Cs' is easy to remember.

Chapter 14

Who will make money?

Cuius regio, eius religio.

— The principle of the Peace of Augsburg (1555)

Cuius regio, eius pecunia.

— David G. W. Birch (2014)

AVING EXAMINED THE issues associated with a cashless economy, considered the roadmap to the post-POS mobile-centric environment, looked at some of the new tools for the democratization of money and decided that the electronic money alternative is better, we can now delve deeper into the fundamental question of who will be issuing that electronic money in the future. Right now, as you will recall, money is 'managed' by central banks but it is created by commercial banks. Most of the money in the economy is in the form of bank deposits created by commercial banks making loans. In essence, whenever a bank makes a loan it simultaneously creates a matching deposit in the borrower's bank account, thereby creating new money (McLeay *et al.* 2014). There's no need to go deeper into this mechanism at this juncture, but it is useful to note the following three key points in the Bank of England's high-level description of the current money-creation regime.

- Rather than banks receiving deposits when households save and then lending them out, it is bank lending that creates deposits.
- Although commercial banks create money through lending, they cannot do so freely without limit. Banks are limited in how much they can lend if they are to remain profitable in a competitive banking system.

- Prudential regulation also acts as a constraint on banks' activities to maintain the resilience of the financial system.

In summary, then, it is currently banks who very literally create money, and the 'rump' of money that is still in the form of state-issued notes and coins doesn't matter and will go away.

The future money makers: 'The 5Cs'

When those rump notes and coins vanish to be replaced entirely by some form of electronic money, there are a variety of different options as to its creation. While there is obviously a wide spectrum of possibilities – and undoubtedly that spectrum spans possibilities beyond my imagination – for the purposes of focusing our thinking I have brought together five realistic options: the 5Cs listed in table 6.

Table 6. Who might make digital currency? The 5Cs.

Who might issue money?	What kind of money?
Central bank	Fiat money I do not include inflation in the definition of risk here, naturally

Commercial banks
  Credit money under political regulation
	Bank money
	  What we have now, essentially: money created by banks under central bank supervision

Companies
  Futures money under commercial regulation
	Private money
	  Currency to be redeemed against future products and services

Cryptography
  There may be political, economic, business, social or technical reasons to give up control of money to mathematics
	Dosh ex machina
	  There is no issuer and no external regulation of issue

Communities
  Reputation money under commercial regulation (decentralized fiat or futures, but no credit)
	Local money
	  Bearing in mind that 'local' means something different in the virtual and mundane cases

We can now look at each of these options in more detail and begin to think about the practicalities of future money.

Central banks

It is natural to look to central banks to replace analogue currency with digital currency, and indeed many people are already studying this option. The Positive Money movement has issued a report on digital currency that provides an excellent review of the issues associated with a central bank alternative to physical currency (Dyson and Hodgson 2016). It recommends that central banks issue digital currency for six main reasons.

- To widen the range of monetary policy instruments by overcoming the zero lower bound on interest rates and enabling new instruments of monetary policy, such as 'helicopter money'.

- To promote innovation in payment systems. When looking at the options for central bank digital cash and when reflecting on our experiences with population-scale schemes such as M-Pesa in Kenya, it seems to me that providing a good API on top of the system and allowing innovators to build new products and services on top of that is transformational and, to my mind, much more likely to lead to real innovation, making the payment system serve the wider economy more efficiently and more effectively.

- To increase financial stability by providing a risk-free alternative to bank accounts. This would increase financial stability by reducing the concentration of liquidity risk and credit risk. Non-bank financial institutions, in particular, would benefit from being able to hold funds in central bank money rather than in the form of an uninsured bank account. Incidentally, Dyson and Hodgson go on to remark that the existence of digital fiat might well exacerbate bank runs as people, for whatever reasons, retreat from other forms of liquidity to risk-free central bank money. The existence of risk-free digital currency in the United Kingdom could plausibly lead to an inflow of funds from foreign banks into sterling digital cash, and that could in turn push up exchange rates.

- To recapture a portion of seigniorage. As discussed earlier, I think that the seigniorage argument is not terribly persuasive one way or the other. It is plausible, though, that the Bank of England might roughly double its seigniorage revenue if most people switch most of their spending from bank accounts to digital cash.
- To create alternative finance. Separating the creation of money from bank loans might mean a reduction in lending, which would have implications for the economy. There are implications for banks in the supply of credit but also implications for the potential for alternative finance to fill the gap.
- To increase financial inclusion. I don't want to get into the complexities of the relationship between financial and social inclusion, and the implications for other regulatory frameworks such as KYC and AML, but I see financial inclusion through ready access to low-value digital currency accounts as one of the main reasons for wanting to move in that direction. Remember, people who are trapped in a cash economy on the margins are the people who suffer most from its existence.

The authors go on to explore the concept of digital cash account providers, which would essentially be something like an Electronic Money Institution is now but with a 100 per cent reserve in central bank money. There are, though, *other implementations* for delivering digital fiat.

Delivering digital fiat

There are two questions we need to ask after reviewing these issues. The first is whether it makes sense for a central bank to issue a digital fiat currency and the second is how the economic, technological and regulatory framework for such a currency might work. Now, it is important to understand that there is a spectrum of opinion on this, with opinions rooted in cultural, not technological, differences. To illustrate this point we can compare the Bank of England with, for example, the People's Bank of China.

Zhou Xiaochuan, then governor of the People's Bank of China, gave an extensive interview at the beginning of 2016 in which he set out the Bank's current thinking about digital currency (Shuo *et al.* 2016). Noting the 'irresistible trend that paper money will be replaced by new products and new technologies', the governor went on to set some broad parameters around just how such a digital currency might operate in China. He is very clear on these considerations, saying that 'a digital currency should be designed in a way that can best protect people's privacy, but we also need to pay attention to social security and social order'.

I couldn't agree more with him about this. Society should set the dial, not technologists, no matter how much we think we know better. The argument isn't about where the privacy dial should be set (I expect I might disagree with the governor's position on that) but about who should set it.

The governor went on to say that it will take about ten years for a digital currency to fully replace cash in China but that he has plans on how to gradually *phase out paper money* (my italics). The costs for cash transactions will increase, as the banks start charging fees for the accounting of physical cash, but he is realistic in saying that digital currency and physical currency will coexist for a long time. As I have written before, I don't think a 'cashless society' means a society in which notes and coins are outlawed: just a society in which they are irrelevant. Under this definition and with the guidance of the central bank, China could easily achieve this goal.

Britcoin and Brit-Pesa

In 2014 the British government held a consultation on digital currencies and in 2015 HM Treasury published the responses to it in a report called 'Digital currencies: response to the call for information'. The government concluded that 'while there are clear barriers to digital currencies achieving widespread use in their current form, the 'distributed ledger' technology that underpins digital currencies has significant future promise as an innovation in payments technology'. This jumbles apples and oranges, since digital currency and cryptocurrency are not the same thing at all (as set out in table 4). A cryptocurrency derives its value from cryptography; a digital currency obtains endogenous value.

One of the organizations that responded was Citi, who said that the greatest benefits of digital currencies can be realized through the government issuing a digital form of legal tender. This currency would be less expensive and more efficient, and it would provide greater transparency than current physical legal tender or electronic methods.

Whether we leave the provision of digital currency to the central bank, as Citi suggests, or to commercial banks is ultimately a political decision, not a technology decision (or even a business decision). David Andolfatto, vice-president at the Federal Reserve Bank of St. Louis, has written that central banks should consider providing digital money services (possibly even a cryptocurrency) at the retail and wholesale level (Andolfatto 2015). As he observes – and I agree with him – there is no reason why, in principle, a central bank could not offer online accounts (which would not need deposit insurance) to provide individuals and organizations with a completely safe place to store money. He also notes that this structure would, of course, give the central bank new monetary policy options, as discussed previously, including the ability to pay interest on low-denomination money (possibly at a negative rate).

I rather think that the creation of money should be under government control even if the government isn't doing it, and I also rather think that there are many reasons for thinking that allowing commercial banks to create money does not always lead to the best possible outcomes for society. But should central bank money be the *only* money? Probably not – and we will discuss the various options for private money provision later in this chapter – but for the time being it is sufficient to note that Andolfatto and others suggest that having competing currency substitutes would serve to act as a bound on government policy options.

If we focus on the issue of the central bank digital currency, the question quickly becomes one of how to implement it. New thinking is needed here – new thinking about the relationship between identity and money (you will be unsurprised to read!) – so let's look at and address three core issues: KYC, censorship resistance and cryptocurrency as an option.

KYC

Clearly anything that is intended to replace physical cash must be inclusive. That means that there cannot be any KYC, nor any other conventional form of account application process. Personally, I do not see this as a negative because society benefits more from having all transactions electronic than it loses from affording a very limited form of economic anonymity for very limited transaction values. Once all of the transactions are in the system, we can use big data analysis and the like to track down criminals. If they're not in the system, this option is not available.

We might, for example, allow people to open digital payment accounts at the Bank of England and store amounts up to £1,000 with no identification at all, perhaps requiring only a mobile phone number or a postal address to activate the account. I see this as being a bit like getting a Gmail account! I log into the Bank of England, create a new account in the name of 'DaveBirch' and get a message telling me that that account already exists so I choose 'DGWBirch' instead. Anyone can then pay me through the national digital payment system by sending money to £dgwbirch. I'd also get another account as 'Lord Tantamount Horseposture' that I could use for gambling or buying drugs or whatever else it is that people do with cash. If I want the account balance to exceed £1,000, then I would have to provide some other form of valid and acceptable identification, such as a Facebook account, and if I want the account balance to exceed £10,000 (the suspicious transaction reporting limit), then I would have to present a passport or something like that. The point is that everyone should be able to get an account. These accounts could pay interest and the interest could be negative. I can easily imagine economic circumstances leading to a tiered system whereby accounts with balances below £10,000 pay 0.5 per cent interest but accounts with balances above £10,000 pay −0.5 per cent interest. Why? Because you want people with surplus money to invest it in productive enterprise but you also want to help the poor at the same time.

Censorship resistance

Neither the central bank nor society wants censorship resistance when it comes to value transfer and I cannot see any reason why this would be implemented. I can certainly see the argument in favour of pseudonymity, which is why I would be allowed to have an account in the name of Lord

Tantamount Horseposture, but of course that account would be linked to my mobile phone number or my Apple ID or my LinkedIn account or whatever, so that if I were to use that account to fund terrorism or evade tax, the authorities would be able to obtain a warrant and uncover that link. This is what I have previously referred to as a 'smash the glass' form of conditional anonymity. So, I might make a bet with someone who doesn't know who £horseposture actually is, but if that bet turns out to be linked with suspicious activity and a Far Eastern betting syndicate, then the police could easily get hold of me.

Cryptocurrency makes no sense for central banks

Given that I am obviously in favour of such an account-based system – which would have minimal transaction costs since the transfer of a hundred pounds between £dgwbirch and £horseposture would use minuscule amounts of resources – and given that I do not see censorship resistance as a requirement, I do not see why cryptocurrency would make sense as a potential implementation. I understand perfectly well that there are arguments in favour: people might, for example, argue that a single point of failure for this important national resource would mitigate in favour of a replicated distributed shared ledger to defend against cyberattack or (as is traditional in the United Kingdom) government incompetence in the procurement and operation of large-scale computer and communication systems. I am open to evidence on this matter, but my first thought is that the cost of maintaining consensus for a system replacing cash on this scale far outweighs the cost of moving from 'five nines' availability to 100 per cent availability. Note also that if censorship resistance is going to be implemented using a cryptocurrency (e.g. Bitcoin), then I simply cannot imagine a scenario in which central banks would allow proof-of-work mining to be controlled by anonymous, largely Far Eastern, mining pools.

Brit-Pesa-ledger it is

Let's summarize, then. A central bank digital currency? This is an entirely reasonable proposition. Imagine something like M-Pesa but run by the Bank of England. Everyone has an account and you can transfer money from one account to another using a mobile phone app (this could use the trusted execution environment (TEE) that is found in modern smartphones: a secure microchip similar to the one on your bank card) or by logging in with two-factor authentication to any one of a number of service providers that use the Bank of England API to access the accounts or by phoning a voice recognition and authentication service. Drawing on my company's experiences from M-Pesa, the Token Administration Platform in Nigeria and other population-scale mobile-centric systems that we have advised on, I think that this API might be the single most important thing that a Brit-Pesa would deliver to the British economy.

In addition to the obvious benefits to trade and industry, and in addition to the obvious benefits to law enforcement, it would mean that the Bank of England would have a real-time dashboard of economic activity that could be added to the real-time retail payment dashboards of the banks (I'm joking of course: they don't actually have these) so that when the Chancellor of the Exchequer gets up in the morning he or she can see exactly what consumer spending was the day before. *Exactly*. So, Brit-Pesa is not only a means of obtaining the cost-effective efficiency that Citi referred to but it ought to be a great improvement in helping to manage the economy.

A digital currency experiment in Ecuador

An interesting case study of digital currency took place in Latin America: the Central Bank in Ecuador (the BCE) has launched a national mobile payment scheme that is designed to handle B2B transactions (along with P2P, top-up, cash in and out, in-store purchases and electronic receipts) with a very low transaction fee (a $50 charge costs four cents: a rate of approximately 0.08 per cent). In essence, a hard electronic currency was created by the BCE: a centralized government solution to that big problem of small change that we discussed earlier (see page 119).

Anyone over 18 could open an electronic money account for free, without the need for physical registration, using a service based on the Unstructured Supplementary Service Data (USSD) system. To open an account, a user called '* 153 #' from their mobile phone with any mobile operator. The service began with transactions such as loading, unloading, delivery of electronic money, personal payments, business payments, consulting and bank transfers and then moved on to electronic money payment of utilities, tax obligations, orders and other things.

A particularly interesting aspect of this otherwise vanilla prepaid value transfer system was that it was denominated in US dollars. The US dollar has been legal tender in Ecuador since 2000, when the post-gold standard 'sucre' was abandoned (apparently, though, the 'centavo' coins are still in use). This, as the economist John Kay has noted (Kay 2013), is in itself an interesting comment on the subject of what is or is not a currency: the 50 cent coin is minted for the government of Ecuador but the United States does not issue 50 cent coins itself (it only issues quarters, nickels, dimes and pennies). So while anyone in the Galápagos or Quito would accept it, no one in Washington would. (Kay also notes that dollar coins, minted for the US Treasury, have not proved popular in the United States but are widely circulated in Ecuador!)

It is important to understand that the US Federal Reserve banknotes that are in circulation in Ecuador, stuffed under mattresses in Ecuador and fuelling the less-formal sections of the Ecuadorian economy are in essence an interest-free loan to Uncle Sam. By replacing these with an electronic currency – or I suppose, more strictly speaking, an electronic currency board – the BCE hoped to reclaim the seigniorage for itself. All well and good, and the ability to transact electronically will also be of great benefit to the country's citizens.

If the central bank had asked for advice from people experienced in the creation of a national non-bank mobile payment systems (Consult Hyperion, for example), I am sure it would have been advised to make the system a platform for innovation and to encourage entrepreneurs to build local solutions on top of it. In the first edition of this book, I said that such a system would also benefit greatly from transparent auditing, as the citizens would not hold the electronic currency unless they were sure that it would remain redeemable at par for US dollars themselves. This is because they would naturally be concerned that if the government were to fall prey to the temptation to put more of the electronic US dollars into circulation than it has (or has the equivalent of) in reserve, then it would simply be creating doomed electronic assignats that would never obtain traction in the wider economy, leaving Ecuador unable to reap the many benefits of its transition away from cash (*Economist* 2014b). This lack of transparency, and the consequent lack of faith from the populace, led to the system being abandoned. In December 2017 Ecuador's National Assembly decommissioned the system and opened the market to mobile payment alternatives from the country's private commercial banks and savings institutions (White 2018), thus providing an enduring case study in the competition between risky central bank deposits and less risky commercial bank deposits!

Commercial banks

The issue of private bank money under what is generally referred to as a 'free banking' regime – which means the unrestricted competitive issue of currency and deposit money by private banks on a convertible basis (White 1989) – is comparatively well known and well understood. The famous case study of Scottish banks before the Bank of England monopoly was extended in Victorian times is illuminating. For a couple of hundred years England had gradually been folding the control of money into the Bank of England monopoly whereas in Scotland private banks continued to issue their own money and competed to keep the value of their money up. The result was a period of incredible innovation when the more tightly regulated London and country banks failed more often than the less tightly regulated Scottish banks (*Economist* 2008). This competition, as noted in the section 'Scotland the Brave' on page 66, resulted in many of the innovations that we take for granted as part of modern banking. Table 1 showed how many of these innovations (coloured banknotes, overdrafts, chequebooks and so on) date from that time. Bank failures in Scotland were fewer and less catastrophic than bank failures in England, supporting a kind of ecological argument that diversity provides strength.

The argument for this kind of private money was developed more recently by economists of what is known as the Austrian School. Back in the 1970s the Nobel-winning economist Friedrich Hayek presented the case for a diverse monetary base, with private banks once again creating money through credit but each creating their own money (Hayek 2007).

Neil McEvoy and I explored this Hayekian view many years ago, arguing that whereas the world's currencies are currently organized on broadly territorial lines, one might imagine a future in which currencies occupy (overlapping) niches according to the virtual, as well as geographic, communities to which people belong and where a vigorous 'foreign' exchange market existed in which people (or, more likely, their computers) trade these currencies (Birch and McEvoy 1997).

Hayek put forward the proposition that the provision of private currency would be more likely to result in sound money than state currency because the issuers of that private currency would have to compete to keep the value of their currency up. It was an interesting thought experiment but it was difficult at the time to see it as anything more than that. Hayek himself discussed the practical barriers, noting the problem of 'cash registers' or 'vending machines' handling notes and coins of differing denominations, sizes and weights, whose relative values would fluctuate. However, Hayek foresaw (perhaps he too had read Bellamy) that:

> Another possible development would be the replacement of the present coins by plastic or similar tokens with electronic markings which every cash register and slot machine would be able to sort out, and the 'signature' of which would be legally protected against forgery as any other document of value.

We now have the digital money and digital identity technologies to make this vision real, cost-effective and desirable and we also have the 'tokens with electronic markings' that Hayek predicted: the mobile phones that all of us now have. Would people use such private digital currencies rather than (or as well as) fiat digital currencies or bank-issued national digital currencies? The Bank of Canada studied this using the Canadian experience with paper money (as well as the comparable

American experience) and concluded that while government-issued digital currency will not drive out private digital currencies, legislation and regulation will be needed for private and government-issued digital currencies to form a uniform currency (Fung *et al.* 2017). The kind of regulation developed in the EU seems to be a step in the right direction, and the regulatory category of Electronic Money Institution is well established; another positive move is the Japanese decision to see cryptocurrencies as a commodity of the kind that can be exchanged for goods, services and legal tender (thereby making it a kind of currency), thus bringing Bitcoin and its ilk into the normal course of business.

Privatization

The weakening of the link between banking and payments, discussed earlier, is a good thing. The fact is that there has never been any sound reason why a single institution should perform both the payments and lending functions. The skills required and the nature of the work are quite different (Brown 1973). Organizations other than banks are perfectly capable of handling payments and there is every reason to encourage a richer ecology in the payments world.

In Europe we have had Electronic Money Institutions and Payment Institutions, India has Payment Banks, and so on. The idea that regulated non-banks could issue money is straightforward. While not of core interest to this book, it is clear that this shift has major implications for banks: while there is no economic principle that inexorably leads to banks providing large-scale payments businesses, they do just that, and these businesses represent a significant fraction of banks' income (Radecki 1999). The management consultants McKinsey say that payments accounted for approximately half of US payment industry revenues in 2011, so if payments are to be provided by non-banks in the future, banks are going to have to work hard to develop alternative revenue sources. One of these sources might well be services relating to identity management and authentication (but that's a topic for another book!).

New technology, new regulation and new business models hint at the potential for a wave of creative destruction – different entities providing different functions all previously put under the heading of banks and money – as the inexorable unbundling of financial services continues. This is not a bad thing.

Companies

The issue of private company money was intriguingly explored by the famous lateral thinker Edward de Bono, who set out his thoughts in a pamphlet for the London-based think tank the Centre for the Study of Financial Innovation back in the early 1990s. His central point was that if the cost of issuing currency falls, it makes economic sense for companies to issue their own money rather than use equities (de Bono 2002); he went on to write that he looked forward to a time when 'the successors to Bill Gates will have put the successors to Alan Greenspan out of business'. De Bono's argument was that companies could raise money just as governments do now: by printing it. He put forward the idea of private currency as a claim on products or services produced by the issuer rather than the bank credit of Hayek. IBM might issue 'IBM dollars' that would be theoretically redeemable for IBM products and services but also practically tradable for other companies' monies or for other assets. To make such a scheme work, IBM would have to learn to manage the supply of money to ensure that (with too many vouchers chasing not enough goods) inflation did not destroy the value of their creations. But companies should be able to manage that trick at least as easily as governments do, particularly as they don't have voters to worry about.

The idea might sound odd at first, but I think it is quite easy to imagine how such a system could work. A start-up launches and, instead of issuing equity, it issues money that is redeemable against some future service. So, for example, a wind farm start-up might offer money in the form of kilowatt hours that are redeemable five years from now. In the early days, this money would trade at a significant discount to take account of the risks inherent in the venture. But once the wind farm is up and running and producing electricity, the value of the money would rise. There might, in this case, be a demand for renewable energy that drives the value of the money higher than its original face value.

With millions or even tens of millions of these currencies in circulation and constantly being traded on foreign exchange markets, it might sound as if the situation would be unbearably complex for anyone trying to pay anyone else. But remember this is not analogous to me taking notes out of my wallet and handing them to you. This is my computer, or more likely my mobile phone, talking to your computer or mobile phone. And our mobile phones are entirely capable of negotiating between themselves to work out the deal. In his original work de Bono puts it quite nicely when he says:

> Pre-agreed algorithms would determine which financial assets were sold by the purchaser of the good or service depending on the value of the transaction. And the supplier of that good or service would know that the incoming funds would be allocated to the appropriate combination of assets as prescribed by another pre-agreed algorithm. Eligible assets will be any financial assets for which there were market clearing prices in real time. The same system could match demands and supplies of financial assets, determine prices and make settlements.

I cannot resist pointing out that de Bono also wrote that the key to any such developments 'is the ability of computers to communicate in real time to permit instantaneous verification of the creditworthiness of counterparties': this is an early vision of what we might now call the reputation economy, which I explored in my previous book, where I noted that identities and credentials are easy to create and destroy but reputations are much harder to subvert since they depend not on what anyone thinks but on what everyone thinks (Birch 2014). Now that the combination of mobile phones, social networks and strong authentication makes the calculation of reputations (including creditworthiness) cost effective even for small transactions, the technology needed to deliver the IBM dollar is in place.

Here the new technology may make a real difference. The de Bono assumption that trading in money (essentially) is cheaper than trading in equities or other kinds of corporate paper is challenged by shifting to shared ledger technology. I can see that the spirit of de Bono's proposals can be implemented in an attractive and practical manner, but not in the way that he imagined. If you can move IBM paper around without expensive clearing and settlement infrastructure, then to all intents and purposes that is the IBM money that he was thinking about – something that hasn't gone unnoticed by pioneers in the cryptocurrency community. Corporate paper that is a cross between private money and a loyalty scheme (so that if you hold the paper you obtain some benefits in terms of products or services) strikes me as being something of an opportunity.

Another factor in favour of this approach is the drive for transparency in company ownership. One might imagine a kind of stock exchange where start-ups launch as previously described but instead of issuing money they create equities that are 'coins' on a blockchain. The trading of these coins is indistinguishable from the trading of electronic cash (because there is no clearing or settlement) but there is an additional transparency in corporate affairs because the transactions are public. And while the company and observers may not know the beneficial owner of the coins (because the wallets are identified only by keys), the stock exchange will be set up to issue wallets after appropriate KYC. In the general run of things transactions are private, but where there is suspicion of wrongdoing the ownership can be exposed under appropriate legal conditions.

Cryptography

The newest category of plausible issuer of the money of the future is, essentially, nobody. The advent of Bitcoin and other cryptocurrencies has opened up the possibility that the money of the future may be intrinsic to the technology and beyond control insofar as it extends to issuing.

It is very interesting to speculate about what this might mean for the political economy of coming generations. If money is placed beyond political control, then we have a return to a sort of 'electronic gold standard', where national economies have very limited options to respond to changing economic circumstances. If those new currencies exploit the technological potential to deliver the anonymity of cash but on a global scale, then one might imagine that the rich and powerful will enthusiastically adopt the new store of value to remain beyond any reach of democratic accountability. Neither of these visions seems particularly appealing to me.

On the other hand, the utopian vision of multiple overlapping currencies beyond political control interacting to create an environment that is much more resistant to shocks and chaos may have something to it. The idea of a richer money ecology is appealing in many ways.

Given our experiences to date it seems to me that the technology of cryptocurrencies, the 'consensus computer' discussed earlier, will undoubtedly have widespread application and cause some disruption as it creates new and better markets. Whether it will also provide the money that those markets use in final settlement is much harder to say but I stick with my prediction that it will not.

I can see may reasons why we might find ourselves using a permissioned shared ledger to implement, for example, a digital currency – or, more interestingly, to allow for the trading of assets – but I can see no obvious reason why we would want to use a permissionless shared ledger to implement a national cryptocurrency. I feel that, as I live in a society, I would like society to have some control over money.

Communities

Fiat currencies are creatures born of the nation state and as such reflect the coincidence of interests that the nation state itself represents, each of which might be enabled by technology to separate and create money. Anthropologist Keith Hart provides a useful categorization of these communities (Hart 2012) that I have used to construct table 7.

While there is a tradition of looking at social, alternative and complementary monies to achieve social good, it has been at the margins of economic thinking. The idea of using such community-based money to, for example, create economic activity where there is none – set out in, for example, Lietaer's *Future of Money* (Lietaer 2001) – is very attractive and there have been a great many such experiments around the world. It appears that digital community currencies have a greater spending multiplier than fiat currency (Groppa 2013), which says to me that we should take them seriously as we continue to reconfigure following the global financial crisis. Historically, however, the ideas were rooted in geography. Technology allows us to 'unbundle' the communities shown in table 7 and look at them individually as potential money issuers.

It is a good time to do so. The issue of community money was given renewed thrust by the global financial crisis and there are examples in countries such as Italy and Greece where the absence of conventional money has pushed communities into thinking more radically. A useful case study is the 'TEM' currency in Volos in Greece (Donado 2011). One TEM is equal in value to one euro, and it can be used to exchange goods and services. Community members start their accounts with zero and get TEMs by offering goods and services. They also receive books of physical currency itself, which are printed with a special seal that makes it difficult to counterfeit. Businesses in the town will accept TEMs (generally in part payment). Individuals can also borrow up to 300 TEMs, but they are expected to repay the loan within a fixed period.

Table 7. Communities.

Type of community	Nature of community
Political	A link to the world and a source of law at home
Place	The territory
Virtual	The constructed cultural identity of citizens
Interest	Subjectively and objectively shared purposes in trade and war
Monetary	Common use of a national monopoly currency

It may be tempting to belittle alternative currencies as limited, unrealistic or maybe a little kooky, but they do work so long as they don't run into counterfeiting problems and supply is intelligently controlled to avoid inflation. Nothing but perception makes the issuing authority of the US government more legitimate than, say, the Ithaca HOURs Circulation Committee. Both try to supply users with real money, and both do their best to wisely steer monetary policy in a way that promotes growth (Wolman 2012).

This is, then, a vision of multiple currencies each of which originates in a different community. I stress again that it is not a vision of a single world or galactic currency! A single currency is more efficient for transactions but it stops economic managers from tailoring the institutions of money to local circumstances (Castronova 2014), hence the attractive notion of more communities tied to specific currencies, thus minimizing their transaction costs between members. If we divide alternative currencies into local and global (Kenny 2014), this perspective tends to privilege the local, and there is evidence to support the idea that such currencies are better suited to supporting growth within communities (Groppa 2013), largely because they mitigate against hoarding (which plagues the nascent Bitcoin economy). Douglas Rushkoff writes that the 'simplest approach to limiting the delocalizing, extractive power of central currency is for communities to adopt their own local currencies' (Rushkoff 2016).

More than economic efficiencies, however, community currencies may embody values (e.g. environmental policies) that are important to the community and therefore drive usage. One might imagine a gold-backed currency for the Islamic diaspora, a renewable energy currency for the Green movement, and so on. Our redesign of money should include values. These might be fun or serious, political or superficial. As I wrote many years ago, people might, for example, want to transact in Manchester United Pounds (they already use Manchester United credit cards and savings accounts) or Microsoft dollars or Islamic e-gold or Cornish e-tin for reasons that have nothing to do with the drivers for the use of traditional means of exchange (World Economic Forum 2016).

Social currencies

I'd like to end this chapter with some thoughts about how the nature of redesigned money might impact society. To use the post-modern visualization of Umberto Eco mentioned earlier, we shouldn't be designing virtual cash, but *hypercash*: not an electronic version of money as it currently is, but an electronic version of money *as it should be* (Eco 1986). If that money is going to embody the values of the communities that create it, we are moving into new realms. Reflecting on the 17th Annual Tomorrow's Transactions Forum, held in London in March 2014,

Wendy Grossman said that 'we are moving from money we understand to money that understands us'.

I was very taken with this encapsulation of a couple of thousand years of monetary evolution, from coins made from precious metals to computations across the social graph. We no longer have money that the normal, typical member of society can understand. The public don't understand how this crucial economic technology works, and they don't care. The debate about what happens when we go from dumb £5 notes with no memory to Bitcoins on a blockchain that know where they have been, and then on to more sophisticated, more intelligent, more connected forms of money, is of the greatest importance and it needs to be opened up so that the public can take part.

Right now, we have money that observes us. Barclays, Visa, MasterCard, Amex, Simple, Loop, Amazon – they all know what I bought yesterday, where I bought it, when I bought it, how often I have bought it and so on. But they don't know why I bought it or who I bought it with. With integration with the social networks, however, they soon will. And they might not be happy! This suggests to me that we will have multiple monies that embody different values, and in a world of shared ledgers and shared ledger applications (what some people still, annoyingly, insist on calling 'smart contracts'), it might well mean a type of money that won't allow you to use it unless you have a track record of upholding its values!

If you think that this is a radical view of the future of money, I have to tell you that it is only the starting point. We can think about this smart money as a vehicle for Szabo-style synthetic currencies (Szabo 1997) that could go even further and be used directly in contracts to substitute for a medium of exchange. This ought to be the science fiction writers' new exchange paradigm. No more 'that will be ten galactic credits, thank you', more 'you owe me a return trip to Uranus and a kilogram of platinum for delivery in twelve months'. This reinvention of a turbo-charged form of barter may, at first, seem to be a step backwards, but it is not. Quite the contrary: it is a consequence of programmable money in a reputation economy.

Chapter 15

Reimagining money

The difficulty lies, not in the new ideas, but in escaping the old ones, which ramify, for those of us brought up as most of us have been, into every corner of our minds.

— John Maynard Keynes in *The General Theory of Employment, Interest and Money* (1935)

A S NOTED EARLIER, we technologists are aware that we overestimate the timescales for adoption of new technologies but underestimate their long-term impact. In other words, it may take longer than people like me think it will for technology to remove cash from our everyday lives, but when it does so the impact on society will be far greater than mass redundancies in the ATM business.

The impending shift will be to a different economy. Mobile phones, shared ledgers and smart money will support multiple identities, use multiple monies (but not cash) through services provided by different entities, and be able to manage our identities (and affinities), our networks and our reputations. There will be social and political implications that are impossible to foresee clearly. What is to be done? Predictions are hard – especially, as the old saying goes, about the future – but it is important to begin developing some ideas for these scenarios now. Next time our banks collapse, or if sterling becomes worthless, we will get a chance to try some of these ideas out.

In chapter 14 I suggested that in the future all money will be local, belonging to the community in which it is used; it's just that 'community' will mean something different in the connected world. Whether the community is Totnes or the Chinese diaspora or World of Warcraft won't matter, but the shared desire to minimize transaction costs for 'us' at the possible expense of transactions costs with 'them' will. Since the overwhelming majority of retail transactions are local, most people's transactions most of the time will be in their local currency, with minimal transaction costs. A small number of transactions will be in 'foreign' currencies (i.e. someone else's local currency).

From this perspective, the widespread view that 'alternative' money can work in isolated local environments but not at scale is wrong, because both locality and globalization will mean something different in the networked world and there's no reason why interconnection between local money of one form or another (via markets) cannot operate globally. Local currencies right now might well be a form of electronic voucher rather than money (Naqvi and Southgate 2013), but in this community-centric vision of the future one can easily imagine London e-shillings, Islamic e-gold or IBM dollars could interconnect through Ripple to provide a seamless global means of exchange. The shared ledger brings a transparency to alternative forms of money.

This is more of a reconnection with the past than it may at first seem. If we look at the history of money management by ordinary people, the relative use of the available money instruments is fascinating. In Britain, for example, right up to the nineteenth century, there were usually several currencies in circulation in addition to sterling. This situation, having been temporarily banished by state capitalism in the post-Bretton Woods world, is likely to be restored (Hart 1999), and I see no reason why people (aided and abetted by their mobile phones and smart watches) could not adjust. This 'new local' version of money must sound as odd to you as the idea of a central bank and cheques did to the inhabitants of Stuart England, but it isn't. Trying to imagine a wallet with a hundred currencies in it and a Coke machine with a hundred slots for those currencies is nuts, of course, but your phone and the Coke machine can negotiate and agree on currencies (or, more importantly, currency markets) in a fraction of a second: the time it takes to 'tap and go' with your iPhone, Samsung MST or Microsoft HCE wallet.

Communities and potential currencies

Let us now try to integrate the economic, technological and artistic perspectives and look at three examples of the different kinds of community that we might imagine creating money and the different kinds of money that they might create to reflect their own values. I've chosen economic, cultural and geographic examples.

Economic communities: the hard e-euro

I remember hearing Alistair Darling, then UK Chancellor of the Exchequer, talking on the radio during the global financial crisis. He referred to the difficulties of currency union and spoke about the problems in Ireland, Greece, Portugal and Cyprus. He spoke about the problems of maintaining monetary policy across currency unions between economies with different fundamentals. All true. But he didn't explain why this is different for the United Kingdom. How is the insanity of trying to maintain a currency union between Germany, Luxembourg and Greece any different to the insanity of trying to maintain a currency union between England, Wales and Scotland? The fact that they are in a political union does not alter the facts on the ground: they have fundamentally different economies. The Chancellor was arguing that if Scotland opted for independence, it would be impossible to maintain a currency union between England and Scotland. But surely if that is true, it is true now! The best monetary policy for England is not necessarily the best monetary policy for Scotland, and technology means that what was optimal for commerce at the time of the Napoleonic Wars may no longer best for the modern economy.

If the argument for currency union is only about transaction costs within economic zones*, then former Chancellor of the Exchequer John Major set out a potential way forward in 1990 (although the idea dates from 1983) with his alternative to the euro, which at the time was labelled the 'hard ECU'. The ECU was the 'European Currency Unit', a unit of account set using a basket of currencies that was intended to help

---

* It isn't, I know, but I am making a different point here.

international business by minimizing foreign exchange fluctuations. Major's idea for the hard ECU was a fully-fledged currency with a 'no devaluation' guarantee (Hasse and Koch 1991). Whereas the ECU reflected the weighted average of inflation rates in the countries concerned, the hard ECU would be linked to the strongest currency (which would have been the Deutschmark, of course). This guarantee would be backed by a commitment from participating central banks to buy back their own currency or make good exchange losses in the event of devaluations.

Imagine what that kind of parallel currency might look like today. It would be an electronic currency that would never exist in physical form but still be legal tender (put to one side what that means in practice) in all EU member states. Businesses could therefore keep accounts in hard ECUs, even in a post-EU Britain, and trade them cross-border with minimal transaction costs. Tourists could have hard ECU payment cards that they could use throughout the EU without penalty. And so on. But each state would continue with its own national currency (you would still be able to use sterling notes and coins in British shops) and the cost of replacing them would have been saved.

This sort of parallel currency does not expect (or indeed ensure) economic convergence. Instead it is about facilitating trade with a community, and I envisage it evolving in parallel with the necessary community reputation system that will serve to facilitate the demand for trade.

Cultural communities: Islamic e-gold

I have long thought that there might be opportunities here. Let us go back to Manchester United Pounds, Cornish e-tin and Islamic e-gold to consider the impact of branding on money. It could be huge! Islamic e-gold could have a billion users and, given the desire to transact with the convenience of a card but in a non-interest-bearing currency, it would seem to be a straightforward proposition to offer a gold card that is denominated in gold. A gold fan tenders their chip and PIN gold card in a shop on Oxford Street to buy a pair of shoes: to the system it's just another foreign currency transaction that is translated into grammes of gold on the statement. If, at the end of the month, the person has used more gold than they have in their account, then they can use some of the bank's gold for a time, at a fee. Hey presto, no interest. And if a gold user wants their gold, then they can, in principle, go to the relevant depository and draw it out (minus a handling fee, naturally). Would interested credit card issuers please form an orderly queue?

Geographic communities: the London e-shilling

Consider a scenario in which cities, not countries, might become the source of money and identity (two of the things that interest me most!). I am sure that many people would see these ideas as being somewhat speculative, and perhaps I did too until I read in the *Financial Times* that 'to make wise decisions, investors and policy makers need to view the world not so much as a collection of countries but a network of cities' (Naqvi 2014). Indeed.

I made a podcast (available at http://bit.ly/2nYWWFu) with Felix Martin (the author of *Money: An Unauthorised Biography* (Martin 2013)) in which he talks about the 'bargain' around technology and money and the bargain between the sovereign and the markets: the bargain that the late Glyn Davies said had always served to weaken the power of the sovereign. In passing, Felix talks about the Bank of England using something like Bitcoin to issue an electronic currency: Bank-of-England-coins or something like that.

Suppose we combine these two sets of ideas and argue for electronic money issued not by countries but by cities or regions? In the podcast, Felix sensibly attempts to refute some of my crackpot theories about London having its own money and Scotland launching the first wholly virtual fiat currency, but I feel that the tectonic plates underlying currency have shifted in my direction. Once again, let's pop over to the *Financial Times* to see what the great and good have said about this, as distinct from wide-eyed techno-determinists like me. What about Martin Wolf? He said that London is far richer than Scotland, and could easily be fiscally self-sufficient (Wolf 2013). If we are recognizing the age of cities, recognizing that there are no national economies, then 'it is high time that London became a true city state'.

How true this is. And the right place to start would be to stop London from distorting the UK economy further by making it have its own money. We already have two economies in the UK – London and everywhere else – so we should recognize that and take London out of the 'Sterling Zone' as soon as possible! I don't see the slightest problem with a 'hard e-shilling' (or whatever a future mayor might select as the currency unit) that would exist in electronic form only. Make the e-shilling legal tender and the only way to pay taxes in Singapore-on-Thames and the whole thing could be up and running in a year.

Art school

A final diversion to help with imagination before we settle on a narrative for post-industrial money is to consider the future of money from a wholly different perspective. For two decades Consult Hyperion has held a forum – the Tomorrow's Transactions Forum – in London every spring to look at the future of transactions. As part of this series, in recent years we organized a Future of Money Design Award for art students.

The idea of the competition is to help us technologists broaden our perspectives by asking artists to think about the future of money, payments, reputation and so on. Just to illustrate the range of possibilities, I thought it would be interesting to highlight a small number of these entries to feed into the thought processes about the future of money, but I hope you will take some time to browse all of the artists' super work at www.futuremoneyaward.com.

Electric Money – Austin Houldsworth (2008)

Austin imagines a dystopian future in which electronic money has been hacked and a new system is implemented. The new system of electric money is an alternative monetary system that uses kilowatt-hours as 'currency'. The benefit of this system is that cryptography isn't required to protect the system as electricity is a form of power that can't be created or destroyed, only converted.

One of the money-generating devices aimed at the homeless is based on a simplified sterling engine: by placing a hand over one of the tin cans, the air inside expands due to the rise in temperature. The expanding air pushes a magnet suspended in ferrofluid through the straw, which in turn creates a small current in the wire.

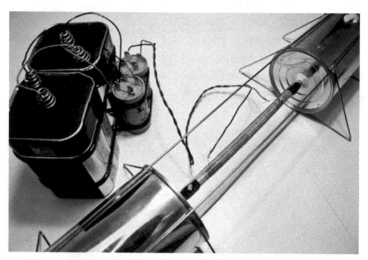

Figure 21. *Electric Money* (courtesy of Austin Houldsworth).

I was struck by this idea because it showed technology and art converging so beautifully. It is easy to imagine a future digital currency based on energy but it took an artist to imagine this decentralization, which, in a strange way, resonates with Bitcoin's electricity-intensive decentralized structure.

Selfie Money – Jonathon Keats (2014)

It's hard times for dollars and pounds. Banknotes are losing out to Square and PayPal. The whole idea of national currencies may become obsolete in the age of Bitcoin.

The Bank of England is fighting monetary obsolescence by updating the £10 note with a portrait of Jane Austen, presumably more enticing to younger generations than Charles Darwin. But it's too little, too late. The only way to successfully compete against the discrete convenience of electronic transactions – let alone the anonymity of cryptocurrencies – is by appealing to flagrant narcissism.

National governments must replace old-fashioned portraits of histor-ical figures with pictures of the people who actually use their banknotes. The new face of paper money must be the selfie.

Given the strong connection between celebrity and wealth in modern society, selfie money should have little trouble gaining popular accept-ance. Moreover, the system should have a beneficial effect on national economies, preventing recession, since the opportunity for people to have their portraits in others' wallets will motivate spending. Narcissism will be the new wealth of nations.

Figure 22. *Selfie Money* (courtesy of Jonathon Keats).

This idea ends fungibility and makes the smart money of the future something like the assignats whose value was determined by the status of the signatories through whose hands it passed. This concept was developed further by another winning entry.

TRAIL$ – Nitipak Samsen (2011)

Have you ever wondered where the money in your pocket came from? Who was the previous owner? Who was the owner before that? Might it have been a famous celebrity?

TRAIL$ imagines the development of a new monetary payment sys-tem: a system specifically designed to replace the easily forged paper banknotes of the twentieth century.

Smart banknotes work by presenting a readable history of ownership on the note itself: an innovation designed to prevent money laundering. Although the system appeared successful, there were loopholes and unexpected instabilities regarding the value of each note, eventually leading to the demise of the story's main protagonist.

The story is presented from the perspective of a civil servant turned entrepreneur: a professional working within the financial industry who explains his personal experiences of the new 'smart' banknote system and its resultant benefits and consequences, from security to intimacy, economic and fanatic perspectives.

(After all, who wouldn't treasure the rare £50 note with both my face and Sergio Aguero's face in its history?!)

Figure 23. A *TRAIL$* card (courtesy of Nitipak Samsen).

This combination of Bitcoin and Facebook – a smart money that remembers where it has been and what it has been used for as well as who has been using it – seems to me to be an interesting vision of a future digital currency. If electronic money is anonymous and fungible, then the future looks very different.

Bigshot – Joe Carpita and Craig Stover (2013)

What happens at the convergence of anonymous routing, crypto-anarchy and crowd funding?

Today the individual is capable of wielding more power than ever before. The proliferation of anonymous, web-based technologies will enable them to yield this power exponentially, creating the potential for devious criminal activity on a scale that has never before been possible. Imagine a world where dangerous minds have a public platform to solicit support from anyone with an Internet connection.

Figure 24. *Bigshot* mock website
(courtesy of Joe Carpita and Craig Stover).

This idea of taking the assassination markets discussed in chapter 10 and opening them up through crowdsourcing encourages us to imagine new sorts of crime (and, in my opinion, new sorts of diplomacy) that we must take into consideration when trying to design the next generation of money just as much as the considerations around technology, economics and banking.

Chapter 16

Back to the future

The electronic money world looks much more like the neolithic world economy before the invention of money than it looks like the market as we have known it in the past few hundred years.

— Jack Weatherford in 'The fiscal frontier'
from *Discover* magazine (1998)

THERE IS THE history of money, which I have dipped into through the book so far and continue to find fascinating, and then there is the history of what people *thought* the future of money would be, which in many ways I find even more fascinating. I am always curious to see what people used to think about the future of money and, where they were wrong, I am always curious to understand why they were wrong. This line of thought led me to an October 1998 article titled 'The fiscal frontier' in *Discover* magazine that asked a number of prominent thinkers to speculate on the future of money. I think it would be helpful to look back at those comments from a couple of decades ago, from the earliest days of the web, to help us to finalize our narrative.

Philip Davis, still professor emeritus of applied mathematics at Brown University, talked about the psychological relationship between the possession of virtual money and the ownership of real property, and spoke about the well-known 'law of unanticipated consequences', with which I am wholly in agreement: money is such a complex nexus that there is a thoroughly anticipated inevitability to the application of the law of unanticipated consequences to its reinvention. Just as tally sticks were invented as a mechanism for deferred payment but the market mutated them into a store of value and then a means of exchange, who knows what the market will do with Bitcoin?

Paul Kocher, president of Cryptography Research Inc., said that breaking a cryptosystem is far more difficult than robbing a physical bank but potentially far more profitable. What an accurate prediction! While cyberfraud spirals out of control, bank robberies have been falling for years and the pickings are lean. Paul, who was (and still is) one of the world's leading experts on cryptography, predicted that the first multi-billion-dollar heist would occur before the year 2010. I'm not sure whether that happened or not. It may have happened and remained a secret. The reported 'heists' are still in the millions or tens of millions but it's entirely possible that much bigger robberies have been kept away from the public gaze.

Chris Gregory, then professor of anthropology and archaeology at the Australian National University (ANU) and now a reader in anthropology at the same institution, said that gold would remain as the sovereign form of money for 'as long as war between people remains a possibility'. At first I thought this was a depressing comment: a reflection of the ongoing narrative of man's inhumanity to man. But it also represents, I think, a streak of profound conservatism about money.

These are interesting and valid observations, but I was looking to obtain a deeper understanding of the complex interrelationship between money and technology, so I read the comments that Jack Weatherford, professor of anthropology at Macalester College, made back then with great interest:

> If we take the long view of history, money was not necessary until very recently. Soon – though not in our lifetime – the money phase of history will pass, and money as we know it will become one of those quaint curiosities of the past.

He went on to say that cash had already 'become the domain of poor people and poor nations'.

He notes that with many new forms of money on the horizon, the difference between barter and money systems will become blurred. Hence his conclusion that the digital money world of the future will look a lot like the neolithic world economy before the invention of money – a conclusion that is all the more surprising to me because he reached it long before the mobile phone reached the furthest corners of the earth and more than 100 million Africans took to Facebook.

I was also very interested in Paul Krugman's comments from that time. The then professor of economics at MIT made several points but I have pulled out four specific ones for exploration here.

Krugman said that there would be a *distinction between electronic cash and electronic money* because of the need for small transactions where neither the buyer nor the seller want the buyer's creditworthiness to be an issue. I used to think that this was true but I don't any more. The 'Internet of things' and always-on connectivity have eroded the cost differential between the two.

He went on to say that there would not be a *universal currency* for a long time. There is a big advantage to separate currencies providing price stability in different parts of the world. I don't think there will be a universal currency *ever*. It doesn't make sense in economic terms, let alone in technological or social or political or business terms.

He further said that corporations would not issue their own *private currency*. I'm not so sure about this. If there are going to be more monies than fiat currencies, then corporations are obvious issuers of transactional medium of exchange currencies, and companies and their customers are a kind of community that has incentives to share a currency. Whether corporations can deliver a store of value is harder to predict, given that they don't (in the grand scheme of things) last that long.

Finally, Krugman said that what everyone wants is *an anonymous, reliable means of exchange*; given a chance, they will always prefer one backed by a government. As he observed:

> One can imagine that a system of purely virtual money might be subject to severe instability.

As discussed earlier, I think a lot of people say they want anonymity (when what they really want is privacy) only because they haven't really though it through (Birch 2013). Do we want to live in a society where transactions are anonymous? That is not obvious to me. A society where all transactions are anonymous is a society that allows the rich and powerful to act with impunity – a society that positively encourages corruption. Hence I specifically use the word 'private'.

Transparency, as I mentioned before, might well be one of the key characteristics of a currency in a community that I would want to belong to. And we will want the private payment systems of the future to be built from open-source software and assembled under public scrutiny to see that the 'privacy dial' is set at a democratically accountable level. Hence the warning from Robert Sapolsky, still professor of neuroscience at Stanford University, who said that

> The very perfection of the identification system will guarantee urban myths about guys bankrupted when some techno-schnook stole their pheromone signature and racked up huge bills buying antique CDs for the Madonna centennial.

This was echoed by Jem Bendell when he wrote for Open Democracy on the 'weaponization' of money (Bendell 2015). We must, in responding to these valid concerns, ensure that society makes some informed decisions about the path taken through the technology roadmap. Fortunately, this roadmap is clearer than the social roadmap, despite the accelerating pace of technological change. Talking of new technology, Marvin Minsky, then professor of computer science at MIT and now at the MIT Media Lab, said that

> With fast computers and huge memories, we could have a nonlinear database that would better understand what each person has and wants. Then, by using complicated game theory-related computations, it might turn out that in general everyone would get more (in terms of their personal values) for the goods that they are willing to 'sell'.

There is a link between Minsky's deductions from the technology roadmap and Weatherford's comments as an anthropologist, but we'll come back to that later. Minsky, incidentally, goes on to make some comments about the relationship between money and taxation:

> Taxes will be lower because of the vast amount of uncollected tax today.

Given that somewhere in the region of a fifth of the economy in developed countries is untaxed and outside the formal financial system, the tax burden falls heavily on those of us who remain wage slaves, and as the post-crisis tax burden climbs to the point where it falls off the demographic cliff, so will the calls for reform grow. Minsky went on to reinforce my observations above by saying that

> The system of electronic currency will never be acceptable unless the laws protecting privacy are greatly strengthened.

With these final building blocks, then, we have an outline of a plausible narrative for the future of money: distributed, private, community-centric and, in the long run, set to vanish. But when will this narrative begin to unfold? If you leaf through the examples from around the world collected together in the book's appendix, you will see that it is already unfolding.

Don't panic

A cashless Sweden! Demonetization in India! The breakup of the euro! The sky is falling! Well, not really.

We've been through monetary change of this magnitude several times before. Around 400 years ago, for example, things were going horribly wrong with money in England. If you had asked people about the future of money at that time, they would have imagined better-quality coins. What in fact happened was monetary revolution and a new paradigm. A generation later Britain had a central bank and paper money as well as a gold standard, current accounts and overdrafts.

We are at a similar cusp now, with a mismatch between the mentality and the institutions of paper money from the industrial age and a new, post-industrial economy with a different technological basis for money. In a generation or so there will be a completely new set of monetary arrangements in place and completely new institutions will manage them. Just as the machine-made, uniform, mechanized coinage introduced by Isaac Newton in 1696 better matched the commerce of the Industrial Revolution, so I have long maintained that we should expect some form of digital money that will better match the commerce of the information age (Birch 2001).

But what will it look like? Are we looking at a world of multiple, overlapping communities with a similar variety of values-based currencies? The ideas of anthropologists like Jack Weatherford and sociologists like Nigel Dodd suggest to me that new technology will re-implement trust-based commerce within reputational groups: the clan of the Neolithic age becomes the global e-clan of the future. There is no need to remember who owes you what, who is good for how much and who owes whom and how much because the machine will do it for you. The technology we have at hand – the dynamic combination of mobile phones and social networks, biometrics and big data – allows us to interact and transact in fluid and shifting ways, essentially using our reputations.

This raises fascinating questions about the use of 'money' within and across trust groups, and those questions deserve further reflection. The more complex and more sophisticated the economy becomes, the more trust matters. The fact that we can now scale trust, because of technologies ranging from digital signatures and mobile phones to social networks and TCP/IP, means that we can both have bigger trust groups and have more of them. If we think of 'money zones' as rather like 'optimal currency zones' for the post-industrial economy, we can see the link between communities that individuals, organizations and governments understand and the trust groups. Perhaps every trust group will have its own money! Rather as the ancient world comprised communities of individuals interconnected by trade, we will see a modern world of trust groups interconnected by transactions facilitated by digital identity, shared ledgers and non-fiat monies.

That back-to-the-future vision may sound odd at first, but it seems congruent with the unfolding roadmaps of technology push, societal pull and business links between the two. A neolithic barter system based on networks of trust couldn't scale into an economy of cities and settlements beyond kinship groups but the arrival of mobile phones and social networks and other new technology changes the dynamic again. As in so many other ways, the wealth of new technologies are reinventing old models (Davidow and Malone 2015).

Chapter 17

The next money

Although central banks have matured, they have not yet reached old age. But their extinction cannot be ruled out altogether. Societies managed without central banks in the past.
— Mervyn King, former governor of the Bank of England (2016)

HOW WILL THE money of the future be organized? Probably not by today's central banks. Looking at the options for the future of money discussed in chapter 14 (central banks, commercial banks, companies, cryptography and communities), considering the visions set out in chapter 15, taking account of the big picture from chapter 16 and considering the pressures for change, it is not at all clear to me that the current central bank option (fiat currency) is the best choice for the post-industrial economy, whether in the form of Britcoin or Brit-Pesa. Central banks might have matured since the global financial crisis of a decade ago, and they may not yet be in their dotage, but as Mervyn King points out this does not rule out their reformation or removal (King 2016d). They can survive (a digital fiat currency is certainly a viable option for the next phase of economic evolution) but it may no longer be optimal for national governments to create and manage money, since national borders no longer define the currency zones that are most effective in supporting the modern economy.

Yet what could replace them? I'm not sure that companies have the trust or the structures needed to manage currencies for the long term. Cryptocurrencies may find a niche but it is hard to see them becoming the mass market medium of exchange. I think that the future of money will be organized around reputation zones rather than currency zones, which is why I have concluded that communities rather than countries will be the natural currency issuers in the future.

If communities are the natural basis for currencies, then there are many communities (both 'real' and virtual) that might incubate the successor to today's fiat currencies. In their book *In Gold We Trust* (Bishop and Green 2012), Matthew Bishop and Michael Green observe that we might reasonably expect many forms of currency to emerge in the post-fiat world, and I agree that there is no compelling argument for a single alternative to hold sway. Further, since we all belong to multiple, overlapping communities, the future landscape is one of multiple, overlapping currencies.

Marginal costs and multiple communities

Why this focus on community? Well, one of the most basic questions asked about the future of money is whether the dynamic of monetary evolution is a tendency towards one currency (that galactic credit beloved of science fiction authors), because the minimization of global coordination costs is the driving factor, or towards an explosion of currencies, because new technology minimizes other transaction costs? As already noted, speaking as a technologist I suspect that there will be more and more different *kinds* of money, not just more currencies, than ever before. This is different from observing that there will be a panoply of payment mechanisms. The cash replacement technologies discussed earlier in this book – PayPal and M-Pesa, iDEAL (which dominates online payments in the Netherlands) and EMV – do not understand that sterling is a 'real' currency and that World of Warcraft Gold is not. Surely a key impact of the transition to efficient electronic platforms, rather than bits of paper, is that currency is just another field in the dataset: I could use PayPal to send Dave's Dollars as easily as to send US dollars.

When we move away from paying at POS (because of our digital identity) and paying in cash (because of our digital money), we enter a money world with very different dynamics, because it is a world where the marginal cost of introducing another currency will be approximately zero. We will then be in the 'let a thousand flowers bloom' mode and might reasonably expect a rash of experimentation. At the end of this period, who knows whether dollar bills or Bill's Dollars (an old joke, beloved of us e-cash types) will be more successful?

What might the post-POS electronic money landscape look like? Hayek pointed out a generation ago that people who lived in 'border areas' in days of old seemed perfectly capable of understanding multiple monies (and surely we are all on the border now: the border between the physical world and cyberspace), so there's no reason to think that they couldn't do so again. More importantly, however, the exchange of medieval moolah took place without mobile phones and 24/7 foreign exchange markets.

If I've already told my mobile phone that I want to collect both US dollars because I'm going to go on holiday to New York and World of Warcraft gold pieces because I feel like a relaxing weekend of orc slaughter, then my mental transaction cost subsequently falls to zero. My mobile phone is perfectly capable of negotiating with yours:

Have you got any WoW gold?

No, will you take British Airways Avios?

Yes, but as they are worthless junk it will be at a 95 per cent discount.

Alright, here you go...

Figure 25. Points mean prizes.

If you think this far-fetched, note that I bought a cup of coffee with Avios on a recent flight (see figure 25). The long-term outcome will surely be that technology is used not to develop replicants – electronic means of exchange that simulate, as perfectly as possible, the current physical means of exchange – but to develop new means of exchange that are better for society as a whole.

Currency in the community

How do we begin to evolve ideas about what this spectrum of future monies might include? I think a good place to start is, again, with *In Safe Hands*, the Long Finance exploration of the world of financial services in 2050 (Ringland 2011). There are four scenarios set out in this report and they seem to me as good a basis as any for constructing narratives about the future of money (figure 26). These scenarios are not random: they are constructed along two axes. The first asks whether the 'Washington Consensus' around central banks and international monetary institutions will continue (I do not think it will) and the second asks whether the communities that redefine money will be wholly virtual or will remain anchored in the mundane.

Thanks to www.longfinance.net

Figure 26. Long Finance scenarios for 2050.

Personally, I think that both community consensus scenarios of cities and 'affinity groups' are plausible visions, but on balance I think that the mundane anchors will remain for any foreseeable future, leaving me to conclude that the 'Many Hands' scenario is the more likely. A world economy built up from cities and their hinterlands will obviously demand different financial services and institutions from one based on national economies. What this means is that the future sense of identity will be city-centric, with people seeing themselves as Londoners or New Yorkers rather than Brits or Yanks. Cities will undoubtedly form defence alliances and trade pacts and so forth with each other but I wonder if they will give up any real sovereignty? It's an interesting and enjoyable area of speculation. This appeals to my long-held appreciation of Jane Jacobs's work on the city as the basic economic unit (Jacobs 1985).

In discussing this scenario, Ringland makes a passing but powerful observation on this future, saying that individuals will protect their 'personal identity, credit ratings and parking spaces' at all costs, and that since monetary arrangements (nation-state fiat currencies) will have collapsed, the commercial paper of global corporations will be used as international currency. I might take issue with Ringland here and say 'social identities' rather than the singular 'personal identity', but I know what she means. Each of these identities will have its own 'credit rating' (referring to the commercial reputation that means that you can buy or sell, whether an individual or an organization) that will be central to economic existence. In the emergent society, this is more likely to be something that comes from the social graph than the conventional credit rating of today, as discussed above. This will be a connected economy and we already know that this real economy is not a market but an exchange (Pentland 2014), animated by trust relationships. To me, then, in the language of digital identity, digital money and digital networks, Ringland is predicting a reputation economy anchored in the mundane. We will have multiple identities, use multiple community currencies (some of which may be related to virtual communities, some physical, some corporate and perhaps even some cryptographic), through services provided by different entities, and we will be defined by our social network and reputation. There will be social and political implications that are impossible to foresee clearly, but we do know that we will, if anything, be underestimating the long-term implications of these changes.

These communities will not be limited by geography, as described in the 'Long Hand' scenario, but will extend to a variety of communities, as I conjectured in chapter 14. The World Economic Forum talks about 'natural identity networks' (World Economic Forum 2016) based not only on traditional national or geographic networks but also on affiliations 'with a supervisory entity' (i.e. the replacement for the central bank, in this context), industries and asset classes (and here I include Ringland's speculation about demographic asset classes).

Here comes the smarter money

So, where does this get us? A fair summary would be that until now, new technology has been driving change in the payments industry; now it is driving change in money itself.

That change is not the change to digital money. That's already here. Almost all of the money in the world is already digital, created by commercial banks under the control of central banks and therefore national governments. It's not the change to cashlessness. There have already been a number of attempts to replace cash ('the last mile' of money) with digital alternatives, in order to create a wholly digital currency. These schemes go back a quarter of a century, to the days of Mondex and DigiCash (Levy 1994), and were conservative: their purpose was to employ new technology to make the existing payments infrastructure more efficient and cost-effective for consumers, retailers and banks (Birch 2015). However, we are now at a point where new money technologies are demanding that society reexamine the issue of money creation and reconsider the central question of the entities that might create money in the future. This book has explored the '5Cs' that might potentially bring new money to the masses. But it is now time to drive down another level and ask ourselves *what* this new money might be. My answer, as you may suspect, is that the new money will be the *smart money* that has been referred to obliquely throughout this book.

Simon Scorer from the Bank of England's Digital Currencies Division has made a number of very interesting points about the transition from dumb money to smart money, and the consequent potential for the implementation of digital fiat to become a platform for innovation (something I strongly agree with) because of the *programmability* of the new forms of money (Scorer 2017). If some new form of digital money were to be managed via some form of shared ledger, then Simon's insight reinforces my feeling that it is not the 'consensus computer' but the 'consensus applications' that will become the nexus for radical innovation. They bring intelligence to money, and some people think this is more revolutionary than it at first appears. One such person is Eric Lonergan, a hedge fund manager, economist and writer. He wrote a great book about money (Lonergan 2009) and he is a source of clear thinking on many issues around this central topic of shared interest. He calls Bitcoin 'intelligent money' because it can self-regulate.

Indeed. But this form of intelligence is only one kind of intelligence, and the Bitcoin self-regulation is only one kind of self-regulation. There are some truly surprising possibilities once you add general-purpose programmability. I have repeatedly bored people to tears with my standard four-hour lecture about why the consensus applications (incorrectly labelled 'smart contracts'*) will be the source of real innovation in the world of cryptocurrency and, indeed, why one of the first uses of such consensus applications (ICOs and tokens) will be much more important to the world of financial services than, say, Bitcoin. But that kind of self-regulation may not be the only thing that intelligent money does. Eric goes on to note that 'intelligence' could also embed social goals, and he says that an 'ethical currency' could in principle be a force for an economy more consistent with our values (which I see as community values). He then goes further, saying that smart money could also help us run the economy better as well (Lonergan 2018).

I agree, and when Eric says, 'my sense is that it [intelligent money] is inevitable – indeed it could be the basis of an edge for digital currency over existing state-backed money', I think it unwise to ignore such a statement from someone who is a thorough student of money. If he

---

*The Ethereum inventor Vitalik Buterin said (on Twitter, 13 October 2018): 'I quite regret adopting the term "smart contracts". I should have called them something more boring and technical, perhaps something like "persistent scripts".'

is right, and money becomes more closely connected with the social goals of the communities that it serves, then the future of money will look very different from both the current Washington Consensus and the Star Wars future (that is, there won't be a 'galactic credit' or whatever, but very many different kinds of money).

Given the magnitude of these claims, we must finish this chapter (and, indeed, this book) by delving down into the technology to ask exactly how this intelligent money might work.

Token money

Cryptocurrencies have delivered the technology platform to deliver the Facebook Florin and the Microsoft Dollar ('Bill's Dollars' rather than dollar bills?). Indeed, cryptocurrencies have provided the technology for literally anybody to deliver their own money. This platform, specifically, is that of 'tokens'. Unlike the underlying cryptocurrencies that have no reality beyond the consensus protocols of shared ledgers, tokens obtain their value by linking to real or virtual assets. Although not specific to the Ethereum blockchain, tokens took off with the development of the ERC-20 standard back in 2015. ERC-20 defined a way to create a standard form of token using consensus applications on the Ethereum blockchain. ERC-20 tokens are simply structured data exchanged between these applications, a practical implementation of digital bearer claims on assets with no clearing or settlement involved in their exchange (and hence a more efficient marketplace for their trading), thus creating a means to make the transfer of fungible value secure without a central authority. There are now a number of different ERC token standards (a sample of them can be found in table 8), and similar kinds of standard are being developed for other shared ledger platforms, such as for R3's CORDA.

Picture this: I want to license some IBM software for IBM$100, so I tell my smart contract to send this value to an IBM smart contract, and the IBM smart contract then creates a permission for me to use the software. Using these tokens, it is possible to implement the smart, programmable money of the future ('this money cannot be used before 1 January 2020' and so on) that we are all excited about.

Table 8. Ethereum tokens.

Ethereum standard	Purpose
ERC-20	Fungible value
ERC-223	More efficient version of ERC-20
ERC-721	Non-fungible digital assets used for 'collectables' (most notably cryptokitties!)
ERC-777	Version of ERC-20 that includes token destruction

The impact of tokens on the financial world must not be under-estimated. Brock Pierce is a well-known cryptocurrency investor who was early into the world of tokens. Here is what he said about initial coin offerings (ICOs) in the middle of 2017 (Chiang 2017):

> I think what I've done is the end of all VC, all private equity, all rates because these are industries that are illiquid... I think the Sequoias of the world will go out of business. I think all the big VCs are done.

That sounds like a fantastic claim – but he may be right. Furthermore, when he goes on to say that Bitcoin, or whatever comes after Bitcoin, will be 'bigger than any government currency', he may be right about that too. When the current craziness has passed and tokens become a regulated but wholly new kind of digital asset – a cross between corporate paper and a loyalty scheme – there will be an opportunity to remake markets in a new and better way. With reputations established as an immutable history of participation in transactions, good behaviour will not be gamed and bad behaviour will be impossible to hide. Market participants will be able to assess and manage risk, and regulators will be able to look for patterns and connections.

What is more, thanks to the counterintuitive behaviour of complementary cryptographic techniques such as homomorphic encryption and zero-knowledge proofs, I will be able to see that your assets exceed your liabilities without necessarily being able to see what those assets or liabilities are. As Salome Parulava and I argued in the *Handbook of Blockchain, Digital Finance and Inclusion*, we will find ourselves in an era of ambient accountability, where the technological architecture means constant verification and validation (Birch and Parulava 2017). This framework takes us beyond 'FinTech' and into 'RegTech'.

At the time of writing, a cumulative $15 billion or so has gone into token sales. Right now, a great many tokens originate in Zug in Switzerland (often referred to as 'crypto-valley') because the issuers use the vagaries of Swiss foundation law to create the tokens. The opinion of the Swiss Financial Market Supervisory Authority (FINMA) is therefore very important. It looks at all kinds of tokens, not only ICOs (i.e. securities tokens), and it looks to regulate them as appropriate (FINMA 2018). In its guidelines, FINMA classifies tokens into three categories: securities, utilities and payments. This is a useful way of looking at tokens and a sound way to regulate the different kinds in different ways. The US Securities and Exchange Commission (SEC) makes a similar distinction, but while the SEC chairman Jay Clayton acknowledged that ICOs 'can be effective ways for entrepreneurs and others to raise funding', he also cautioned that neither payment nor utility tokens have a safe harbour if they function as securities (Achilles et al. 2018).

The use of tokens to create new kinds of money, as shown in figure 27, is logical precisely because tokens link values on the shared ledger to traders and tradeable assets. To my mind, these links must be created and maintained by regulated institutions. If you tell me that a string of bits represents a dollar, an ounce of gold or a square foot of the Empire State Building, I couldn't care less. But if Citi tells me (this is the institutional binding in figure 27), then that string of bits has a real value to me. Similarly, if you tell me that a string of bits represents a Citi account holder, I don't care. But if Barclays tells me, then I will happily trade with that account knowing that all relevant regulations will be taken care of.

It seems to me, then, that digital money might be best implemented in this way, using tokens, even though some communities will want to use the underlying cryptocurrencies. This form of digital money is the smart money of the future, in contrast to the dumb money of today (see table 9). It is programmable money, where apps can choose to move value under certain conditions. It is money with a memory (banknotes have no history; Bitcoins do). It is money that is a platform for innovation – money with an API.

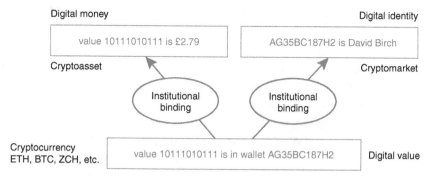

Figure 27. From cryptocurrency to cryptomarkets.

Table 9. Dumb money and smart money.

Dumb money	Smart money
Money is bits	Money is an application
Money is standalone	Money has an API
Money that substitutes for memory	Money that *has* a memory
Money that you can make decisions about	Money that can make decisions about you
Money that is a static creation of the nation state	Money that is a dynamic property of communities

Personally, I focus on tokens rather than the underlying crypto-currency because tokens link to real-world assets and because the ability of cryptocurrencies themselves to become mass-market stores of value remains to be proven. While the technology of tokens implemented using consensus applications may have issues yet to be resolved (around scale, for example), the concept clearly works (Birch 2017). This means multiple monies that embody different values, and it might well mean a type of money that will prevent people from using it unless they have a track record of upholding its values.

More than economic efficiencies, however, community currencies may embody values (e.g. environmental policies) that are important to the community and therefore drive usage. One might imagine a gold-backed currency for the Islamic diaspora or a renewable energy currency for the green movement, and so forth. In fact, the distinguish-ing characteristic of the money of the future might well be that it has values. These might be fun or serious, political or superficial. People might want to transact in Manchester United pounds (indeed, they already use Manchester United credit cards and savings accounts) or Microsoft dollars or Islamic gold e-dinars or Cornish e-tin for reasons that have nothing to do with the drivers for the use of traditional means of exchange (World Economic Forum 2016) – and I, for one, look forward to seeing experiment and exploration in these monies of the future.

Chapter 18

Coda: the story of money

Cash, I think, in ten years' time probably won't exist. There is no need for it, it is terribly inefficient and expensive.

— John Cryan, CEO of Deutsche Bank, at the
World Economic Forum in Davos in 2016

THIS, THEN, IS our narrative. We need money to transfer value between individuals and organizations. This money, depending on your point of view, either originates from the tokenization of barter goods or from the 'monetization' of debt. Let's put that debate to one side for the moment (although I'm happy to advance my own theory that money originates in the creative tension between debt obligations and technological evolution: in other words, technology enables the use of debt as a store of value and a means of exchange) and focus on the historical arc.

In the predawn of civilization, the only technology available was the human memory. Hence the observation that money is in fact simply a primitive form of that memory (primitive because it has limited use). As civilization evolved and new technologies came along, so those technologies gradually replaced the human memory that had proved adequate to the task for the Neolithic clan but could not scale to the tribe, the city or the nation. Over a period of a few thousand years civilization settled on a set of monetary arrangements that worked well with the available technology. The past bequeathed the present a gold standard to support international trade (the basis of prosperity in an industrial age): currencies that were organized on the basis of the relatively new institution of the nation state, money that was provided largely by the other relatively new institution of the central bank, a wide variety of flexible and effective paper instruments to effect the transfer of value (such as cheques and letters of credit), and a variety of banknotes and coins to facilitate retail payments.

As the industrial age began to give way to the information age, the monetary arrangements that had been forged in the crucible of the Industrial Revolution began to break down. The gold standard faded and what we think of as the Bretton Woods set of arrangements based on international institutions (e.g. the International Monetary Fund) replaced it. Fiat currency (from the Latin, as in *fiat lux*: 'let there be light') became the normal form of money even as it began to dissociate from the nation state (with the euro), banks became the primary creators of money so that in most advanced economies almost all of the money in circulation is in the form of bank deposits, bits about atoms replaced atoms in the marketplace as electronic payments came to dominate by value (and now, in some countries, by volume), and standardized state-provided notes and tokens remained as the mundane rump.

While the great majority of people (and politicians, as mentioned in a British parliamentary debate in 2014 on the topic of money creation[*]) do not understand money, they do retain the monetary paradigms of the brief diversion in monetary history that was the century from 1871 until 1971. Hence, while the future began back in 1971, with the previously noted severing of the ties between money and atoms, it has not yet begun to reshape the collective consciousness. Or, at least, it had not until recently. While experiments and discussions and pilots using many forms of alternative currency had been underway for years (everything from time banks to Bristol Pounds) and while a number of people had been studying money and considering alternative arrangements (Hayek springs to mind), it took the global financial crisis and the emergence of Bitcoin to begin to reset thinking and make discussion of the future of money less of a philosophical diversion and more of a subject for polite conversation among strategists and policy mavens.

While the future began more than a generation ago, it's still hard to say how it will evolve. Looking at these money eras in more detail

---

[*] 'Money creation and society', *Hansard*, 20 November 2014, Column 434.

will, I hope, help to tease out some threads in the relationship between technology and money that we can use to construct a narrative about where technology will take money. This book attempts to understand those threads, to reflect on the relationship between technological invention and monetary innovation and to make a prediction about the future of money that may, I think, appear surprising at first but sensible on reflection. That prediction is that the newest technologies will take money back to where it came from: a substitute for memory to record mutual debt obligations within multiple overlapping communities. This time, however, the money will be *smart*. It will be money that reflects the *values* of the communities that define it. It will know where it has been, who has been using it and what they have been using it for.

Looking backwards redux

The seatbelt sign came on and I glanced out of the window as I buckled up. I could see the M25 out of the window: a strangely beautiful ribbon of tarmac winding its way through the Surrey countryside. I thought I saw a rainbow over Woking in the distance but I couldn't be sure if it was real or just a reflection of my fevered excitement as I returned home, New York already fading from memory. Without thinking what I was doing, I picked up the in-flight magazine and started to leaf through it. I don't know what came over me that day, because I knew full well that in-flight magazines are only to be used in case of emergency. If the plane is going down, then you start reading and pretty soon you will be in an induced coma that gives you the best chance of survival when you hit the deck. I knew that the safe exposure level was only four or five pages maximum. But in the excitement of coming home I finished the article on Morocco's hidden treasures and started reading about the East End that Phil Mitchell would have grown up with.

I slumped down in my seat, the magazine slipping through my fingers as my cerebral cortex went into a power-saving shutdown mode that is normally only available to mystics who find themselves on deserted mountaintops. In a moment there was nothing but the warm, comforting, enveloping darkness of eternity. Then, after what seemed like just a few seconds, I saw the light. It said 'Exit or Whatever' and it was over a door opposite the bed that I was lying in.

All the muscles in my body ached – a deep-seated ache that I'd never experienced before. I didn't know what it meant but, determined to defeat it, I spent an agonizing few minutes trying to sit up. Then I realized that there were tubes connecting me to equipment by the side of the bed and that there was a light flashing on one of the displays. Footsteps. Behind me I heard a door open and a man's voice.

'Nurse, he's out of bed!'

I lay back down exhausted. When I open my eyes again a younger man of kindly disposition was looking down at me.

'This is astonishing', he said over and over again, and then, realizing that my eyes were open, he looked straight at me and said, 'Can you hear me, David?'

'Where am I,' I said slowly.

He told me that I was in a Research Institute. I asked him how long I'd been there: 'Have I been here overnight?'

'Oh no,' he said, 'you've been in a coma for a hundred years: it's 2117 according to the old calendar.'

It turned out that I'd been moved to the Research Institute that was studying the long-term impact of celebrity gossip and fake news on the human brain but because I hadn't recovered for so long they'd moved me to a side room and sort of forgotten about me apart from some periodic physiotherapy. Now that I'd woken up I was a celebrity! And not only to the medical staff: the mainstream social media feeds all sent bots to interview me and within a couple of hours I was on a billion phones worldwide.

The next day they decided that I was well enough to get out of bed and go for a walk, so they decided to take me down to the shopping mall nearby to get some clothes and other essentials. It was fun. I walked into the clothes booth in the mall and took off what I was wearing. There in the mirror in front of me was me standing in what looked like pyjamas made out of wicker. As soon as I thought how much I didn't like them, the clothes changed. In a moment I realized that I could direct the choices in front of me merely by thinking about them, and within a couple of minutes I'd found an outfit that I liked. I stepped out and a disembodied voice told me that it would take a few minutes for the replicator to produce the clothes and I was entitled to a free drink in the meeting centre while I was waiting.

While we sipped our genetically engineered energy coffee with quinoa milk, I asked the doctor how we'd paid for the clothes.

'You can have a look if you want,' he told me, and the table changed into a screen that showed a series of incredibly complicated negotiations involving parking places in London, Facebook Florins, Nuclear Electricity and some sort of interest-free loan instrument from the Free State of Wessex. The negotiations seemed to involve my headband, the table standing between us, the booth in the mall, and the Vodafonica chip that I'd had implanted in my neck that morning. I was curious how this all worked.

'Are digital currencies used by people, as well as by things?'

'Certainly,' said the doctor, 'it's just that nobody ever bothers. Best just to leave it to your stuff. After all, money is pretty boring, isn't it?'

Appendix: around the cashless world

The value of money is settled, like that of all other commodities, by supply and demand, and only the form is essentially different.

— Walter Bagehot, *Lombard Street: A Description of the Money Market* (1873)

PAYMENT CARDS AND clearing houses, standing orders and giro slips put cashlessness back on the agenda. Not as a utopian hypothetical but as a near-future revolution brought about by mobile phones that, as chapter 10 showed, needs policy and planning. Just how near is that future though? If we look around the world, we can see that some countries are on the verge of cashlessness while others are a long way from it. By cashlessness, incidentally, I do not mean that every single banknote and every single coin has been ritually cursed and then hurled into Mount Doom: I mean that cash has ceased to be relevant to monetary policy, has become irrelevant to most individuals and has vanished from most businesses. As we look to the future we can begin to ask, quite reasonably, whether developments in digital payment technology and changes in payments and banking regulation will bring us to the point of cashlessness within, say, a generation. Here are a few snapshots from around the world to illustrate how things are changing.

The United Kingdom

Let's use the United Kingdom as a snapshot of a developed economy as we begin to think about the future. According to the Office for National

Statistics, consumer spending in the United Kingdom is around £300 billion per quarter, accounting for some two-thirds of the country's total GDP of £2.3 trillion. In 2016, £647 billion was spent on cards in the United Kingdom (469 transactions per second!).

There were some 39 billion payments made in 2017, according to the trade association UK Finance, of which nine in ten were made by consumers; of these, 85% were for spontaneous purchases and 15% for regular bills and other commitments.

Almost all adults (98%) have a debit card, and two-thirds have a credit card. Retail spending on cards was almost £75 billion per quarter, and around three-quarters of this was spent on debit cards. About a quarter of this spending is online, and e-commerce sales continues to grow faster than overall retail sales. In terms of volume, just under half of all retail transactions are cash, which is in slow decline. While cards have long accounted for the majority of retail spending by value, 2016 was the first year in which they also accounted for more than half of all transactions. Debit cards have now overtaken cash, ahead of previously predicted timescales, largely because of contactless. Debit cards account for 42.6% of all transactions, putting them ahead of notes and coins, at 42.3%. Analysis by UK Finance suggests that in 2017 there were some 13.4 billion debit card payments, of which 5.6 billion were contactless, making it the crossover year when the volume of card payments exceeded the volume of cash payments. The latest figures show that 2018 will be the crossover year for contactless, as there are now more contactless transactions than 'chip and PIN' transactions.

While the decline of cash has been steady to date, there are reasons for thinking that it might accelerate. The 120 million contactless cards in circulation, the high penetration of contactless terminals in retail, high smartphone penetration and instant payments all point in the same direction. We see retail chains going cashless already, especially in London. As the last redoubts of cash begin to fall, I've personally heard a taxi driver complaining about cash and lauding contactless and mobile solutions, a sandwich shop owner talking about the problems of managing a cash float (and change), and frequent complaints about parking machines. I think many people in the United Kingdom are beginning to challenge the assumption that the inertia around cash means an insurmountable barrier to change. It does not. Honest retailers also want it to vanish in favour of more efficient electronic alternatives.

One big change to note is the expected growth of account-to-account credit transfers because of the success of the Faster Payments Scheme, the enhancements coming with the New Payment Architecture, and the potential impact of open banking (which began at the start of 2018 in the UK). There were 1.6 billion such payments in 2017. UK Finance are predicting 50% growth over the next decade, but I feel that may be an underestimate of open banking's potential to bring new products and services based on strongly authenticated credit transfers.

The United States

The situation in the United States is, in many ways, rather strange. By volume, most US paper currency is used domestically, with the $1, $5, $10 and $20 notes making up a majority of transactional notes. However, as the dollar is widely held overseas, especially the $100 bill, most US currency by value is exported. This may explain why, according to the Federal Reserve Bank of Richmond, there are now more $100 bills 'in circulation' than $1 bills. The Federal Reserve Board reports that, while the use of cash in retail transactions has fallen, the volume of notes in circulation has more than doubled (from 13.5 billion to 31.3 billion) in the past twenty years and the value of US cash has more than tripled, to just over a trillion dollars (Oliver 2012).

How much is exported? It used to be thought that some two-thirds of US cash was held overseas – indeed, the Federal Reserve Bank of Richmond's estimate is 70% – but other studies have estimated that that fraction is now far lower, observing that there has been a decline in the holding of US dollars coinciding with a rise in the holding of euros. It is still $100 bills that are stuffed under corrupt politicians' beds in the Americas, but on Europe's periphery the €500 note is making a fist of it. Whether this will continue, who knows, but it must have significant implications for US government policy with respect to cash, assuming that it has such a policy (Fiege 2012).

As a result, the United States has far more cash 'in circulation' as a proportion of GDP than, for example, the United Kingdom, but the dynamics of that cash tell us less about the trajectory of cash use. What we can say about the United States is that non-cash payments in the retail sector are dominated by the debit card and that business payments are dominated by credit transfers, as shown in figure 28.

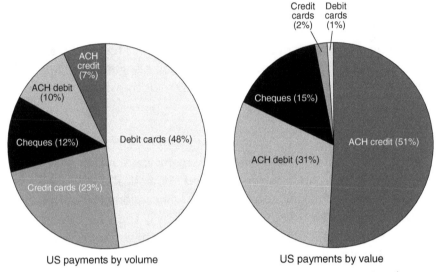

Figure 28. US non-cash payments. (*Source*: Federal Reserve, 2016.)

With the rising popularity of the mobile phone person-to-person scheme Venmo among millennials and the launch of the banks' own Zelle scheme bringing mobile-initiated account-to-account transfers to Main Street, the aggregate figures may be misleading. Perhaps America is moving closer to cashlessness than the broad figures for notes 'in circulation' suggest.

The most recent figures available (Federal Reserve Payments Study 2016) show total non-cash payments growing by 5.3% in volume and by 3.4% in value per annum.

Kenya

A decade on from the then-radical step of allowing a non-bank payment scheme (discussed in detail in 'The M-Pesa story' in chapter 7), Kenya has more than 33 million mobile money users and 174,000 mobile agent locations. Figures from the Central Bank of Kenya show an astonishing trend. Between February 2013 and September 2016 the number of monthly M-Pesa transactions almost tripled, going from 53 million per month to 131 million, while the number of card transactions fell from 34 million per month to 18 million. While mobile money use was tripling, card use was halving. I am told by reliable sources that one of the key reasons for this – apart from the fact that M-Pesa is now accepted at some 150,000 retail outlets in a country with only around 10,000 card terminals – is that when it came time to reissue EMV cards for Kenyan bank customers, the customers had to go to their local branch, with identification, and stand in line to get their new card. Many of them just didn't bother, especially since they had already started to use mobile money instead of cards.

At the time of writing, mobile money continues to boom, with person-to-person use growing a quarter year-on-year and retail use growing two-thirds year-on-year. M-PESA continues to dominate (with an astonishing 96% of Kenyan households having at least one M-Pesa user), accounting for three-quarters of the market, with Equity Bank accounting for most of the rest.

As a Deutsche Bank report on electronic payments noted (Mai 2014), a preference for electronic payments as an alternative to cash payments is not the sole driver of cashless payment growth: changes in population, economic activity and regulation are also likely to influence transaction numbers. I think that that 'economic activity' category deserves more attention. You can see the effect very clearly in Kenya, where for most people there are only two payment choices: cash or M-Pesa. A raft of economic activity is now floating on the M-Pesa river of money – businesses that simply could not exist in a cash-only economy – so it is always interesting to try and understand why.

This means understanding the social, cultural and economic factors around electronic money uptake. An excellent paper on this topic by Iazzolino and Wasike says that a 'rational calculative approach' is not adequate to understand people's decision making (Iazzolino and Wasike 2015), which is something that I learned back in the days of Mondex (see 'The Mondex story' in chapter 1). One clear message from the paper, incidentally, is that different groups will have different reasons for wanting to shift from cash to digital alternatives. One man the authors quote, for example, came up with a very specific use that I'm sure we can all understand:

> If you go drinking, it's better to use M-Pesa because it's safer. Maybe you get drunk and lose your money. If you find yourself unable to dial the number, it means that it's time for you to go home.

This kind of non-rational, non-calculative approach helps to explain the dynamic in the country, where mobile money is replacing cash but cards are not. Kenya, after ten years of M-Pesa development, helps us to understand the embedding of 'financial devices' in social structures, so that we can develop theories about how cash, payment cards and mobile money are used and what they stand for. (The paper noted above uses the case study of *chama* gatherings, where Kenyans want to be seen to be pooling money.)

Sweden

Sweden provides a useful case study of the journey through debit cards and into the world of cashlessness. In the old days there were domestic debit cards in Sweden: Bankkort and Sparbankskort. These were free to customers, who mainly used them to get cash from ATMs. Credit card volumes were low. By comparison with their Nordic neighbours, the Swedes were heavy users of cash (and hence saw far more armed robberies than their neighbours).

In 1995 the Swedes decided to ditch their domestic debit cards and replace them with scheme cards. So Visa Sweden and EuroPay Sweden sprang up with a system of bilateral interchange fees (there are now twenty-nine issuers and ten acquirers who have these agreements, which are not seen, as I understand it, by Visa or MasterCard) and began to market cards as an alternative to cash. And they had significant success. Today, there are no paper cheques and debit card transactions dominate at point of sale.

If you look at Swedbank as an example, they saw debit card transactions soar from 12 million in 1995 to over a billion by 2012, while ATM transactions only went from 50 million to 85 million. A pretty successful effort by any measure. More than 97 per cent of Swedes have debit cards (these are issued to citizens from the age of seven years up, with parental permission) and more than 99 per cent of merchants accept them, the consequence being that more than 80 per cent of retail transactions use the cards (it's about half in the United Kingdom and about two-thirds in the United States).

The goal of the Riksbanken, Sweden's central bank, has begun to be achieved, in that Sweden is one of the few countries in the world where the cash 'in circulation' is actually falling. According to the most recent Bank for International Settlements figures (September 2015), cash is 2 per cent of the Swedish economy (compared to 10 per cent for the eurozone as a whole) and accounts for only a fifth of retail transactions.

However, as the Riksbanken said back in 2012, even in Sweden the use of cash is still far too high compared with where it should be on the basis of social costs (because debit cards have the lowest total social costs). They want to drive cash usage down still further, and as a result Niklas Arvidsson of the KTH Royal Institute of Technology in Sweden has predicted that paper money and coins will disappear from Swedish society 'but probably not before 2030' (see Foss 2013). Not everyone is heading down this path, though. While most of the bank branches in Sweden are now 'cashless', there are still reactionary forces at large. For three of the four major Swedish banks, 530 of their combined 780 offices no longer accept or pay out cash; in the case of the Nordea Bank, 200 of its 300 branches are now cashless; and three-quarters of Swedbank's branches no longer handle cash. While the other banks are going cashless, though, Handelsbanken is expanding cash handling. Let's see how the competition pans out.

Cards will not, of course, be the final nail in the coffin for Swedish cash. That honour belongs to the mobile phone. But there is still work to be done at the social planning level to prepare. Niklas goes on to say:

> [Digital currency] would also have to meet several requirements, such as good emergency backups. People would need to be able to pay even during power cuts, or when electronic systems crashed or were hacked. Currently cash payment is the only system that never fails, so it's difficult to see how we could go totally cashless.

I think he's wrong about this (see the section on 'Disaster' on page 143) but you can see his thinking.

Anyway, the main reason that I wanted to detail the situation in Sweden is that their anti-cash alliance is a broad church, embracing not only banks and law enforcement but also trade unions and retailers. And they have a great figurehead too: Bjorn from ABBA. Listen to him: he is spot on!

- Go Bjorn! 'It is completely incomprehensible why Sweden's central bank is to issue a new series of notes from 2015.'
- Go Bjorn! 'Who needs 500 Kroner or 1000 Kroner notes?' (As far as I understand the situation, Sweden's banks have said essentially the same thing to the central bank.)
- Go Bjorn! 'The problem of begging isn't a problem of payments or payments technology.'

He's even made the ABBA museum cashless! And when asked about that, he said 'some people asked did we want to frighten away the Russians with their bundles of notes', which might well be a more general comment about activities in a number of European capitals and nicely makes the point that if Sweden were to go cashless, one export that might increase is Eastern European criminals (Rugaard 2014). All of which makes me wonder why the general public, in Sweden and elsewhere, are not more outraged about the use of cash to support (indeed, subsidize) a variety of nefarious activities.

It is interesting to observe that there has been something of a backlash against cashlessness more recently. This seems to be centred on the marginalization or exclusion of certain groups, which suggests that cashlessness needs to be planned for, rather than just happen.

China

In China it is mobile payments that are leading the charge against the mundane. China has a very vigorous mobile payments market: in 2015 two-thirds of Chinese retail payments were non-cash and soon something like a third of all retail payments by value will be Internet or mobile payments, with cash under a fifth. In 2017, some $16 trillion in mobile payments were made in China: almost half of all the mobile payments made in the world. (For comparison, PayPal handled under half a trillion dollars.)

This is a colossal industry, with revenues heading towards $100 billion, fed by the simple and widespread use of QR codes and dominated not by banks but by Ant Financial's Alipay and Tencent's WeChat. At the time of writing, Alipay has just over half of the mobile payments market and WeChat almost 40%, although it is in large part thanks to WeChat that Chinese consumers have long been able to navigate their day without banknotes or bank cards (*Economist* 2016).

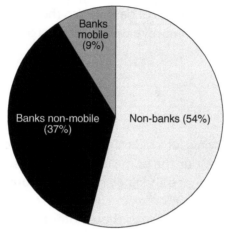

Figure 29. Chinese e-payment volumes, 2Q16.
(*Source: China Daily*, November 2016.)

Tencent and Alipay have created not merely payment systems but entire ecosystems with payments as an integral part. The result has been that in some cities there are shops, markets and event stalls that will accept only mobile payments.

Meanwhile, as shown in figure 29, banks are not doing too well out of the mobile-centric electronic payments revolution in China. The country provides a window into the 'cardmageddon' (the time at which cards will cease to dominate non-cash retail payments by volume) that is approaching in developed markets. Since Chinese consumers switched to using those third-party QR code services, the banks lost something in the region of $20 billion in fees income in 2015 (Wildau 2016).

If you think about it, though, there's a much bigger problem looming. It's one thing for banks to lose interchange income (they are losing that anyway because of the downward pressure on interchange everywhere), but hey, it's only money. The truth is that they are losing something far more important. When the banks don't see the payment transactions, they don't see the data either. This presents a major problem for them when their traditional lending business is under pressure from interest rate deregulation and rising defaults. Big data is vital to their ability to expand into new business lines. As the *Economist* noted in a special report of 28 June 2018, mobile payment ecosystems generate 'immense amounts of data, which the companies then use to target advertisements, improve their e-commerce services and power AI offerings'.

India

India has been carrying out a radical experiment with cash. On 8 November 2016 Narendra Modi, the prime minister, addressed the nation and announced that 500 rupee and 1,000 rupee banknotes were being withdrawn from circulation in order to combat corruption and terrorism.* The result was pandemonium, as these notes represented 85 per cent of the cash in circulation. There were queues at ATMs (wealthy people paid poor people to stand in line for them!) and widespread protests from merchants, who saw trade collapse.

Why was there no Kenyan- or Chinese-style infrastructure in place? I think it is fair to say that the Indian emerging payments environment and what the Reserve Bank of India called its 'calibrated' approach to mobile payments regulation, beginning with its very strict regulation back in 2009, failed to unleash the latent demand from Indian consumers or the inherent enterprise and creativity of Indian businesses. Figures from the World Bank's Consultative Group to Assist the Poor show that while India has a fifth of the world's unbanked population and nearly a billion mobile phone connections, in 2016 less than a -third of 1 per cent of Indian adults used mobile money services.

---

* See 'Text of prime minister's address to the nation' from the Press Information Bureau, Government of India (8 November 2016).

A couple of years ago it was clear to many people that India was missing out because of this and that something would have to be done to allow the multiple benefits of mobile payments to spread in the country. Mobile payments have a key role to play in financial inclusion and this is vitally important to India, so the lack of progress was becoming a social and political issue. Back in 2013 there was an article in the *New York Times* titled 'Mobile payment startups face reluctant Indian consumers' (Bergen 2013) that I suggested at the time should really have been titled 'Mobile payment startups face reluctant Indian regulators'!

The regulatory environment finally began to change back in 2015. Carol Realini and Karl Mehta have looked at the issue of financial inclusion in India in some detail (Realini and Mehta 2015). They note that the previous approach towards national financial inclusion there was to use 'business correspondents' (or BCs). The idea was that banks were to use third-party non-bank BC agents to deliver services. Realini and Mehta have an interesting case study on Eko, one such BC. I couldn't help but notice that the most widely used Eko service is domestic remittance, which is a payment application in my eyes and not a banking application at all. While, as Realini and Mehta note, India may have relatively few bank accounts but a lot of mobile phones, it is not in my view the natural corollary to imagine that getting people to open bank accounts and then access those bank accounts using those mobile phones is a way forward. This isn't just my opinion: the figures show that it is not the optimum route to inclusion. More than half of the 160 million bank accounts created in the Indian government's most recent account opening drive have never been used, and at a cost of $3–$4 to open and maintain that is a lot of wasted money. Most consumers, most of the time, need payments not banking.

The regulatory situation finally began to change in 2015 with the decision to create a new category of financial institution (similar to the approach adopted in Europe), with licences being issued to these new 'payment banks'. Payment banks can

- accept deposits from individual customers with a maximum limit of Rs 1 lakh (around €1,300);

- issue debit and ATM cards for transactions, but not credit cards; and
- allow transactions through Internet and leverage technology to offer low-cost banking solutions.

Importantly, a key to overall systemic risk evaluation is that a payments bank cannot undertake any lending activity. This makes it possible to expand the systemically less risky payments business while keeping the more systemically risky core banking credit activities under tight control.

The Reserve Bank of India granted the first eleven licences in this new category to a variety of fintech, tech and telecoms companies and consortia. Among the successful bidders were the mobile operators Vodafone M-Pesa and Bharti Airtel, the technology companies Fino PayTech and Tech Mahindra, the Department of Posts, and Vijay Shekhar Sharma, the founder of m-commerce outfit Paytm. By the time of the Modi shake-up, Bharti Airtel had only just begun operations, having launched its payments bank in Rajasthan. The Airtel Payments Bank launched with banking points at 10,000 Airtel retail outlets in the state and hoped to have 100,000 merchants on board within a couple of months (Aulakh 2016).

The combination of the regulatory regime and the parallel introduction of the Universal Payments Interface (UPI) to the banks has energized the sector. Street vendors accept Google Pay, WhatsApp Pay, Paytm, PhonePe and the bank UPI app 'BHIM', while Credit Suisse is now forecasting that Indian mobile money volume will reach $1 trillion in 2023, up from $200 billion in 2018 (Rai and Antony 2018).

Paytm is an interesting case study. It had been up and running for a while and it did indeed see volumes double in the immediate aftermath of Modi's announcement and added 20 million users in just five weeks. It subsequently obtained investment from Alibaba and has 7.5 million merchants signed up. But rivals (e.g. Google with Tez) have entered the market to build on the banks' UPI. Bank solutions transfer some $3 bilion per month this way, compared with half a billion for Paytm, and WhatsApp (which has 200 million Indian users) is entering the marketplace as well.

If India does accelerate its shift to a less-cash economy (a cashless India is still some way off), and if that does indeed deliver the expected economic efficiency, then other countries are sure to study the process carefully.

South Korea

A central bank survey shows that South Koreans carry an average of 1.91 credit cards, 2.03 mobile cards and 1.26 cheque or debit cards. In other words, they will soon have more cards in their mobile phones than in their wallets. Four out of ten respondents to the survey picked credit cards as the means of payment they use most, up from three out of ten the previous year. The ratio of those picking cash, meanwhile, continues to fall.

As South Koreans are carrying less cash – with the average standing at 74,000 won last year, down 3,000 won from the previous year – the central bank is also issuing less cash. It released 12.3 per cent fewer 10,000 won banknotes last year than in the previous year, while the issuance of 5,000 won and 1,000 won notes dipped by 5.9 per cent and 3.7 per cent, respectively (Ja-young 2016).

The Bank of Korea is planning a 'cashless society' by 2020. If a shopper buys a 9,500 won item and pays with a 10,000 won banknote, for instance, the shopper will be credited 500 won to his or her prepaid card instead of getting a 500 won coin in change. This makes obvious sense in a developed economy where the cost of coin production (the big problem of small change, remember) already outweighs any economic benefit from coin circulation.

As South Korea is a hotbed of cryptocurrency activity and with the mayor of Seoul having recently called for the city to issue its own 'cryptocurrency', it seems to me that the country may become one of the key laboratories for monetary experiments in the coming years.

Denmark

As with Sweden, Denmark is getting serious about the war on cash, and the government has proposed getting rid of the obligation for selected retailers to accept payment in cash (Reuters 2015). The Danish government's ambition was that businesses such as clothing retailers, petrol stations and restaurants should no longer be legally bound to accept cash, as they are currently: a situation specific to Denmark. In common law countries (e.g. the United Kingdom and the United States) there is no requirement for retailers to accept any form of payment at all, cash included. It's a misunderstanding of what 'legal tender' means to imagine that they do. But in Denmark the law says that certain types of retailer must accept cash. (My good friend Kristian Sorensen tells me that to accommodate strong opposition from the government's right wing coalition partners, the proposal was eventually replaced with a more lightweight approach, where only certain types of merchant during specific times of the day are allowed to refuse cash. Petrol stations can refuse cash at night, for example.)

Once again, it's the mobile phone that is the enabler. Most of the adult population of Denmark use MobilePay, the mobile-initiated account-to-account immediate-payment service (the equivalent of Zelle in the United States or Pingit in the United Kingdom), which was introduced by Danske Bank in Denmark. It was launched in 2013 and has attracted more than 3.4 million users out of a population of 5.7 million, which, when you look at the demographics, means that it already has around 70 per cent of its total addressable market (i.e. Danish smartphone users aged fifteen and up). Right now it is processing around 500,000 transactions per day, with an average value of around €33. This frequent use makes MobilePay the third most used app in Denmark (surpassed only by Facebook and Facebook Messenger).

At the time of writing, MobilePay is accepted in more than 40,000 shops across Denmark and at close to 10,000 webshops. Many smaller merchants have signed up for a 'small business acceptance' app, allowing them to accept electronic payments without a POS terminal. Merchants are charged between 0.3 and 0.75 Danish krone for payments (depending on the number of transactions per year), and I'm told (by a very reliable source) that the fraud levels through this channel are significantly lower than they are on cards. They have extended the app to provide a contactless NFC and Bluetooth option for point of sale.

What interests me most about their roadmap is that they have a very good API and are now trialling it with some merchants because, as we all know, merchants want their own apps to deliver the best customer service and the future is 'app and pay'.

In the United Kingdom we have two mobile A2A front ends to interbank payments: the aforementioned PingIt, offered by Barclays, and Paym, offered by everyone else. Paym has around 2 million people registered and it transferred around £26 million in 2014. We happen to be a Barclays-centric household so I use PingIt all the time and find it very convenient. I was very excited, therefore, back in February 2015 when they extended their addressing from mobile phone numbers to Twitter handles!

(If you want to try this out for yourself while supporting a good cause, by the way, simply fire up the PingIt app on your mobile phone, select a modest amount for test purposes – say, £250 – and send it to @dgwbirch. I will let you know as soon as your payment reaches the 'Dave Birch Holiday Home in the South of France' emergency appeal fund.)

While neither PingIt nor Paym is close to being used by half the adult population of the United Kingdom, or to edging cash out of the way for the person in the street, across the North Sea MobilePay is playing a key role in bringing Denmark closer to cashlessness.

Somaliland

Somaliland gained independence, with Somalia, from Britain in 1960 (it became part of the British Empire back in 1888). It has a population of some 3.5 million and sits on the Horn of Africa. It announced its secession from Somalia in 1991 and has operated as a more or less independent country ever since. It has its own president, parliament and constitution. It even boasts a central bank that prints its own currency, the Somaliland shilling (*Economist* 2011), in contrast to Somalia, which has had no currency for twenty-five years.

Like many other poor countries in Africa, it has a vigorous mobile sector, and within that vigorous mobile sector mobile money transfer is a thriving value-adding service. For example, Zaad is a mobile money-transfer service offered by Telesom, the country's largest network operator. Telesom has 500,000 subscribers and it estimates that 40 per cent of the territory's population has a mobile phone. More than 300,000 Somalilanders use Zaad, which was first launched in May 2009. The service limits standard users to transfers of $500, while merchants are allowed to transfer up to $2,000 at a time. What Somaliland Telecoms calls 'special arrangements' are made for its wealthier users, depending on the amount in their bank accounts.

Mobile is growing there by leaps and bounds. There are no ATMs in the country and credit cards are regarded as ridiculous by local people (Munford 2012). I suspect, although I've never been to Somaliland, that one of the reasons that Zaad and the telecommunications systems are so successful is precisely because the government hasn't been able to control them. Munford thinks that the vigour, inventiveness and dynamism that accompany the private sector approach to providing the market with an appropriate means of exchange (shades of George Selgin's Birmingham button makers here (Selgin 2008)) may have a surprising outcome. It is entirely possible that Somaliland will be the world's first cashless country!

New Zealand

New Zealand is steadily moving towards cashlessness. As far as I can tell from my visits, virtually no one uses cash and the overwhelming majority of retail transactions are on cards. When I last arrived at a hotel in Auckland and unpacked my suitcase, I discovered that I'd forgotten to pack my deodorant so I strolled out of the hotel to see if there was a nearby pharmacy or convenience store. I wandered into the first one I saw and picked up a deodorant stick. I walked over to the clerk and proffered a $20 bill alongside the deodorant. To my surprise and delight the clerk told me that they *did not accept cash after 7 pm* and that it was cards only, so I bought a large chocolate bar as well to reward the store for their forward-thinking policy. There was not a single shop, restaurant, taxi or fast-food joint that I visited on my trip that needed cash.

I saw plenty of contactless terminals and even a couple of vending machines that accepted mobile payments, contactless cards and (bizarrely) coins. I wanted to give a local QR code payment service,

QuickTap, a try as well because it looked quite interesting but when I tried to download the app nothing happened. Maybe you have to be logged in to the NZ iTunes store or something ridiculous like that. Anyway, now that banks and the mobile operators have got together to launch an NFC service, I'll use that instead.

New Zealand is an advanced country that illustrates one of my all-time favourite quotes, from William Gibson's 'cyberpunk' masterpiece *Count Zero*, about a future in which 'it wasn't actually illegal to have [cash], it was just that nobody ever did anything legitimate with it'. The future may well be unevenly distributed, but some of it is in New Zealand.

Germany

Germany is an outlier when it comes to retail payments. The average German wallet contains 103 physical euros, according to European Central Bank estimates in 2017: more than three times the figure in France. Cash accounts for around 80% of German POS transactions by volume (although only 48% of the value), compared with less than half that next door in the Netherlands.

Perhaps it is that Germans are just naturally conservative people. The Roman historian Tacitus (55–117 CE) wrote in his history *Germany and Its Tribes* that the barbarian inhabitants of that land had traditionally exchanged weapons, slaves, cattle, women and such like to settle up between themselves but that the Romans had introduced them to money. Having changed their medium of exchange once in the last two millennia, perhaps they just don't want more change for change's sake.

Although I have long suspected that much of the cash in Germany is stuffed under mattresses rather than circulating in the economy, it is still surprising to hear from the Bundesbank that nine in ten of the euro banknotes that they print are never used in transactions. That's right: nine in ten. Nearly all of the cash printed in Germany is never used. Not rarely, not occasionally, but never. Can it really be that the German predilection for holding some of their money in the form of cash accounts for these billions of euros in inert paper money?

Given the current unusual circumstances with respect to interest rates and so forth, it is certainly a plausible hypothesis. The European Central Bank interest rate for bank deposits is currently *minus* 0.4%. Conventional economic theory would predict that at a minus rate, depositors would prefer to hold cash rather than pay the banking system to look after their money for them. Now, it clearly costs something to manage cash over and above the cost of managing an electronic deposit, so it is interesting to speculate what the German 'crossover' negative interest rate might be: the modern version of the old 'specie point' at which it was cheaper to hold bullion for monetary purposes rather than paper instruments.

The current negative interest rate costs German banks about a quarter of a billion euros per annum. The Bavarian Savings Bank Association distributed a circular to their members some time ago setting out their calculation of the crossover rate, which they worked out to be something like −0.2%, or half of the current negative rate. However, this isn't really a serious calculation because (as the association itself says in its circular) it doesn't take into account the significant costs of cash in transit or the additional security expenditure that would be needed to guard cash hoards. But it does make a fun point, at least to me, which is that the existence of €500 notes has an impact on that crossover rate. Now that the European Central Bank has decided to stop printing the €500 notes, banks will have to store masses of €200 bills, so the cost of storage and transport will be higher (which, in turn, will put a premium on the €500 notes in circulation, so that they will trade above par). Just as an indication, 2 billion euros in €200 notes weighs about 11 tonnes.

As far as I know, no banks have to date decided to store their squillions under the mattress rather than leave them on deposit. That Bavarian estimate must, therefore, be too low, and the costs of transport, security, insurance and so on must be quite high, so the European Central Bank should be able to push interest rates further into negative territory before it gets close to a genuine crossover point that would see banks investing in larger mattresses.

Bibliography

Achilles, J., K. Larsen and M. Selig. 2018. The US SEC asserts its regulatory enforcement power in the ICO space. In *Payments & Fintech Lawyer,* February.

Agence France-Presse. 2013. Denmark frees Chinese duo held in 'fake' coin mix-up. URL: http://bit.ly/2nTnOFX (accessed 10 April 2017).

Andolfatto, D. 2015. Should the Fed issue its own Bitcoin? *Newsweek,* 31 December.

Ardizzi, G., C. Petraglia, M. Piacencza, F. Schneider and G. Turati. 2013. Money laundering as a financial sector crime—a new approach to measurement with application to Italy. Working Paper, Centre for Economic Studies & Ifo Institute.

Aulakh, G. 2016. Bharti Airtel launches payments bank in Rajasthan. *The Economic Times,* 23 November.

Badev, A., and M. Chen. 2014. Bitcoin: technical background and data analysis. Staff Working Paper, Divisions of Research & Statistics and Monetary Affairs, Federal Reserve, 7 October.

Barrdear, J., and M. Kumhof. 2016. The macroeconomics of central bank issued digital currencies. Bank of England, July.

BBC. 2013. Chinese tourists detained in Paris over one-euro coins. URL: www.bbc.co.uk/news/world-europe-24524699 (retrieved 14 October).

Bellamy, E. 1946. *Looking Backward 2000–1887.* Cleveland, OH: World Publishing.

Bendell, J. 2015. What happens to democracy in a cashless society? *Transformation,* openDemocracy, 8 April.

Benson, C., and S. Loftesness. 2012. Core systems: ACH. In *Payment Systems in the US.* San Francisco, CA: Glenbrook.

Bergen, M. 2013. Mobile payment startups face reluctant Indian consumers. Blog, *New York Times*, 4 October.

Birch, D. 2000. Reputation not regulation. *The Guardian*, 2 November.

Birch, D. 2001. Farewell then, Beenz. *The Guardian*, 27 September.

Birch, D. (ed.). 2007. *Digital Identity Management: Technological, Business and Social Implications*. Farnham: Gower.

Birch, D. 2013. Talking 'bout your reputation. *Crossroads: The ACM Magazine for Students*, Fall, p. 32.

Birch, D. 2014. *Identity Is the New Money*. London Publishing Partnership.

Birch, D. 2015. What does cryptocurrency mean for the new economy. In *Handbook of Digital Currency* (ed. D. L. K. Chen). Academic Press.

Birch, D. 2017. The importance of ICOs to the future of money. In *Payments & Fintech Lawyer*, October.

Birch, D., and N. McEvoy. 1996. DIY cash. *Wired UK*, April.

Birch, D., and N. McEvoy. 1997. Technology will denationalise money. In *Financial Cryptography*, pp. 95–108. Springer

Birch, D., and S. Parulava. 2017. Ambient accountability. In *Handbook of Blockchain, Digital Finance and Inclusion* (ed. D. Lee and R. Deng), pp., 375–388. London: Elsevier.

Bishop, M., and M. Green. 2012. *In Gold We Trust? The Future of Money in an Age of Uncertainty*. London: Economist Newspaper Limited.

Blas, J. 2014. Africans face $2 billion yearly 'remittance supertax' says report. *Financial Times*, 16 April.

Blomfield, A. 2009. Global currency 'could save world economy'. *Daily Telegraph*, 26 March.

Boyle, D. 2002. *The Money Changers*. London: Earthscan.

Bray, H. 2014. *You Are Here*. New York: Perseus.

Bremner, C. 2014. Playboy Saudi prince 'blackmailed' after Paris ambush. *The Times*, 21 August.

Brown, J., and P. Duguid. 2000. *The Social Life of Information*. Boston, MA: Harvard Business School Press.

Brown, R. 1973. The bank clerk goes electronic. *New Scientist*, 9 August, p. 307.

Bruno, G., and J. McWaters. 2016. The future of financial infrastructure: an ambitious look at how blockchain can reshape financial services. World Economic Forum, August.

Buiter, W. 2009. Negative interest rates: when are they coming to a central bank near you? *Financial Times* blogs, Maverecon, 7 May.

Calder, N. 1956. Automation in banking. *New Scientist*, 29 November, p. 18.

Cameron, K. 2005. The laws of identity. Microsoft, 11 May.

Castronova, E. 2014. *Wildcat Currency*. New Haven, CT: Yale University Press.

Chittenden, O. (ed.). 2010. *The Future of Money*. London: Virgin.

Chown, J. 1994a. Money in the commercial revolution. In *A History of Money from AD 800*, pp. 23–31. London: Routledge.

Chown, J. 1994b. The development of banking and finance. In *A History of Money from AD 800*, pp. 129–137. London: Routledge

Chiang, C. 2017. The wizard behind the ICO model that's changing venture capital. URL: https://btcmanager.com/the-wizard-behind-the-ico-model-transforming-venture-capital/ (6 June).

Christensen, C. 1997. *The Innovator's Dilemma: When New Technologies Cause Great Firms to Fail*. Boston, MA: Harvard Business School Press.

Christensen, C., S. Anthony and E. Roth. 2005. Competitive battles. In *Seeing What's Next*, pp. 29–51. Boston, MA: Harvard Business School Press.

Cleland, V. 2015. Working together to deliver banknotes for the modern economy. Bank of England, 2 September.

Cockburn, P. 2015. We can all get by quite well without banks – Ireland managed to survive without them. *The Independent*, 12 July.

Cohen, B. 2006a. New frontier. In *The Future of Money*, pp. 179–202. Princeton University Press.

Cohen, B. 2006b. *The Future of Money*. Princeton University Press.

Conway, E. 2014a. Bedlam. In *The Summit: The Battle of the Second World War*, pp. 121–150. London: Little, Brown.

Conway, E. 2014b. The Bretton Woods system. In *The Summit: The Battle of the Second World War*, pp. 365–385. London: Little, Brown.

Coyle, D. 1997a. *The Weightless World: Strategies for Managing the Digital Economy*. Oxford: Capstone.

Coyle, D. 1997b. *The Weightless World*. In *The Weightless World: Strategies for Managing the Digital Economy*, pp. 1–25. Oxford: Capstone.

Coyle, D. 2001. *Paradoxes of Prosperity: Why the New Capitalism Benefits All.* New York: Texere.

Coyle, D. 2002. Sex, *Drugs and Economics: An Unconventional Introduction to Economics.* London: Texere.

Coyle, D. 2014. *GDP: A Brief but Affectionate History.* Princeton University Press.

Daley, J. 2008. Who cares if cheques become extinct? *The Independent,* 2 February.

Davidow, W., and M. Malone. 2015. How new technologies push towards the past. *Harvard Business Review,* 8 May.

Davies, G. 1994. *A History of Money from Ancient Times to the Present Day.* University of Wales Press.

Davies, G. 1995a. From primitive and ancient money to the invention of coinage. In *A History of Money: From Ancient Times to the Present Day,* pp. 33–64. Cardiff: University of Wales Press.

Davies, G. 1995b. The Treasury and the tally. In *A History of Money: From Ancient Times to the Present Day,* pp. 146–152. Cardiff: University of Wales Press.

Davies, G. 1995c. Aspects of monetary development in Europe and Japan. In *A History of Money: From Ancient Times to the Present Day,* pp. 547–592. Cardiff: University of Wales Press.

Davies, G. 1997. Monetary innovation in historical perspective. Consult Hyperion Digital Money Forum, London, 7 October.

Day, J., and J. Reed. 2001. A brand new line. In *The Story of London's Underground,* pp. 158–173. London: Capital Transport.

de Bono, E. 2002. The IBM dollar. In *The Money Changers* (ed. D. Boyle), pp. 168–170. London: Earthscan.

Del Mar, A. 1885. *A History of Money in Ancient Countries from the Earliest Times to the Present.* London: George Bell & Sons. (Reprinted by Kessinger Publishing.)

Desan, C. 2014a. Money reinvented. In *Making Money: Coin, Currency and the Coming of Capitalism,* pp. 11–22. Oxford University Press.

Desan, C. 2014b. Priming the pump: the sovereign path towards paying for coin and circulating credit. In *Making Money: Coin, Currency and the Coming of Capitalism,* pp. 231–265. Oxford University Press.

Dodd, N. 2014. Utopia. In *The Social Life of Money*, pp. 318–384. Princeton University Press.

Donado, R. 2011. Battered by economic crisis, Greeks turn to barter networks. *New York Times*, p. A8, 2 October.

Drehmann, M., and C. Goodhart. 2000. Is cash becoming technologically outmoded? Or does it remain necessary to facilitate 'bad behaviour'? An empirical investigation into the determinants of cash holdings. London School of Economics.

DuPont, Q., and B. Maurer. 2015. Ledgers and law in the blockchain. *King's Review*, 22 June.

Dyer, C. 2002a. The growth of the state. In *Making a Living in the Middle Ages: The People of Britain 850–1520*, pp. 50–57. New Haven, CT, Yale University Press.

Dyer, C. 2002b. Making a new world. In *Making a Living in the Middle Ages: The People of Britain 850–1520*, pp. 265–270. New Haven, CT, Yale University Press.

Dyson, B., and G. Hodgson. 2016. Digital cash: why central banks should start issuing electronic money. *Positive Money*, January.

Dyson, E. 2001. Who am I talking to? *New York Times Syndicate*, 21 May.

Eco, U. 1986. *Travels in Hyper Reality*. San Diego, CA: Harcourt Brace.

Economist. 2008. Under threat. *The Economist*, 7 February.

Economist. 2011. Mo money mo problems. *The Economist*, 24 July.

Economist. 2014a. The treasure of darkness. *The Economist*, 11 October.

Economist. 2014b. Money from nothing. *The Economist*, 3 September.

Economist. 2016. WeChat's world. *The Economist*, 6 August.

Edgerton, D. 2006. Significance. In *The Shock of the Old: Technology and Global History Since 1900*, pp. 1–27. London: Profile Books.

Einzig, P. 1966. Maize money of Guatemala. In *Primitive Money: In Its Ethnological, Historical and Economic Aspects*, pp. 177–178. Oxford: Pergamon.

Ellinger, B. 1940. The deposit banks. In *The City*, pp. 111–236. London: Staples Press.

Ellis, D. 1998. The effect of consumer interest rate deregulation on credit card volumes, charge-offs, and the personal bankruptcy rate in bank trends. *SSRN Electronic Journal*, March.

Evans, C. 2015. The blind economists and the elephant: Bitcoin and monetary separation. *Southwestern Journal of Economics* **11**(1), 1–19.

Fallows, J. 2013. The 50 greatest breakthroughs since the wheel. *The Atlantic*, November, p. 56.

Ferguson, N. 2001. The money printers. In *The Cash Nexus*, pp. 137–162. New York: Basic Books.

Financial Times. 2015. The case for retiring another 'barbarous' relic. *Financial Times*, editorial, 23 August.

FINMA. 2018. Guidelines for enquiries regarding the regulatory framework for initial coin offerings (ICOs). Report, FNMA, 16 February.

Foss, A. 2013. The cashless society is closer than you think. *ScienceNordic*, 7 May.

Freeman, C., and F. Louca. 2001. *As Times Goes By*. Oxford University Press.

Friedman, M. 1992. *Money Mischief: Episodes in Monetary History*. Orlando, FL: Harcourt Brace Jovanovich.

Friedman, M. 1991. *The Island of Stone Money*, p. 5. Hoover Institution.

Friedman, M. 1992. Bimetallism revisited. In *Money Mischief*, pp. 126–156. Orlando, FL: Harcourt Brace Jovanovich.

Fung, B., S. Hendry and W. E. Weber. 2017. Canadian bank notes and dominion notes: lessons for digital currencies. Staff Working Paper, Bank of Canada, February.

Gardner, J. 2009. Innovating in banks. In *Innovation and the Futureproof Bank*, pp. 67–106. Chichester: Wiley.

Giraudo, A. 2007. The beginnings of the paper economy at the medieval fairs. In *Money Tales* (ed. M. Westlake), pp. 112–117. Paris: Economica.

Glasner, D. 1998. An evolutionary theory of the state monopoly over money. In *Money and the Nation State* (ed. K. Dowd and R. Timberlake), pp. 21–46. New Brunswick, NJ: Transaction.

Goetzmann, W. 2016. Financial architecture. In *Money Changes Everything: How Finance Made Civilization Possible*, pp. 46–64. Princeton University Press.

Graeber, D. 2011a. The Middle Ages. In *Debt: The First 5,000 Years*, pp. 251–306. New York: Melville House.

Graeber, D. 2011b. Primordial debts. In *Debt: The First 5,000 Years*, pp. 43–72. New York: Melville House.

Greenberg, A. 2011. Crypto currency. *Forbes*, 9 May, p. 40.

Greenberg, A. 2013. Meet the 'assassination market' creator who's crowdfunding murder with Bitcoins. *Forbes*, 18 November.

Groppa, O. 2013. Complementary currency and its impact on the economy. *International Journal of Community Currency Research* **17**(A), 45–57.

Hanson, N. 2004. *The Confident Hope of a Miracle: The True History of the Spanish Armada*. Corgi.

Harari, Y. 2014. The cognitive revolution. In *Sapiens: A Brief History of Humankind*, p. 466. New York: Vintage Digital.

Hart, K. 1999. The future of money and the market. In *The Memory Bank*, pp. 294–326. London: Profile.

Hart, K. 2012. A crisis of money: the demise of national capitalism. *openDemocracy*, 14 March.

Hasse, R., and T. Koch. 1991. The hard ECU – a substitute for the D-Mark or a Trojan horse? *Intereconomics* **26**(4), 159–166.

Hayek, F. A. 2007. *Denationalisation of Money*. London: Profile.

He, D., and 10 others. 2016. Virtual currencies and beyond: initial considerations. International Monetary Fund, January.

Hill, K. 2014. 21 things I learned about Bitcoin living on it a second time. *Forbes*, 15 May.

Hock, D. 2005. House of cards. In *One from Many: VISA and the Rise of Chaordic Organization*, pp. 75–88. San Francisco, CA: Berret-Koehler.

Hockenhull, T. (ed.). 2015. The shekel. In *Symbols of Power: Ten Coins that Changed the World*, pp. 12–23. London: British Museum Press.

Home Office. 2016. Action Plan for anti-money laundering and counter-terrorist finance. Home Office, April.

Hudson, M. 2000. How interest rates were set, 2500 BC–1000 AD. *Journal of the Economic and Social History of the Orient* **43**(Spring), 132–161.

Iazzolino, G., and N. Wasike. 2015. The unbearable lightness of digital money. *Journal of Payment Strategy and Systems* **9**(3), 229–241.

IBSintelligence. 2013. In the fast lane. *IBS Journal*, 4 April, p. 22.

Issing, O. 2000. New techologies in payments: a challenge to monetary policy. European Central Bank, 28 June.

Jacobs, J. 1985. *Cities and the Wealth of Nations*. Toronto: Random House.

Jacomb, M. 1998. The city to come. *The Spectator*, 8 November, p. 17.

Jansen, M. 2013. Bitcoin: the political 'virtual' of an intangible material currency. *International Journal of Community Currency Research* **17**(A), 8–18.

Jay, P. 2000. Globalisation: boats not bytes. In *Road to Riches or The Wealth of Man*, pp. 130–178. London: Weidenfeld & Nicolson.

Ja-young, Y. 2016. Korea shifting to cashless society. *Korea Times*, 1 March.

Jevons, W. 1884. Representative money. In *Money and the Mechanisms of Exchange*, pp. 102–105. New York: Humboldt.

Josset, C. 1962. Bank notes until the early nineteenth century. In *Money in Britain*, pp. 112–115. London: Frederick Warne.

Kahn, R. 2015. Currencies are easy, policies are hard. Macro and Markets, Council on Foreign Relations, 5 July.

Kay, J. 2013. A currency is anything that two people agree is a currency. *Financial Times*, 6 August.

Kelleher, T. 2015. Ripple's overlooked path to decentralization. *American Banker*, 23 July.

Kenny, C. 2014. Alternative currencies. Parliamentary Office of Science and Technology, August.

Kenny, C. 2015. Why the world is so bad at tracking dirty money. *Bloomberg News*, 23 February.

Keohane, D. 2015. Buiter on the death of cash. *FT Alphaville*, 10 April.

King, B. 2013. Bank 3.0. Marshall Cavendish International, Tarrytown, NY.

King, B. 2014. Why kids don't have signatures. *Medium*, 5 May.

King, M. 2016a. *The End of Alchemy*. London: Little, Brown.

King, M. 2016b. The good, the bad and the ugly. In *The End of Alchemy*, pp. 15–50. London: Little, Brown.

King, M. 2016c. Innocence regained: reforming money and banking. In *The End of Alchemy*, pp. 250–289. London: Little, Brown.

King, M. 2016d. Heroes and villains: the role of central banks. In *The End of Alchemy*, pp. 156–210. London: Little, Brown.

Klein, M. 2000. Banks lose control of money. *Financial Times*, 15 January.

Kobrin, S. 1997. Electronic cash and the end of national markets. *Foreign Policy* **107**(Summer), 65.

Lanchester, J. 2016. When Bitcoin grows up. *London Review of Books* **38**(8), 3–12.

Lanier, J. 2013. *Who Owns the Future.* London: Allen Lane.

Lascelles, D. 2016. A walk on the Wilde side. *Financial World,* April, p. 34.

Leigh, D., J. Ball, J. Garside and D. Pegg. 2015. HSBC files reveal mystery of Richard Caring and the £2m cash withdrawl. *The Guardian,* 9 February.

Leighton, B. 2014. How smart was that? *Swindon Evening Advertiser,* 21 May.

Lelieveldt, S. 1997. How to regulate electronic cash. *American University Law Review* **46**(4), 1163–1175.

Lessin, S. 2013. Identity+30. South-by-Southwest Interactive, March, Austin, TX.

Levinson, T. 2009. The undoing of the whole nation. In *Newton and the Counterfeiter,* pp. 109–116. London: Faber & Faber.

Levy, S. 1994. E-money (that's what i want). *Wired,* December.

Lewis, M. 2003. *Moneyball.* New York: W. W. Norton.

Lietaer, B. 2001. Work-enabling currencies. In *The Future of Money,* pp. 125–178. London: Century.

Lonergan, E. 2009. *Money.* Durham: Acumen.

Lonergan, E. 2018. What if your money had a mind of its own? *Prospect,* June.

Mai, H. 2014. US payments keep going electronic. Deutsche Bank Research, 18 February.

Malkin, L. 2008. *Krueger's Men: The Secret Nazi Counterfeit Plot and the Prisoners of Block 19.* Boston, MA: Back Bay Books.

Mar, A. D. 1885. Supply of materials suitable for money, and development of coinage and printing. In *A History of Money in Ancient Countries from the Earliest Times to the Present,* pp. 1–13. London: Kessinger.

Martin, F. 2013. The great monetary settlement. In *Money: The Unauthorised Biography,* pp. 109–122. London: Bodley Head.

Maurer, B., and L. Swartz. 2014. The future of money-like things. *The Atlantic,* 22 May.

Mayer, M. 1998a. The nature of money. In *The Bankers: The Next Generation,* pp. 37–62. New York: Plume.

Mayer, M. 1998b. What money does. In *The Bankers: The Next Generation*, pp. 63–94. New York: Plume.

McLeay, M., A. Radia and R. Thomas. 2014. Money creation in the modern economy. *Quarterly Bulletin*, Bank of England, January.

McWilliams, D. 2014. Prostitutes and software developers: a short history of the Italian black economy. Gresham College Shorts Lecture, 14 February.

Mougayar, W. 2016. Lighthouse industries and new intermediaries. In *The Business Blockchain*, pp. 109–123. Wiley.

Munford, M. 2012. Somaliland's mobile payments boom. *The Kernel*, 18 May.

Murphy, A. 1978. Money in an economy without banks. *The Manchester School* **46**(1), 41–50.

Naim, M. 2010. *Illicit: How Smugglers, Traffickers and Copycats are Hijacking the Global Economy*. Random House.

Naqvi, A. 2014. Cities, not countries, are the key to tomorrow's economies. *Financial Times*, Comment, 25 April.

Naqvi, M., and J. Southgate. 2013. Banknotes, local currencies and central bank objectives. *Bank of England Quaterly Bulletin*, Q4, p. 317.

New Scientist. 1961. How far have the banks gone with automation? *New Scientist*, 29 April, p. 278.

Nilson Report. 2013. Global card fraud losses reach $11.27 billion. Nilson Report, August, p. 1.

Nocera, J. 1994. Here come the revolutionaries. In *A Piece of the Action: How the Middle Class Joined the Money Class*, pp. 89–105. New York: Simon & Schuster.

Norman, B., R. Shaw and G. Speight. 2011. The history of interbank settlement arrangements: exploring central banks' role in the payments system. Bank of England, June.

Nuvolari, A. 2004. Collective invention during the British Industrial Revolution. *Cambridge Journal of Economics* **28**(3), 347–368.

Odlyzko, A. 2011. The collapse of the railway mania, the development of capital markets, and Robert Lucas Nash, a forgotten pioneer of accounting and financial analysis. *Accounting History Review* **21**(3), 309–345.

Omwansa, T., and N. Sullivan. 2012. *Money, Real Quick: The Story of M-Pesa*. London: Guardian Books.

Pantaleone, W. 2014. Italy seizes 556,000 euros in fake coins minted in China. *Daily Mail,* 12 December.

Peck, M. 2013. Ripple credit system could help or harm Bitcoin. *IEEE Spectrum,* 14 January.

Pentland, A. 2014. Social physics and the human centric society. In *From Bitcoin to Burning Man and Beyond* (ed. D. Bollier and J. Clippinger), pp. 3–10. Boston, MA: ID3.

Perez, C. 2005. The changing nature of financial and institutional innovations. In *Technological Revolutions and Financial Capital*, pp. 138–151. Cheltenham: Edward Elgar.

Postman, N. 1993. The judgement of Thamus. In *Technopoly*, pp. 3–20. New York: Vintage.

Pringle, H. 1998. The cradle of cash. *Discover,* October, p. 52.

Radecki, L. 1999. Banks' payments-driven revenues. *Federal Reserve Bank of New York Economic Policy Review,* July, p. 53.

Rai, S., and A. Antony. 2018. Banning rupees didn't work, this might. *Bloomberg Businessweek,* 15 October.

Raphael, A. 1994. Coffee house to catastrophe. In *Ultimate Risk*, pp. 17–41. London: Bantam.

Raymaekers, W. 2015. Cryptocurrency Bitcoin: disruption, challenges and opportunities. *Payments Strategy and Systems* **9**(1), 22–29.

Realini, C., and K. Mehta. 2015. Mobile phones are a potent solution. In *Financial Inclusion at the Bottom of the Pyramid*, p. 256. Victoria, BC: Friesen Press.

Reuters. 2015. Denmark moves step closer to being a cashless country. *Daily Telegraph,* 6 May.

Ringland, G. 2011. *In Safe Hands? The Future of Financial Services*. Newbury: SAMI.

Roberds, W. 1997. What's really new about the new forms of retail payment? *Economic Review,* 1 January.

Roberds, W. 1998. The impact of fraud on new methods of retail payments. *Economic Review,* Q1.

Robinson, J. 2014. BitCon: the naked truth about Bitcoin. Amazon Digital Services, 26 September, p. 149.

Rogoff, K. S. 2017. International dimensions and digital currencies. In *The Curse of Cash: How Large Denomination Bills Aid Tax Evasion and Crime and Constrain Monetary Policy* (paperback edition). Princeton University Press.

Rosner, M., and A. Kang. 2016. Understanding and regulating twenty-first century payment systems: the Ripple case study. *Michigan Law Review* **114**(4), 648–681.

Rugaard, M. 2014. Money, money, money – but not in cash. *Digital Values*, January, p. 16.

Rushkoff, D. 2016. Reimagining money. *The Atlantic*, 7 March.

Salter, J., and C. Wood. 2013. The power of prepaid. DEMOS, 30 January.

Sands, P. 2016. Making it harder for the bad guys: the case for eliminating high denomination notes. M-RCBG Association Working Paper Series, Number 52 (February).

Sargent, T., and F. Velde. 2002. Our model and our history. In *The Big Problem of Small Change*, pp. 373–374. Economic History of the Western World Series. Princeton University Press.

Sayers, R. 1965. Computers and money. *New Scientist*, 1 April, p. 13.

Schewe, P. 2007. *The Grid: A Journey Through the Heart of Our Electrified World*. Washington, DC: Joseph Henry Press.

Schlichter, D. 2011. Beyond the cycle: paper money's endgame. In *Paper Money Collapse*, pp. 221–240. Wiley.

Schmeidel, H., G. Kostova and W. Ruttenberg. 2012. The social and private costs of retail payment instruments: a European perspective. European Central Bank, September.

Schneier, B. 2000. *Secrets and Lies: Digital Security in a Networked World*. New York: Wiley Computer Publishing.

Schneier, B. 2011. Unanticipated security risk of keeping your money in a home safe. *Schneier on Security*, 15 April.

Scorer, S. 2017. Beyond blockchain: what are the technology requirements for a Central Bank digital currency? In *Bank Undergound*. URL: https://bit.ly/2y9g7Se (updated 13 September 2017).

Seabright, P. 2005. *The Company of Strangers: A Natural History of Economic Life*. Princeton University Press.

Seidensticker, B. 2006. *Future Hype: The Myths of Technology Change*. San Francisco, CA: Berrett-Koehler.

Selgin, G. 2008. Britain's big problem. In *Good Money: Birmingham Button Makers, the Royal Mint, and the Beginnings of Modern Coinage 1775–1821*, pp. 4–37. Ann Arbor, MI: Univerisity of Michigan Press.

Shafik, M. 2016. A new heart for a changing payments system. Bank of England, 27 January.

Shenton, C. 2012. Worn-out, worm-eaten, rotten old bits of wood. In *The Day Parliament Burned Down*, pp. 40–57. Oxford University Press.

Shepard, W. 2016. A cashless future is the real goal of India's demonetization move. *Forbes*, 14 December.

Shorto, R. 2013. The company. In *Amsterdam*, pp. 89–127. New York: Vintage.

Shuo, W., Z. Jiwei and H. Kan. 2016. Zhuo Xiaochuan interview. *Caxin Online*, 15 February.

Sinclair, D. 2000. Bankers' hours. In *The Pound*, pp. 171–188. London: Century.

Sofsky, W. 2008. *Privacy: A Manifesto*. Princeton University Press.

Solomon, E. 1997. *Virtual Money: Understanding the Power and Risks of Money's High-Speed Journey into Electronic Space*. Oxford University Press.

Solove, D. 2007. *The Future of Reputation: Gossip, Rumour and Privacy on the Internet*. New Haven, CT: Yale University Press.

Spang, R. 2015a. Conclusion: money and history. In *Stuff and Money in the Time of the French Revolution*, pp. 271–278. Cambridge, MA: Harvard University Press.

Spang, R. 2015b. Liberty of money. In *Stuff and Money in the Time of the French Revolution*, pp. 135–168. Cambridge, MA: Harvard University Press.

Spang, R. 2015c. Making money. In *Stuff and Money in the Time of the French Revolution*, pp. 97–134. Cambridge, MA: Harvard University Press.

Spufford, P. 2002a. From court to counting house. In *Power and Profit: The Merchant in Medieval Europe*, pp. 140–173. London: Thames & Hudson.

Spufford, P. 2002b. Helps and hindrances to trade. In *Power and Profit: The Merchant in Medieval Europe*, pp. 174–223. London: Thames & Hudson.

Spufford, P. 2002c. The transformation of trade. In *Power and Profit: The Merchant in Medieval Europe*, pp. 12–59. London: Thames & Hudson.

Standage, T. (ed.). 2005. *The Future of Technology*. London: Profile.

Steil, B. 2007a. Digital gold and a flawed global order. *Financial Times*, 5 January.

Steil, B. 2007b. The end of national currency. *Foreign Affairs*, May.

Swan, M. 2015. Limitation. In *Blockchain: Blueprint for a New Economy*, pp. 83–91. Sebastopol, CA: O'Reilly.

Szabo, N. 1997. Formalizing and security relationships on public networks. *First Monday* 2(9).

Thornbury, W. 1878. The Bank of England. In *Old and New London*, volume 1. British History Online (retrieved 29 December).

van Hove, L. 2006. Why fighting cash is a worthy cause. *ProChip*, October.

Vigna, P., and M. Casey. 2015. Genesis. In *The Age of Cryptocurrency*, pp. 41–68. New York: St. Martins.

Wallace, B. 2011. The rise and fall of Bitcoin. *Wired*, November.

Wandhofer, R. 2016. Ready in an instant. *Financial World*, February, p. 44.

Wang, Z. 2010. Regulating debit cards: the case of ad valorem fees. *Federal Reserve Bank of Kansas City Economic Review*, First Quarter, p. 71.

Watson, R. 2010. *Future Files: A Brief History of the Next 50 Years*. London: Nicholas Brearley.

Watson, R. 2011. Scenarios for the future of money. Consult Hyperion Digital Money Forum, London, March.

Weatherford, J. 1997. *The History of Money*. New York: Three Rivers.

White, L. 1989. Free banking as an alternative monetary system. In *Competition and Currency: Essays on Free Banking and Money*, pp. 13–47. New York University Press.

White, L. 2018. The world's first central bank electronic money has come – and gone: Ecuador, 2014–2018. In *Cato at Liberty*. URL: www.cato.org/blog/worlds-first-central-bank-electronic-money-has-come-gone-ecuador-2014-2018 (updated 2 April 2018).

Whittaker, M. 1996. Welcome to Mondex city. *The Independent*, 11 May.

Wiesmann, G. 2009. ECB warns of eastern Europe risk as demand for euro cash rises. *Financial Times*, 10 July, p. 8.

Wildau, G. 2016. China banks starved of big data as mobile payments rise. *Financial Times*, Financials, 29 August.

Wolf, M. 2013. Capital gains fuels visions of a breakaway London. *Financial Times*, 17 May.

Wolman, D. 2012. Time for cash to cash out? *Wall Street Journal*, Life & Culture, 11 February.

Wood, G., and A. Buchanan. 2015. Advancing egalitarianism. In *Handbook of Digital Currency* (ed. D. L. K. Chen), pp. 385–402. Academic Press.

World Economic Forum. 2016. A blueprint for digital identity: the role of financial institutions in building digital identity. World Economic Forum, August.

Zinnbauer, D. 2012. 'Ambient accountability': fighting corruption when and where it happens. Transparency International, 29 October.

Index